# Chasing Conrad

## A tale of the sea and a glimpse into the abyss

## Simon J Hall

Whittles Publishing

Published by
**Whittles Publishing Ltd.,**
Dunbeath,
Caithness, KW6 6EG,
Scotland, UK
www.whittlespublishing.com


© 2015 Simon J. Hall
ISBN 978-184995-155-5


Also by Simon J. Hall: *Under a Yellow Sky*

Printed by
Latimer Trend & Company Ltd.,Plymouth

# Contents

# *Acknowledgements, thanks and apologies*

First, in writing this book I give unrestrained appreciation and thanks to:

Butcombe beer and Doom Bar bitter, Châteauneuf-du-Pape, a very occasional cigarette, Tetleys tea, junk TV, Ibuprofen, sherbet lemons, Admiralty charts 1263 and 748B, my discharge book, all the letters I wrote home (which my mother kept), pictures of my father, Roget's Thesaurus, the Oxford English Dictionary, *The Third Man*, directed by Carol Reed, *Hold My Hand I'm Dying* by John Gordon Davis, Joseph Conrad, Rudyard Kipling, Alfred Noyes, Robert Louis Stevenson, Somerset Maugham, *The Principles of Ethics, Volume 1* by Herbert Spencer, Jack London, the Internet, *Cosi fan Tutte* by Mozart, *Silver Machine* by Hawkwind, Apple, my PC, Microsoft Word, William Shakespeare, *Under Pressure* by Queen, Friedrich Nietzsche, Whittles Publishing, my seafaring friends – John, Jimmy, Barry, Dick, Charlie, Moz, Patsy, Shooey, Des *et al.* – all of you who gave me compliments about my first book, all the people I will offend with this second book, my kids who provide the context, my beautiful and ever-encouraging wife Antoinette … and all the gods that move us all.

This is a casual sequel to the book I wrote on my experiences when I first went to sea; *Under a Yellow Sky*. Several readers who were not blessed with a seagoing life were mildly baffled by some of the nautical terminology used in this earlier book. To address this shortcoming, I have now included a guide to seafaring language.

All the shipping companies I served with were decent and honourable organisations. I have not mentioned the names, although many who read this and who were at sea at the time might believe they recognise those organisations I am writing about. There is no intended criticism expressed or implied, and I apologise for any offence any might choose to take. Any failings are mine and mine alone.

Even if you sailed with me, you will be lucky to recognise yourself in the pages of this book. I have made deliberate changes, not only to people's names but also to the order of events. I have sometimes transplanted occurrences between different ships to confuse the trail. The reason for this clouding is to avoid embarrassment to those who would prefer to keep their past to themselves, nothing more.

So, if you come across an unpleasant or stupid shipboard character and think: 'My God! That's me!' Take heart – it might not be. Whilst this book is intended as a true account, those of you who remember the details and chronology in a different way should make allowances for these changes. Of course, some may just remember events in a completely different way.

Last, I have been brutal in my descriptions of some of the British ports in the 1970s, although this represents my experience. These places have all changed now, and many are veritable garden cities. I hope my words do not cause any modern-day inhabitants to become too exercised – there were some very mean corners of the country at that time.

There is no embroidery in these pages, beyond my choice of words.

# A Guide to Seafaring Language

| | |
|---|---|
| AB | Able seaman |
| Abaft | Behind |
| Abeam | Out to one side of the ship, at right angles to the fore-and-aft length |
| Aft | Backward (as a direction on board a ship); or the back area of the ship |
| Aldis lamp | Very bright hand-held lamp that flashes: used for signalling |
| Ape | Deck cadet |
| Ballast | Weight, usually water in tanks, put into the bottom of an empty ship to make her stable |
| Bilges | Bottom-most inside part of a ship, where water (usually filthy) accumulates |
| Bits | Steel bollards on the poop deck and fo'c'sle head |
| Bollards | Steel posts on the dock for securing ships' ropes |
| Bosun | Chief petty officer in charge of the deck crew |
| Bow | Front of the ship |
| Bridge | Command and navigational centre of the ship |
| Bulkhead | Wall |
| Bumboat | Small boat that ferries supplies and people between the shore and ships at anchor |
| Bunker fuel | Fuel oil for ships |
| Cabin | Room |
| Cargo blocks | Pulley-wheel mechanisms with steel wires running through |
| Casab | Deck storekeeper (Chinese crew), a petty officer |
| Chief | Chief engineer officer |
| Chief mate | Chief officer |
| Choff | Chief officer |
| Clutter | Waves close to the ship picked up by radar |
| Coaming | Raised lip around a HATCH, to help keep water out |
| Deadweight | Measurement of a ship's capacity, mainly applicable to tankers |
| Deck | The floor on a ship, as well as a particular level on it; e.g. the boat deck |
| Deck boy | Uncertificated deckhand under age 18 |
| Deck storekeeper | PETTY OFFICER on deck, junior to the BOSUN |
| Deckhead | Ceiling |
| Dogs | Securing lugs on HATCHES and watertight doors |
| DHU | Deck hand uncertificated |
| Dodger | Curved steel plate on the BRIDGE wing that deflects the wind |
| Draft / draught | Depth of a ship under the surface of the water |
| DR | Dead reckoning: an estimate of the ship's position |
| DR | Declined to report – a black mark on a seaman's discharge record |
| Dunnage | Wooden planking to protect cargo from steel decks and bulkheads |
| ETA | Estimated time of arrival |
| Fathom | Six feet: traditional measurement of sea depth |
| Fireman | Engine room worker |
| Fiver | Fifth engineer officer |
| Flying bridge | On a tanker, the raised walkway between accommodation blocks |

| | |
|---|---|
| Fo'c'sle head | The raised deck at the front of the ship (*pron.* **foke**s'l, short for 'forecastle') |
| For'ard | Forward (as a direction on board a ship); or the front area of the ship (*pron.* **forr**'d) |
| Foreign Going Arts. | Agreement (Articles) signed when someone joins a deep sea ship |
| Fourth | Fourth engineer officer |
| Fourth mate | Fourth officer |
| Gross tonnage | The way ships are measured, except tankers (which are measured by DEADWEIGHT) |
| Gunwales | Stiffened top edges of the hull of a wooden boat (*pron.* gunnels) |
| Hatch | Large square or rectangular covered opening in a deck for cargo to be loaded and unloaded |
| Her | Don't forget that ships are female |
| Holystoning | Scrubbing a wooden deck with a cement block, water and sand |
| Hook | Anchor |
| Home Trade Articles | Agreement a seaman signs when joining a coastal waters ship |
| *Kung hei fat choy* | Cantonese for 'Happy New Year' |
| Knot | Measurement of speed: one nautical mile per hour. ('Knots per hour' is a useful indication of an unreconstructed landlubber.) |
| Leci | Electrical engineer officer (*pron.* **leck**y) |
| Marks | Maximum load lines painted on the side of a ship near the waterline, aka Plimsoll Line |
| Mate | Chief officer |
| Midships | On a tanker, the accommodation block in the centre of the ship |
| Monkey island | Deck above the navigating bridge |
| MV | Motor Vessel |
| Old Man | Captain or master |
| Petty officer | Senior crew member positioned between the officers and the crew |
| Pilot | Someone employed by a port authority to guide ships into and out of the port |
| Point | 11.25 degrees (directional, relating to a compass bearing; one point is 1/32 of a circle) |
| Poop deck | Top deck at the aft end of the ship |
| Port | Left side of the ship, when looking FOR'ARD |
| Pratique | Permission for a ship to enter port, after it has confirmed that there is no infectious disease on board |
| Q Flag | The plain yellow flag flown when a ship is requesting inward port clearance (PRATIQUE) |
| Quartermaster | Helmsman |
| Ralston | Analogue stability calculator, for checking a ship's stability |
| Roads | Anchorage area in a port |
| Second | Second engineer officer |
| Second mate | Second officer |
| Sparks | Radio officer |
| SS | Steam Ship |
| Starboard | Right side of the ship (when looking FOR'ARD) |
| Stays | Wire ropes that brace the masts |
| Stern | Back end of the ship |
| Stevedore | Someone who loads and unloads ships in port |
| Stores | Deck storekeeper (British crews), a PETTY OFFICER |
| Supercargo | Someone hired by the shippers to supervise cargo work in port |
| Taffrail | Polished wooden rail around the outer edges of the upper accommodation decks |
| Telegraph | Device to indicate engine speed requirement: e.g. 'Full Ahead' |
| Third | Third engineer officer |
| Third mate | Third officer |
| Truck | Cap on the top of a mast |
| Tween decks | Cargo storage decks under the main deck |
| Wharfie | New Zealand slang for STEVEDORE |
| VLCC | Very large crude carrier |

# Preliminary

When my twentieth birthday arrived, I was studying for my Second Mate's Certificate of Competency, having just served three and a half years as a deck cadet in the British Merchant Navy. Phew, that was the hard part over, I told myself, now for the good life. A good life it was, too, but no less hard, on reflection. The problems and pressures that tested me were just different, and I remained forever handicapped by the confines of my own personality and the errant foolishness of my notions. Older and wiser; but not wise.

For the next six years I served as a junior officer across a range of ships, across the range of the world. My life was both halcyon and turbid. I am comfortable in writing of what happened, not only of the good things but also of my fecklessness and waste.

Most young men look forwards, they look for change, they look for new things. Not me. I had a reverse gene; I looked backwards. The life I wanted and the life I sought had started to die out before I was born, although there were still scraps of it left, if you looked hard enough. So I looked for it and I chased for it: Chasing Conrad.

# 1

# School for the Almost Serious

In the 1970s, when I was a young man in my teens and twenties, my nautical life and my lifestyle placed me outside the ring of most gatherings of normal society. My conversation was founded on the experience of having called into places around the world that were off the well-trodden track. I mixed with eccentric people, I visited shady and savage parts of the world, I was commonly found in the company of the unsavoury and I spent my relaxation time in dockland bars that were frequented by the strange and the unnerving. I drank too much, I was caught up into violence too often, I rubbed shoulders with rough people, the brutish, louts, bar girls, drug addicts, madmen. On balance, I also met extraordinary people, the brave, the committed, those who lent a hand, people who shined a light wherever they went. My very job was to travel the world away from the tourist corners, and by doing so I journeyed beyond the social map. This life all too often made social interaction awkward when I came home. Young men who were younger than me asked me questions of my life at sea, the majority of which were leeringly designed to flush out some licentious tale. 'Girl in every port, eh?' 'Every girl loves a sailor, right?' and so forth. I would reply with a shrug or a nod and a smile. Sometimes, they asked naive questions in such an earnest manner that I felt I was unable respond without mocking them: 'I'd love to be in the middle of a hurricane. Is it fun?' 'Do you kill pirates?' and such like. Young men who were older than me found it more difficult to ask questions because they were keen not to underline their own more passive and sedate lives. They kept quiet when I spoke of some occurrence in a far-flung part of the world and just gave knowing nods, to let everyone know they had their own hidden depths of excitement.

In the world in which I existed, I was worked to excess, but I was young and strong and healthy, which allowed me to stay up all night to drink the wine and then work the next day without a break. I had no hobbies, and few interests beyond the job that I did and the appetites of a young man seeking the things that most young men seek: girls, drinking, the company of other like-minded men, excitement. I just performed on a larger stage as I travelled the world, 'serving my time' as a deck cadet in the British Merchant Navy. Part of me was a latter-day Sydney Carton caricature; increasingly dissolute while building up to a meaningful gesture yet unknown. The other part was post-empire schoolboy, resolutely seeking out adventure in what I believed were dark and mysterious lands, even though everyone else around me knew the lamps had now been lit.

To become a deck officer in the Merchant Navy, you have to serve your time – three and a half years of it to be precise, under the contract I signed. Until the late 1960s, trainee officers were known as apprentices, a name that had endured for two centuries; the derogatory term in common usage was 'ape.' Then one day, the powers that shaped the shipping world decided that the word 'apprentice' was a bit too industrial, too menial-sounding, it was a bit too grubby. It didn't evoke the right image. The immediate post-war period had passed by, and a more modern age had arrived which called for a sleeker and more professional term. So, the Merchant Navy apprentice was consigned to the history books and the cadet was born. Those who aspired to work on the bridge and run the ship became deck cadets, those who worked down in the oily inferno of the engine room became engineer cadets. When I was at sea as a deck cadet in the early 1970s, not a lot had actually changed in the life of a cadet, though, when compared to the life of an apprentice; the pattern of work continued unbroken and we were still known as apes. The cadet was still rooted at the bottom of shipboard life, the lowest of the low, destined to do the jobs no ordinary crew member would ever be asked to do, and destined to go into disgusting shipboard places where few had gone before. The cadet's position remained as it was before the change of name, which meant that he ranked somewhere between the most junior deckhand and a dog. It was only after the cadet had served his time and had gained a range of ancillary certificates that he would become eligible to sit his professional examinations, the passing of which would grant him access to the holy grail of officerhood.

My time was all served on deep sea ships with one of the big London tanker fleets. There were a lot of smart new vessels in the fleet at the time, but I only ever sailed on old and battered steamers, rusty, dirty, damaged, unsightly. Most of them were older than me. My illusions of a life on the ocean wave were sharply broken within the early days on board my first ship as I found myself being harnessed to the wheel of hard labour with a forty-two-month sentence. When I arrived in Hamburg to sign on for the first time, I was expecting to be taken in hand by square-jawed, fair-minded officer mentors who would see to it that I was trained to become one of them. My expectations, childlike and trusting, were that my life would be to shadow the officers and learn their wisdom, me in my smart gold-braided uniform, them in theirs. I was confident that I would soon learn to become wise and learn to order people around, and I was confident that I would be pretty good at it.

But that was not to be. For three voyages as a cadet, I sometimes felt as if I was enslaved, or as near as it was possible to be. I had to wear rough work-clothes most of the time, not my smart uniform. I was made to work like a beast of the field and was probably treated with less compassion. The work was hard and the hours were long, but the most challenging aspect to absorb was the grinding relentlessness. After the initial shock, I found I could cope with most things that were thrown at me, however dirty and degrading. The work was tiring, sometimes exhausting, often working sixteen or twenty hours non-stop, but I could do that too. What I found unsettling, though, was the slow turn of the wheel, whereby I never seemed to make any progress. I just rose in the morning, worked, worked, slept, rose the next day, worked, worked, slept.

If that all sounds like a picture of misery, it wasn't. The days were full; I became fit and strong and tanned, my companions were mostly vibrant people who wanted to engage with life, and I visited strange and exotic parts of the world. I learnt not just about the sea but I learnt about people, about how to conduct myself, I learned how to cope. I had adventures beyond my imagination and I met people who were so different and contrary to my experience they might have been cast from another species. And in between all of my times at sea I was despatched to a maritime college, to the School of Navigation in Plymouth, where I learnt other things. I learnt how to stretch my mind with studying, I learnt how to live in a semi-militarised environment, I learnt how to march and sail and survive in the open water. I learnt Morse code and celestial navigation and how to tie obscure knots. I learnt how to fight fires and rescue people from awkward places. I learnt rudimentary medicine: how to strap a broken limb, give an injection, clean a wound and drill the skull to relieve pressure after a blow to the head.

On my fourth voyage, three years into my time, I became a senior cadet and started to spend more of my days at sea in uniform, being polished up in the final phase. The grim and dirty jobs were mostly behind me – mostly, but not completely. I learnt the way of the bridge, how to navigate, how to plot the course, how to avoid colliding with other ships. I learnt how to use the radar, the echo-sounder, the directional finder, the Decca navigation system, the radio.

And in amongst all of this I discovered the pithier things of life. I was taught how to drink, I learnt of drugs, I roved through the seedy side that surrounds us all, I encountered violence, prostitution, cruelty, exploitation. I met all manner of characters, from the good and inspiring to the treacherous and loathsome. In my three and a half years, I grew from callow youth to strong young man, from unconfident to unstoppable. The last phase at sea was my final schooling before I went ashore to take the Board of Trade examinations.

In 1973, the School of Maritime Studies in London was housed in a soulless building at the south end of the Minories, a few hundred yards from the Tower of London. I arrived there one damp grey morning in March, checked in at the reception area and found my way to the classroom that had been allocated for those of us studying for their Second Mate's Certificate, the first of our professional examinations. There were twenty-five on the course, although only half that number were there when I walked in. They were a mix of characters, standing around, leaning against desks, talking, smoking. Most were my age although some were a lot older – a couple looked old enough to be my father. I scanned them to determine those who I liked the look of, those I disliked on sight and … the rest. I couldn't see anyone at either extremity; they were all the rest. There was no one I knew, which disappointed me.

I took a seat near the front by the window, where I thought I would be able to look down into the courtyard and ogle the female students as they walked by. A very black man with skin the colour of burnt cork came in and asked if he could sit next to me. He told me his name was Marvin and he was from Ghana and worked for the Black Star Line. He had the whitest smile I had ever seen. The room filled up and became noisier. I half-chatted to Marvin while keeping my eye on the arrivals in case anyone came in who I knew. No one did.

The head of the Maritime Studies Department came in and gave us a dull speech. He droned, we fidgeted. No one had any questions, we all wanted him to go. There was an attendance register that we would be asked to sign every day. Two or three people hadn't turned up. We were given a timetable and a list of books to buy, and were told of the behavioural expectations the college had of us. Lessons ran from nine to five with an hour for lunch. The work covered the gamut of subjects we had to master: navigation, electronics, naval architecture, hydrostatics, meteorology, mathematics, physics, seamanship, ship-handling and communications. The day was divided into four lessons, two in the morning and two in the afternoon.

The London School of Maritime Studies had an alien feel. My previous spells at a maritime college had been in Plymouth during my cadetship. There, we had lived in small dormitories that housed between six and twelve cadets. The life was ordered in a way that was absurdly nautical: the dormitories were called cabins, the floors were decks, the walls were bulkheads, going out at night was known as shore leave. We lived a semi-military existence in uniform, we had to march every morning, we had daily inspections, there was a high degree of discipline. In London, it couldn't have been more different. The college was attached to what was then known as the City of London Polytechnic. There was no discipline as I had known it. We wore civilian clothes of our choice, although there was a general expectation that we wore jackets and ties, which most of us did. Smoking was permitted in class, tin ashtrays were scattered about, and a blue fog hung over the room for most of the time. Two thirds of the class smoked. A couple of people, many years before their calling, tried to rouse the non-smokers to get the habit banned during lessons, but they were either shouted down or ignored. Sleeping was allowed but snoring wasn't. Barracking and rowdy behaviour was strictly out. The lecturers were a mixed bag – some were engaging, although others were so paralysing in the dullness of their delivery that I wanted to thud my head against the desk.

The first lecture on the first day would be after lunch, giving us the morning to deal with the completion of the bureaucratic necessities such as payment and formal registration. We would also be given a tour of the building. I was being sponsored by my shipping company, which was paying all the fees, although the less fortunate had to fork out the money themselves before they were accepted. The tour was given by a youngish and over-eager lecturer who made us troop round one identical lecture room after another. We looked at each other in disbelief after being taken into a large room full of books and told, with a flourish, that this was the library. Someone put his hand up and asked if he could go to the toilet, which made us all snigger, but the young lecturer took the question seriously and we set off in a crocodile to learn where the washrooms were. At lunchtime I walked down the Minories with a few others to the Kelvin Hughes nautical chart and bookshop to pick up the required textbooks. We all had a swift pint in the Three Lords on the way back and swapped war stories.

With Plymouth as my baseline, this was a very different college experience for me, the main difference being that we didn't live in the college. The camaraderie instilled by a group of young men living together in extreme conditions like some big dysfunctional family was not there. This lack of camaraderie, together with the weaker ambiance that comes with low-level discipline and greater institutional freedom, meant that I didn't feel tied to the college in any way, I didn't feel I belonged. Home for me at that time was in West London, in Ruislip, where I was staying with my parents. Ruislip was at the end of the central line, a forty-five minute commuter crush on the underground twice a day. I had never thought my life would be like that. I rose in the morning, walked down to the tube station and sat packed among a grim and silent crowd until my destination. I always sat in one of the two smoking carriages. I didn't like the experience at the start, and I grew to despise it by the end. I could have taken my Second Mate's Certificate in Plymouth, as most of my colleagues did, but I wanted a change, I wanted something different, I wanted to be in London.

The School of Navigation in the Minories took centre stage in 1969 when the venerable King Edward VII Nautical College in Stepney merged with the Sir John Cass Department of Navigation in Aldgate and relocated to the new building near the Tower of London. This was shortly after another renowned Merchant Navy training establishment came to an end; HMS Worcester, a floating sea school that had been around on different ships of the same name since 1862. The demise of these traditional nautical training grounds, with the subsequent shoehorning of all future London training of Merchant Navy officers into the Minories, caused bitterness among both lecturers and students at the time. They resented lowering themselves, resented having to leave institutions that were specialised maritime learning centres in their own right, places of great historical context, to locate as a single department within a polytechnic. Most of the lecturers who took our courses made frequent references to the 'bricklayers and hairdressers' who populated the same building; it was plain to see that this fallen status still cut deep. Not that we saw much of the other polytechnic students, be they bricklayers, hairdressers or rocket scientists, because we were penned into a different part of the college. After the first fortnight, I started to regret going to London to study, and pined for my friends and the familiarity of Plymouth – but the die was cast, the fees were paid and London was where I was going to stay.

I fell in with several similar-minded souls. Max was normally a quiet man but he drank a lot and often made a spectacle of himself. At the close of the second college day, we went to the pub to get to know each other, after which he fell down between the train and the platform at Tower Hill underground station and became wedged. People became frantic in case the train started moving although they started to laugh as he was levered out by two guards. Max had served his time on chemical tankers and intended moving to general cargo ships, which mirrored my intentions.

Glenn was a well-spoken old-fashioned man, a few years older than the rest of us. He dressed fastidiously and spent his time chasing girls who would inevitably reject him. He lacked natural charm and rarely made any headway. Early in the course, he became smitten with a girl he could see from the window of the classroom, who worked in the college administration across the courtyard. He would spend hours staring in her direction with a pained expression. A few days after he had discovered her, as we were strolling along the Crosswall one lunchtime, we passed a flower seller. Glenn bought a huge bunch of blooms and rushed into the administration centre. We watched from below: shrieks from the girls through the open window, then torrents of laughter. Glenn emerged, shamefaced, glum, dragging his flowers behind him.

The last person in our band was Jacky, a shrill cockney who lived in Wapping, which was walking distance from the college. He was a Bank Line man and had spent the past four years tramping the world on older general cargo ships that rarely came home. The four of us went well together.

Marvin from Ghana rarely came out of the classroom. At lunchtime and in the breaks between lessons, he would read his books and besiege me with questions when I returned. I felt he had little chance of passing the exams, as he was excruciatingly slow and his English was stunted, but I helped him as best I could. Sometimes he liked to press me on social issues and was forever asking me how I would feel if I were a white man in a room full of black men. I was uncomfortable with discussions of this nature and always replied lightly to the effect that I had often been in that situation in different parts of the world and it hadn't caused me a problem. He told me that he would become chief officer once he passed his Second Mate's Certificate and would eventually be given a senior port management job in Tema, the port for Accra, capital of Ghana. He said he would even be given command of a ship for a few weeks so he could call himself captain in his new port management job. I congratulated Marvin on his future success, although there was something in the depths of his eyes I didn't like. I felt that deep down he disliked me and everyone else in the room.

As the course took shape, the lecturers often succeeded in driving us to drink by lunchtime. There were two pubs we frequented, The Angel and The Three Lords. The Angel was the closest and the rowdiest. There was a wild lady DJ upstairs on selected days and we all flocked in to see her. She wore jeans and a bikini top, and drove the male clientele into a frenzy with her blue jokes and innuendos. We used the Three Lords when we wanted to talk and drink without having to fight for the bar all the time, which was always the case in the Angel. On most days we would have two or three lunchtime pints and then go back to college, mixing our beery breath into the fog of cigarette smoke. Sometimes we would cut out the second morning lecture and spend a good three hours in the pub, after which we would then become too drowsy to comprehend the afternoon lecture and would fall asleep at our desks, our heads resting upon our folded arms.

The first few weeks was taken up repeating exercises that I had done thoroughly as a cadet at Plymouth and in subsequent correspondence courses. This was much the same for most of the class, who, like me, had recently finished their time and were now taking their Second Mate's Certificate for the first time. There was a cadre who had been sailing

*Royal Albert Dock London in its heyday in the mid-1960s.*
*Used with the kind permission of www.pandosnco.co.uk.*

as uncertificated third mates, now aware that they were in danger of becoming too long in the tooth to continue in a rank they couldn't break out of, who had come back to college for another attempt. Mixed in with them were several long-term serial failures who were much older and who made periodic returns to the college. Because of this mixed bag, the course started at the bottom in an endeavour to make sure no one was left behind. This allowed me and others who had recently been cadets and whose minds were still sharpened, to coast in the early weeks and take days off without the danger of missing anything meaningful.

Sometimes our band of four would award ourselves a day's holiday and go down the West End to spend lunchtime in the Shakespeare's Head in Carnaby Street, which was a grand place to while away the middle hours. Dark panelled wood, smoky, noisy, full of people making fools of themselves. Actors and scriptwriters wandered through, wrapped in insincerity. They were good company although they could turn waspish at any perceived slight. We would sometimes see a half-famous person, and others we almost recognised from a television event, on their way to becoming half-famous. On occasions we would go to Leicester Square and try to pick up European girls on holiday, with offers to show them the town. More often than not we failed to impress, although we sometimes struck lucky.

Not every day was a pub day. When we felt we needed to work in the afternoon we would have lunch in the café under the railway arches in the Minories, which was run by an Italian family, an old widowed mama clad in black, who was helped by her daughter and husband. The daughter's husband used to beat her; she often had a black eye or a marked up face. She served the diners while he slammed about in the kitchen. Mama looked after the tea and coffee behind the counter and didn't speak much. We never ate in the college refectory, having inherited a disdain for the lowly students who we regarded as inferior company to us professional men.

Sometimes, when I wanted to be alone, I would wander down to St Katherine's Dock, which was just downriver of Tower Bridge. St Katherine's Dock had closed to commercial shipping in 1969, after operating for nearly 150 years. The dock had never been a great success; even when it was built it was too small for the larger ships, which had to call further downriver at the West and East India Docks or further down still at the Royal Docks. St Katherine's had been badly damaged in the war and had struggled to recover before finally closing. In the 1970s, the place was being taken apart to build the marina and the smart flats and hotels and restaurants that stand there today. I watched in dismay as the old character and heart was ripped out to be replaced by pretty things. I always loved the feel of decaying dockland, it had a wistful pull for me. I felt my stomach jump as I watched the cranes and bulldozers smash and shatter what was there. All the history, all the tens of thousands of ships that had called there, all the tales that could be told by the millions of sailors who had passed through, everything broken into dust. I hated the thought of the new marina and would traipse back to the college feeling glum.

When I was feeling up for a longer walk, I would go down East Smithfield and along the Wapping Highway to the Limehouse Link. The East India docks at the north end of the Isle of Dogs had been the first of the London docks to close, and were in a terrible state of collapse, gradually being pulled down and filled in. The West India docks were still active, although only just. I walked by quickly. It was too painful to linger by the corpse of these places that had pulled in the wealth of the empire for nearly 200 years.

Eventually I came to the Royal Docks: the King George, the Albert and the Victoria. They were still operating and would do so for another decade. The traffic was shifting downriver to the more modern complex of Tilbury, although in the early and mid-1970s there was still a fairly healthy flow of general cargo liners from the big British shipping names: Ben Line, Port Line, Blue Star Line, Union Castle, Bank Line, Clan Line, Palm Line and many others. They were mostly conventional general cargo ships plying their trade. This was the past, but it was my future, it was where I wanted to be before it disappeared forever. My plan was to do a final trip on tankers after I passed my Second Mate's Certificate and then move into general cargo ships while they were still there. I walked the Royal Docks and watched the ships work, lost in my thoughts and plans. I loved the bustle of the quays and the smell of the ships as they unloaded their cargoes of goods from Africa and the East.

On a conventional general cargo ship, goods were loaded directly into the ship. The holds would be crammed with every imaginable type of cargo: crates of tea, un-crated cars, textiles, coffee, steel ingots and bags of grain would fill one hold, while in the next there would be rubber, animal skins, cloth, beer, drums of wire and rolls of paper. Meat would be loaded in the freezer rooms, palm oil in separate side tanks, alcohol and wine and valuables in lock-up stores, fruit and fresh foods in the chilled compartments. The deck cargo would be the larger items: railway engines, boats, trucks, plant and machinery. The loading plan for a general cargo ship was an intricate patchwork where weight and space was calculated, and each piece of cargo needed to be compatible with its neighbour to avoid taint and spoilage.

I would often while away a whole afternoon watching the docks at work, ambling from ship to ship. The security at the dock gates was rudimentary and easy to slip though. Sometimes, I would go aboard one of the ships to strike up a conversation with the third mate. I would then get a tour, which fired up my enthusiasm even more. General cargo life had the romance, and I wanted to be a part of it.

But general cargo ships were feeling the relentless push of the containerisation that had begun in the 1960s. This new shipping method allowed that cargoes were pre-packed in twenty-foot containers, which were then loaded aboard and stacked within the ship. The loading and unloading process was quick and sleek. It became almost immaterial what was actually in the container. The chief mate was only concerned with the weight of each unit to make sure that the heavy ones were not all on the upper levels, because that could cause the ship to become unstable and topple over. Container ships were hunting down the main trade routes: they were the future and we all knew it.

I found it necessary to remind myself from time to time that I was in London for a purpose: to obtain my Second Mate's Certificate. These examinations were the first serious ones I had to take. They were still known among us as the Board of Trade exams, despite the Board of Trade having morphed into the Department of Trade and Industry four years beforehand. I didn't find the work hard, I was just bored by the end of the first term, bored, bored, bored. And I loathed the commuting. The twice daily journey on the tube was becoming increasingly hellish for me. I started to recognise my fellow passengers each morning, although we never spoke or even acknowledged each other. I started to silently hate them, for no reason other than I hated being there. I couldn't concentrate on the lessons because I was becoming numb with the whole experience. Max and Jacky and Glenn were decent enough people and I enjoyed our jaunts but we weren't close, we lived in different quadrants of a vast city. I wanted to be back at sea. I craved the sea.

The majority of the college work was science based. In the navigation there was a lot of mathematics, some calculus although mostly trigonometry. This was not ordinary trigonometry; ours was spherical trigonometry, the basis of celestial navigation. Spherical trig was mysterious maths to all but the select few. No one had a calculator, we all used Norie's Tables, a massive tome of logarithm tables written by the famous hydrographer and mathematician John Norie in the early 1800s and in continuous print ever since. Physics: this included electronics, which I hated, and mechanics and hydrostatics, which I was good at. Meteorology was a big subject: weather and water and pressure and all things in the air and above it. Naval Architecture showed us how ships were built; there was a lot of precision drawing, cross-sections of tankers and cargo ships and reefer ships and passenger ships. Then there was seamanship and ship handling, anchoring procedures, emergencies. Some parts of the studies I enjoyed, and there was nothing I really struggled with, apart from my enthusiasm.

The examination itself was in three parts: orals, writtens and communications. Communications was colloquially known as 'signals'. Signals was sending and receiving Morse code, semaphore and flags, along with radio procedure. The signals lesson was an enjoyable interlude. It was easy fare to most people, although Marvin struggled badly. He had difficulty in either sending or reading. He was so hopeless that the rest of us were embarrassed. Orals was a one-hour grilling by three wise nautical men who could ask you anything and everything to do with the sea. The failure rate was high in orals. Writtens was the meat of the course, though, and was what it was all really about. Everyone would be quite happy to fail orals and signals as long as they passed the writtens. In writtens you had to get at least 65 per cent in each subject, otherwise you failed the whole lot and had to do every single exam again. The single exception to this was a 'referral'. A referral in writtens would sometimes be given if someone obtained a good pass in every subject except one in which they had a very narrow fail, 2 per cent or less. Someone might then be granted a referral in that one subject and so be allowed a year to take it again. A referral was like gold dust.

As the second term wore on, I was finding it difficult to continue. I loathed the commuting more and more, I disliked the classes. I hated being ashore. My friends were either at sea or down in Plymouth. I stayed with my parents in West London. I irritated them, they irritated me. On the weekends I prowled the pubs of Ruislip and surrounding towns, restless, bored, striking up conversations with strangers. I had no girlfriend, just the occasional pick-up from the oily charm I managed to dredge up, although I never saw anyone more than twice. I wanted to meet a decent girl who I was really attracted to, although never managed to find anyone, which was just as well because I wasn't deserving at that stage of my life and would have been a poor catch.

I didn't have the money to buy a car and hadn't yet passed my driving test anyway. I bought a motorbike though, a mean-looking Yamaha with a 250 cc engine, the largest I was legally allowed to have on my licence. I bought it from a dodgy-looking man in a garage in Wandsworth. I set off home, I had never ridden a motorbike before in my life. The journey was dreadful, I struggled to understand the gears. I stopped at a traffic light and the bike tipped over, it fell on top of me, passers-by had to lift it off as I flapped and floundered beneath the weight. Later, I crashed into a wall. A mile from home I ran out of petrol and had to ignominiously push my bike the rest of the way home. After that, my motorbike worked sporadically, it worked when it felt like it. I was mechanically hopeless and when it wouldn't start I was perplexed and had no idea what to do. I asked other people for help but to no avail. My brother Peter laughed and told me I had bought a heap. I took it to a garage and they tinkered and tutted and charged me lots, and still it only worked sporadically. I would shout and swear at my Yamaha bike in my incompetent frustration and sometimes I would beat it as punishment for its antics.

I decided to give up all the classes apart from signals and orals. For everything else, I would work through old exam papers. I scrounged over twenty papers for each subject. I worked through them all, I worked through them all again. I memorised every answer. I went to the library every day for five hours and did two exams. Then I read the answers and corrected my mistakes. I memorised all the correct answers. I identified my weak areas and read the books and filled the gaps. Nothing is new, everything comes up again, I told myself. All the questions that would come up in my exams would have been asked before, in one way or the other. I scrounged further old exam papers. My twentieth birthday passed, I hardly noticed.

The college wrote to me and asked why I was not attending classes. I ignored them. They kept writing although I binned the letters. My shipping company wrote to me and asked why I was not attending college. They threatened to stop my study leave pay. I lied to them. I told them I was working, I told them the college was mistaken. They were only partially convinced, but I had booked my exams by then and the date was only three weeks away. I started going into the classroom in the morning on a few occasions and signed the register, then left for the library. I used different libraries, I became a library traveller: the college library, Ruislip Library, the British Library, various City libraries. I went on occasional lunchtime beanos with Max and Jacky and Glenn. The three of them were content to continue plodding through the college course. Jacky said that his study leave pay would stop in a flash if his company had reports that he was not turning up. Marvin tried to convince me to come back. He said he was lonely sitting by himself and no one would talk to him because he was black. I told him no one else would talk to him because he wouldn't talk to anyone else. He predicted my downfall and said I would never become an important man in life like him if I didn't apply myself properly. I told him I would have to live with my obscurity. He shook his head in pity. I read and re-read the collision regulations, learning the more important rules *identidem*. I sat in the libraries and did the same old exam papers again and again and again and got drunk at the weekends and searched for girls in the pubs of Ruislip.

The examination centre for Certificates of Competency was in an old and shabby building in an old and shabby part of town. It was situated in Ensign Street, which lies parallel to Dock Street and forms a junction with the notorious Cable Street, scene of the famous Cable Street battle in 1936. The battle was between Oswald Mosley's fascists, the police and a coalition of Jews, Irish, Socialists, Anarchists and Communists. It was a full-scale riot; the police and the fascists were pelted with rotten fruit and the contents of chamber pots. Stones and clubs were used as weapons by the rioters. Several policeman were badly hurt; they retaliated by thrashing the rioters they took into custody. By the time the riot ended, nearly 200 people had been injured.

There were no riots when I turned up to take my examinations, just street-corner loafers, small children playing in the road, some dogs, other exam attendees. Everywhere was grubby, the pavements were cracked, litter blew in the wind, crude graffiti marred brick walls, plant life grew through the concrete in abandoned wastes. The place looked as if little had been done since the Mosley riot. I arrived early and sat in the café on the corner of Cable Street and Dock Street, scene of thousands of cases of pre-exam nerves. I refuelled on sweet milky tea and a greasy fry-up, watching the world limp by through the fogged windows.

I was the first of my class to sit the exam. It was a Monday and I had two exams a day for four days. Orals and signals were to be held the following week. The examination hall was big, high-ceilinged, wooden floors. The paint job was ancient, dark cream and dark green; it looked as if leftover military paint from some forgotten issue had been used. The room echoed. Desks were set out one behind the other in lines of ten, six feet apart, each with an uncomfortable chair. A big clock was high on the wall at the front of the room; as each minute went past the hand jumped forward with a mechanical thud. We sat at our desks and listened to a lecture about conduct, timings and the perils of cheating. The exam papers were placed on the desks upside down. The invigilator started to prowl, the clock thudded onto the hour, we were told to start.

The orals exam was on the following Wednesday. I faced a trio of wise men, Department of Trade officials, all ex-mariners, all ex-Masters. One was kindly and doddering, one was blank-faced, one was sneering. I wondered if this was a calculated blend, or if it was how they had developed, or if my over-active imagination was just conjuring the images. I was grilled and pressed for an hour on what I knew. It was not just a matter of giving the right answer, it was a matter of giving the right answer in the right manner. When I was asked what action I would take if a ship was bearing down on me three points off the starboard bow, I would answer by saying: 'I would observe Rule 19, which says *when two power-driven vessels are crossing, so as to involve risk of collision, the vessel which has the other on her own starboard side shall keep out of the way of the other.*' This verbatim recital told them I knew my Collision Regulations. If anyone attempted to simply explain what they would do, they ran the near certainty of failing unless they were remarkably convincing. The three wise men wanted to hear the rules quoted. After hearing the rule quote and only after hearing the rule quote, they would then move into the practicalities of how I would alter course, when I would start the manoeuvre and all the other aspects involved. Only then would they be satisfied. The major part of the oral examination centred around the Collision Regulations; it took at least half of the time. Every lecturer had said the same thing: 'If you don't know your collision regs off by heart, don't even bother to turn up; you'll fail.' Good advice; I made sure I could spout off all twenty-nine rules word for word. Some of the rules were small, like Rule 19, although some were more than a page long. I knew that if I could put on a good show in collision regs I stood a decent chance of being forgiven some stumbles on cargo work, ship handling, crew management and the other areas they might delve into. I was proved right on both counts: my handling of collision regs was pristine and I bungled my ship-handling and seamanship. I passed.

Signals was a breeze. I passed the tests on Morse and the light recognition without breaking step. People rarely failed signals; you had to be backward or woefully unprepared to fall down on that. Obtaining a Second Mate's Certificate also required that I had an up-to-date eyesight and colour test, which I did, and had passed the week before the exams.

There was a wait for a couple of weeks for the written results, which I filled by riding my motorbike around the countryside on the occasions it chose to work, taking the tube and exploring London when it didn't. I felt I had done a fairly good job on the writtens, although the cold finger of failure was forever on my shoulder, a spectral voice whispering worrying prophecies into my ear. The thought of having to do all the exams again was crushing. The brown envelope arrived one Saturday morning, my mother woke me up, I tore it open, I whooped. The result was a referral in meteorology. My parents couldn't understand why I was celebrating if I hadn't passed. I explained that my referral meant I had narrowly failed meteorology and therefore I was being given twelve months to pass that one subject again. I was confident because I felt that in a year I could probably read every book on meteorology on the planet. In my mind I couldn't fail, and in the meantime I would serve as uncertificated third mate because the industry was crying out for Merchant Navy officers. That was why I was celebrating.

I phoned the company on Monday morning and was put through to the Personnel Department.

I said: 'I passed orals and signals and got a referral in meteorology.'

The Personnel Officer on the other end of the line said: 'Well done. You're in; no one fails a referral. When can you leave? We need third mates now.'

'I'll go straight away,' I replied. 'I just need a few days to buy some kit.'

'Good. We've got an H Class ship where the current third mate is desperate to get off because he's getting married soon; we haven't been able to find anyone to relieve him. You'll go as uncert third mate.'

'Suits me. Which ship is it, and where is she trading?'

'The *Horomya*. She's due in Houston on Sunday. You can fly out on Saturday with the new second mate. We'll send you a ticket; you had better get some stripes.'

The *Horomya*: my previous ship, the last one I had sailed on as cadet. I knew her like the back of my hand. My first trip as third officer couldn't get any easier.

I went into town at lunchtime to share the news of my referral with Max and Jacky and Glenn. They shook my hand and slapped me on the back and gave up the afternoon's work to celebrate. We all went over the road and got smashed in the Angel, while the lady DJ danced on her podium like a madwoman. Glenn told her of our celebration news and she played me a dedication record, 'Waterloo Sunset'. Several of the others came over from the college to join us, including Marvin.

Max said: 'Marvin's locked onto me now you've gone; he's such a pain.'

I said: 'Look after him. He'll see you right if you ever go to Accra.'

'Who the bloody hell wants to go to Accra?' said Jacky.

We all laughed. Who in their right mind would want to go to Accra? I did actually, but I didn't tell them.

After the lunchtime bell at the Angel, we stepped outside, blinking into the bright afternoon and decided to keep the party going. Jacky knew a West End club that served all day and which would let us in, so we jumped on the tube to Tottenham Court Road. The club was in Greek Street, off Soho Square. It was grim and dim, expensive to get in and expensive to drink in, but nobody cared because I was paying. I didn't care because I had a referral in meteorology.

As soon as opening time arrived we drifted south-west through Soho, stopping at different pubs as we came to them. At eleven o'clock after last orders there was only Max and me left.

We vowed to go on through the night. On the club circuit, we began at the noisy and vibrant places that shut at two o'clock, then moved to the serious ones that stayed open until four, after that to the sad places that kept going until breakfast. I was spending money like a sailor on a spree, which was what I was. I didn't care about the money for three reasons. First, I was entitled to six months' study leave and one month of ordinary leave and I was going back to sea after only four and a half months, which meant the rest of my leave would be liquidated and converted to extra pay at third officer rate. Second, I never cared about the money anyway. Third, I had a referral in meteorology.

At six o'clock in the morning we were back in the same Greek Street club we had started in. It was dark and almost deserted. A crumpled couple were groping each other in one corner, some middle-aged men in suits were grinding the last drop of enjoyment out of their night out. We sat at the bar, dull drunk by then. 'Waterloo Sunset' struck up on the turntable and we sang along heroically, waving our pints of Worthington E. We decided it would freshen us up if we walked to Waterloo Bridge and watched Waterloo Sunrise before going home. We strolled down to the Embankment in the early morning quiet and sat on the river wall and watched the dark grey morning become a paler shade of grey. It started raining and it became clear that there would be no sunrise to see. It rained harder. We gave up and walked to the Strand and caught early tube trains to our respective destinations. I fell asleep and woke at the end of the Central Line, the guard shaking me by the shoulder.

A couple of days later, I hopped on the tube and went to Fenchurch Street where I called in at Miller Rayner, the naval tailor, to buy the gold braid that designated an uncertificated third officer – a half diamond, together with shoulder epaulettes for my tropical uniform. I picked up some new shirts and a few other uniform sundries to make sure I would be well turned out. I then went to the Kelvin Hughes shop in the Minories and bought a good quality Tamaron sextant and a pair of Russian binoculars, my badges of office, plus four books on meteorology. When I walked past the Three Lords I looked through the window and saw Max and Jacky in there, hunched over the bar. It would have been rude to pass on by, so I took out my epaulettes, balanced them on my shoulders then walked in with an exaggerated swagger to join them. We had a few drinks although I made a point of not staying too long as I had no intention of getting plastered and losing all my expensive new kit.

I arrived home at teatime. An envelope was waiting for me on the hall table; my ticket to fly to Houston on Saturday morning. My mother sewed on my new gold stripes that evening and cut off the cadet collar flashes. I played with my sextant for the next couple of days, then packed at leisure, thinking all the time: 'Houston, then back to sea.' Anticipation and excitement made creatures squirm inside me. I clock-watched all day Friday.

# 2

# *War and Pisces*

I flew out to Houston on the Saturday morning flight from London with BOAC, travelling with Brian, the replacement second officer. He was much older than me, a stout man in his early thirties who was losing his hair. I speculated that he was stuck as second mate because he couldn't pass the examinations for his master's certificate. He never said this directly although the situation seemed clear from the bits I picked out of our conversations.

The newly introduced Boeing 747 we flew in was comfortable enough. I was keen to sink a few cans of beer during the first half of the flight but Brian was more reserved and just wanted to read then watch the film. I ended up at the back of the plane for most of the flight, drinking and making a racket with some American oil men who were returning home from working in the North Sea.

Houston is the biggest city in Texas and the fourth largest in the United States. At that time, the Organisation of Petroleum Producing Countries, OPEC, was preparing to announce an oil embargo against the West, which would cause oil prices to quadruple. The USA wasn't even a member of OPEC despite being a big producer. Most US oil was in Texas. Houston and Dallas were kings of the oil business. The rest of the USA would be driven into recession by the oil price rise and Congress would impose a 55 mph speed limit, the long-term effects on most industry of the USA would be profound. In the Texas oil cities however, big money would be made.

Brian and I were picked up from the airport by a gnarled and ancient man who took us to our hotel in the biggest car I had ever been in. The 1000 flight from London took eleven hours, although Houston time was six hours behind so we arrived at three in the afternoon local time. The gnarled man told us the *Horomya* wasn't due in until Tuesday now, so we would be staying in a hotel for three nights; we were booked into the Downtown Houston Motel. He told us our hotel booking was for bed and breakfast only, so we asked for food money and he said the allowance was $30 a day, $90 in total. He peeled off $100 for each of us from a fat wad of money, saying that the additional $10 was for sundries and emergencies. We protested that the additional $10 wasn't enough to cover anything and we bickered outside the hotel until he gave in and handed us another $50 each, under protest.

The Downtown Houston Motel was a light and airy place built around a courtyard where residents parked their cars. There was an attached restaurant, the Sunshine Café, which sold light meals. There was also a dark bar and an underground nightclub. The weather outside was blazing hot at over 100°F, although inside the air was polar.

We did some sightseeing over the next couple of days. Brian wanted to see Houston's giant sports stadium, the Astrodome, which I found marginally interesting although a two-hour tour to view artificial turf was too long for me. My choice was the Budweiser brewery, which Brian found as dull as I had found the Astrodome.

The Houston ship canal is a natural watercourse, rather than a man-made canal, although it does need regular dredging. The canal allows big ships to progress up to Port Houston, not far from the city centre and nearly thirty miles up from Galveston Bay off the Gulf of Mexico. But on Monday morning the gnarled agent arrived and told us there had been a change of orders and the *Horomya* was now bound for Lake Charles, Louisiana, 150 miles east as the crow flies. He had booked us on the lunchtime flight with Texas International Airways. The flight with Texas International was memorable. The plane was small and cramped and propeller-driven, the stewardess was a six-foot blonde in purple hot pants and the safety announcement was in a drawl so Texan that I couldn't understand what was being said. The in-flight meal was a bag of peanuts and a bottle of Coke.

Lake Charles has a mixed history. Named after a French settler following the War of Independence, the place had become a hotbed of slave trading and contraband in the early nineteenth century. Renowned pirate Jean Lafitte supplied slaves to the local plantation owners, including Jim Bowie, hero of the Alamo. Lake Charles grew fat and rich on the timber business, coming relatively unscathed through the Civil War of the 1860s, and continuing to flourish until 1910, when it suffered a disastrous fire which saw one-third of its population made homeless. Nevertheless, it recovered, and through the 1930s and 1940s boomed again as a timber centre. By the 1970s it had become an important inland port, one of the busiest in Louisiana, with a lot of petrochemical interests. When we arrived at the tanker berths there was no sign of the *Horomya* – in fact there were no ships there at all. The driver who had brought us from the airport told us he had to go, and we were left in the afternoon sun to wait for our ship to arrive. We sat on bollards in the shade of a crane, the port was deserted, a thick silence hung over the reclaimed swampland, insects clicked in the nearby undergrowth. The *Horomya* came nudging round the headland two hours later, flanked by a pair of tugs.

Having already sailed on the *Horomya* as a cadet, I knew her well. I had also sailed on one of her sister ships prior to that and so my working knowledge was as sound as it could be. The *Horomya* was a white oil tanker of 18,000 tons deadweight. The deadweight is essentially the carrying capacity of the ship. In other words, if the ship was weighed full of cargo and then weighed empty, the deadweight would be the difference between the two. Ships are measured in different ways, and it is only tankers whose primary reference measurement is the deadweight. White oils are among the earlier extractions from crude oil, after it has been carefully cooked in the refinery. The first substances to escape from crude in the refining process are the high grade methanes and propanes. Next come the white oils: high octane jet fuel, petrol or gasoline, kerosene, naphtha and similar light high-grade liquids. After that come the heavier black oils: diesel, industrial burning oils, lubrication oils. What then remain are the tars and sludges: bitumen and asphalt. Many people think that white oil ships are the most dangerous because they carry high octane cargoes, but in fact crude oil carriers are the bigger potential hazard, because crude oil still contains everything.

The officers and crew had all changed since I was last aboard the *Horomya* and everyone was new to me. The third mate I was relieving was happy I knew the ship; he gave me a lightning handover and rushed off to get changed and packed so he could be home in time for his own wedding, which was on the coming Saturday. The chief mate was equally pleased I knew the ship; he had been waiting with dread to see who was going to arrive. With a new second mate and a new third mate, it would be a nightmare for him if neither of us were familiar with tankers. Brian hadn't sailed on H Class ships before; he had a general cargo background but he did have two tanker trips under his belt on V class ships, which were bigger vessels although not dissimilar in operation. The captain, the Old Man, was a big stern character who I didn't like the look of at first. In time we settled into a reasonable relationship although initially he was sharper than he needed to be. I expect his nerves were a little on edge in having a first-trip third mate with no certificate.

The ship was half-laden and we were to complete the discharge in Lake Charles before heading back out into the Gulf of Mexico to steam south-west to the Caribbean and to Curaçao, a small island off the coast of Venezuela, which mainly functioned as an oil refining centre. Curaçao was governed by the Dutch, part of the Netherlands Antilles along with Aruba and Bonaire and a couple of other islets.

We Lake Charles left at midnight and it took us ten hours to complete the seventy-mile journey up the canal to the mouth of the Gulf of Mexico, where we dropped the pilot. I had the eight-to-twelve watch and it was mid-morning when the pilot left. The day was clear and bright and the wind was light, turning up small wavelets on the blue waters. We could see a few ships crossing well ahead although traffic was generally light. Oil rig platforms dotted the sea in clusters.

The Old Man said: 'Put her on auto and send the second man down to the bosun,' then went through to the chartroom.

I said: 'Aye, aye, sir,' then dismissed the AB quartermaster from the wheel and clicked the lever on the Sperry gyro system through to autopilot, watching the compass settle down. The AB went out to stand on the bridge wing with the second man of the watch. When going in and out of port the ship was always taken out of autopilot and a second man was put on the watch because it was not considered safe for someone to steer for more than an hour at a time. The two quartermasters would then do hour and hour about, one steering, one as lookout. I stood the second man down, telling him to report to the bosun for general duties.

*The SS* Horomya *at sea.*

I then told the remaining AB to get a broom and sweep the bridge wings and start washing down the dodgers.

The Old Man stuck his head out the chartroom door: 'Third Mate. Come in here.'

I went in there.

He pointed to the thin grey pencil line on the chart heading south-west. The engineers had wound the ship up to full revs now and the mast stays were rattling on the monkey island above the bridge housing.

'It looks clear enough ahead. There are a couple of ships about ten miles off the starboard bow but they'll be crossing well ahead. See this oilfield here?' he tapped the chart. 'Keep well off; do not let us drift east of the line.'

I nodded.

'Call me if you're in any doubt. Don't hesitate.'

I nodded.

'I said call me if you're in any doubt!'

'Aye, aye sir!'

'Any problems?'

'No sir. I'm fine.'

'It's all yours.' The chartroom door closed and I heard him clumping down the stairs.

'It's all yours.' Every junior officer hears those words for the first time only once, and they are profound. After three and a half years of crouching on the deck, chipping, painting, tank cleaning, doing every filthy job known to men who worked on ships, I was now up with the gods, a watch-keeping officer in charge of an 18,000-ton ship. I didn't know what to expect – trumpets sounding from the sky perhaps. But like many things we wait for in life, it was rather ordinary when it arrived. There was an assumption that I could do the job I was being paid to do and so I was left to do it. There was no one to talk to; the sailor was sweeping the decks and I couldn't chat to him anyway. I was tightly strung and anxious not to be unmasked as a fraud, so I plotted the course, made sure we kept well clear of shipping, kept us west of the line as we passed the oilfield and generally got on with things.

The Old Man came back up to the bridge on several transparent pretexts for the rest of the watch, asking me if he had left his pipe up here, telling me to tell the second mate to work out an ETA and call him with it, asking me if we had passed the oilfield yet and sundry other excuses. His grey eyes scanned the horizon as he spoke, he stuck his head into the radar hood, he checked the position on the chart. I was aware that he had a duty to ensure he wasn't leaving an utter imbecile in charge of his ship and I wasn't offended.

The first watch went off without any snags; I even had to alter course for a crossing ship before I handed over to the second mate.

The first night watch, from eight in the evening to midnight, was more tense. The night was clear and black and moonless, lights dotted the horizon: oil rigs, rig supply boats, fishing boats, big deep sea ships, smaller short sea coasters. I paced the bridge, the lookout called out a running commentary on new lights: 'Light two points off the port bow, Third Mate.'

'Light one point abaft the port beam, Third Mate.'

'Light dead ahead, Third Mate.'

I acknowledged. I looked at each new light through my binoculars. In most cases I had seen it before the lookout anyway. I would watch the light and assess it. I enjoyed night watches, they were quiet, I was alone in the dark apart from the lookout. I had to plot the ship's position every thirty minutes and make sure we safely avoided other ships. That apart, I was free to pace and I was free to think.

A light ahead showing red and green was a ship coming straight towards us. Both ships had an obligation to alter course slightly to starboard, so that we passed port to port. I would wait until the other ship was about five miles away before altering 5 degrees to starboard. I would then watch the other ship carefully to see if she did the same. If she hadn't made a move at three miles I would turn another 5 degrees, possibly more. Five miles sounds a long way off, but two ships steaming at 15 knots have a closing speed of 30 knots, which means that five miles is ten minutes from collision impact. And ships take time to change direction. Ships often have to close to much less distance when navigating in congested inland waters and might not alter until less than two miles off, but anyone who aims for a close encounter in open seas at night is acting recklessly.

A red light on the starboard side was a crossing ship that we had to give way to if she looked as if she was not going to cross sufficiently far ahead or astern of us. This entailed taking regular compass bearings to see if she was pulling ahead or dropping astern. If a crossing ship was first seen two points off the bow and five minutes later she was closer and still bearing two points, she was on a collision course. If she had moved ahead to only one point, then she was safely crossing ahead. Ships crossing from starboard to port (that's from right to left for you landlubbers) were not unwelcome. I saw them, I knew what to do and I would act in plenty of time, altering to starboard and swinging round their stern to let them cross safely ahead.

The ships to fear, the ships that set every watch keeping officer's pulses racing, were ships crossing from port to starboard, from left to right, ships on the port side showing green. Every time I encountered one, every single time, I would feel myself snap into concentration. If I was dozy I would become wide awake, if I was idly dreaming I would come back sharply on focus. These were the danger ships, these were the ships that could take you down into the green depths.

Not all ships are well manned and have well-trained bridge officers. Some have half-trained ones, some have untrained ones, sometimes they are asleep, or drunk. Sometimes there is no one on the bridge at all. Sometimes they just don't know what to do. It is a status mark and a matter of national pride for a country to have its own ships under its own flag; it is a statement from that country that it is indeed a country. That is all very well for long-established maritime nations such as Britain or Holland or Norway. But for the scores of third world countries, or newly independent countries, more often than not there wasn't the training infrastructure in place to produce competent officers on the bridge. Even the captain might have only been at sea a short period of time, witness Marvin for example.

So, when I saw a ship crossing port to starboard, my mouth would go dry and I would watch her very, very carefully. The danger lay in the fact that I couldn't alter course to port to let the ship slide across ahead, because if she was at that moment about to alter course to let me pass then I would be altering straight into her. So it was necessary to hang on and hope until the last safe minute, and then, if it looked like the ship was going to keep on coming, I would come out of autopilot, put the sailor on the wheel, give three short blasts on the whistle as a wake-up, wait thirty seconds, give three more blasts if she hadn't started to alter course, go over hard to starboard to swing the ship away from her, right round in a full circle. Every watch-keeping officer has to do that manoeuvre at some time. When I judged the time was crucial, I would reach for the direct phone to the captain's cabin as I started the manoeuvre and shout: 'We're about to go hard-a-starboard sir; there's a ship crossing that's not going to move!' then slam the phone down. I always phoned because three short blasts would bring the Old Man up to the bridge to see what was going on anyway. The Old Man would arrive and we would watch the other ship to see if she moved and we would swear at her and shout over the VHF radio. Sometimes she would alter course at the very last minute, although on several occasions I was forced to take evasive action. As we started to swing, our ship would heel right over, because a ship thrown hard over at full speed is going to lean when she turns sharply, and I would hear the crashing of crockery and other objects from below. When it was over and the rogue ship was safely past, I felt a collapse of relief, quickly followed by a surge of exhilaration which made me laugh out loud. I felt as alive as it was possible to be. The Old Man and I would laugh together as we swore at the ship that was getting smaller as she continued on her way, oblivious.

☆   ☆   ☆

We exited the Panama Canal on the Pacific side after loading a full cargo in Curaçao , then headed west across the Pacific Ocean, bound for a clutch of ports in Japan. A Pacific crossing was relaxing and would allow us to put the ship in good order, provided the weather stayed fair. It was a long haul from Panama to Yokohama, 7,685 nautical miles to be precise, which meant that the voyage would take over twenty-one days if we averaged 15 knots. The Pacific is a vast body of water, the biggest of the three great trading oceans at 60 million square miles, which is one and a half times the size of the Atlantic and twice the size of the Indian Ocean. It's also the least populated by shipping traffic, and we would go days without sighting anything. Although there are main shipping routes, because the shortest distance between two ports will always be the shortest distance between two ports, ships will spread out, drifting off as the current and seas push them, never sticking to the precise line. On a 50-mile journey from A to B, most ships would track the same course, but on a journey of nearly 7,700 miles, there will be a lot of spreading. In addition, the captain of each ship will have their own preferences based on experience, their interpretation of potential hazards, avoiding perceived weather patterns, or simply having an inclination to go north of an island when others might go south. Some companies had specific rules laid down by the owners about which routes their ships would take, which added to the mix of directions. Occasionally, we would pass within a few miles of another ship, although there were days when we would get excited if we saw a smudge on the horizon. Officers would crowd on the bridge to study a passing ship, discussing what sort of ship she was, what shipping line it might be, where she was bound and what she might be carrying.

There are two line crossings at sea that cause a ship's crew to get exercised. The first is the crossing of the equator and the second is the transit of the 360-degree meridian, the International Date Line. Both the Panama Canal and Yokohama were in the northern latitudes so there would be no crossing of the equator, which meant no crossing the line ceremony. This was a mixed blessing for the younger crew members who had not crossed the line before. On the one hand they would not have to undergo the gruesome and humiliating ceremony, while on the other they still had it to face at some future crossing. The crossing the line ceremony was a ritual that has run for centuries and which had evolved mostly to stave off the boredom that sets in on long passages, giving the crew some light relief. The first-time line crossers were blindfolded and brought before Neptune, a crew member appropriately dressed up and holding something resembling a trident. Neptune's assistant was Davy Jones, who was decked out in similar fashion. Those being initiated were granted permission to enter Neptune's kingdom, subject to being pelted with rotten fruit, doused in garbage or some other appropriate muck and then given a good salt-water soaking with a fire hose or tossed in the swimming pool. At the end of it all, the newly initiated were given a certificate to prove they had indeed crossed the line.

In most cases the ritual was given and taken in good spirit, but then man can be brutish and sometimes the ceremony could get out of hand. In was not uncommon for people to be stripped naked and daubed with sticky oil-based paint and grease and then have their head shaved before being hosed down. The victims might also be poked with sticks and whacked with lengths of hose, as well as suffering other miscellaneous abuse. And all of this was in the civilised twentieth century of course. In the early nineteenth century, it was really rough. The culmination to the ceremony then was that the new initiate was thrown overboard tied to a line and dragged behind the ship. This was after he had been force-fed slops from the housings of the pigs and chickens that were carried on board, tarred and coated with sweepings, shaved and then thrashed with a rope end. The eventual heaving overboard must have come as something of a relief. Death was not unknown.

The line we did cross was the 180 degree meridian, the International Date Line, two weeks out from Panama. The date line is at the opposite side of the world from the meridian of 0 degrees, which runs through Greenwich and is the reference point for lines of longitude. The earth turns anti-clockwise when viewed from above the North Pole, which means that as you go further east from Greenwich the sun rises earlier. Each 15 degrees of longitude represents one hour, and so the clocks advance. By the time you reach 180 degrees east, you will be twelve hours ahead of Greenwich time. Conversely, if you travel west from Greenwich then the clocks will be retarded by one hour for each 15 degrees of longitude, meaning that by the time you reach 180 degrees west the time is twelve hours behind Greenwich.

If someone on one side of the date line was looking across at someone on the other side of the date line, there would be twenty-four hours' difference in their times, one being twelve hours ahead of Greenwich and the other being twelve hours behind. When you cross the line, the actual date has to shift and you either gain a day or lose a day, depending upon whether you are going west or east. It was always a cause for celebration if someone ended up with two birthdays. It was still a celebration, in fact, if someone lost the day of their birthday and could thus proclaim themselves a year younger.

There was a shameful incident when we crossed the 180-degree meridian. When crossing the date line, there is no tradition of ceremony, there is just the crossing, although on the *Horomya* a ceremony was afoot. We carried six engineer cadets, one of whom, known as Porky, was deeply unpopular. Porky was short and pink and plump, he wore glasses as thick as bottle ends and had chronic halitosis. He washed rarely and his body odour was rank and repellent. If that wasn't bad luck enough, Porky suffered further by having a tedious and unpleasant personality, a smirking manner that made most people immediately dislike him. His real name was Peter, but when he came on board and first introduced himself, he said he liked to be called Pisces, because that was his birth sign. That was a bad opening move. If someone at sea is going to carry a nickname, it is going to be a nickname chosen by others, which is how nicknames work. People don't invent their own nicknames, otherwise the world would be full of people with names like Rocky, Flint, Blade and sundry other heroic and machismo handles. Peter started off by being called Peter the Porker and then it was changed to Porky Pisces, with a subsequent shortening to Porky.

Porky was picked upon by everyone who worked down the engine room, particularly by the fourth engineer, a pockmarked mean-looking man who tormented him mercilessly. The fourth organised the most horrific 'crossing the date line' ceremony for Porky. I was working on the lifeboats one afternoon, checking the equipment, when I heard screaming coming from the main deck. I climbed down and walked over to the rails to see what was going on. Porky was being heaved down the deck naked by a group of engineers: the group comprised the fourth, a couple of fivers (fifth engineers) and several engineer cadets. Porky was half dragged and half marched along by the two fivers, while the others walked behind and flicked towels at his backside whenever he resisted too much, causing him to howl with pain and leap forward. When they reached the big manifolds used to connect the hoses to pump the cargo ashore, they pushed him down onto on the deck so that he was sitting in a patch of sticky oil. Two cadets held his head securely, while the fourth engineer took out a pair of scissors and proceeded to hack off Porky's hair in chunks. Porky screeched, they all laughed. When the barber work was done, Porky looked like a badly plucked chicken. One of the fivers then took a tub of alvania grease and used a large brush to coat Porky's newly cropped head. Alvania is a thin khaki-coloured grease that can get into every pore. Once Porky's dome was greased, his legs were pulled apart and the fiver gave a liberal coating to his genital area, before they flipped him over and stuffed a large plug of grease into his anus. As a finale, two buckets of filthy water were heaved over him. They let him go, they scattered. Porky howled with rage and humiliation. He lurched to his feet, he skidded on grease, he crashed back down with a solid whack that carried up to the boat deck. He lay there winded and wounded and weeping. The ceremonial party stood back a distance. They laughed cruelly although the laughter started to die in their throats as they looked at the pitiful sight that Porky had become. They turned and went aft into the accommodation. I walked down the ladder to check if he was injured, but a couple of sailors were already standing over him. Porky waved his arms furiously and screamed obscenities, telling them to get away. He got back to his feet and dragged his greasy, bruised body back to his cabin. We didn't see him in the bar or the dining saloon for several days.

It was a harsh and unpleasant episode. The fourth engineer had shown his nasty side by organising it, but the others were just as bad for joining in. And perhaps I was too, for watching, along with most of the other officers who had been looking on. Although there was an unspoken rule not to interfere with high spirits, I felt diminished and grubby that day.

The voyage across the Pacific drifted from one quiet day to another; the crossing the Date Line ceremony was the only really enlivening event. I relaxed into my position. It wasn't that stressful. There was no traffic and very few landfalls: celestial navigation was the order of the day.

Celestial navigation works like this. Imagine the world is wrapped within a giant sphere 1,000 miles away from the surface. Actually, it doesn't have to be 1,000 miles away – it could be 50 miles or a million miles away; the distance is not the point, just imagine the sphere. Imagine then, all the heavenly bodies are sitting on the surface of the sphere as if they were the same distance away from the Earth: the sun, the moon, Venus, Polaris, Canopus, Sirius, Alpha Centauri, Saturn, every star, every planet, the whole lot. First, we would estimate the ship's position is on the chart. Second, we used a sextant to measure the angle between the horizon and a heavenly body as it sat on the surface of the sphere. Third, we calculated what the angle should be if we were at the estimated position. Last, the difference in the two angles was how far away we were from our estimated position. What we ended up with was a line on the chart on which we were positioned somewhere.

In the day we used the sun as the celestial body, and sometimes the moon. At dawn and dusk we used the stars. At night we didn't use anything because we couldn't see the horizon, because it was dark. When we measured the angle, it was known as a 'sight.' Star sights were more accurate because we would take half a dozen in a few minutes and then produce a lot of lines that would cross to give an accurate position. Sun sights were accurate enough, although we were only using one celestial body, taking sights progressively as the sun's relative movement tracked across the sky to give position lines that gradually changed direction, which in turn allowed us to get a cross and fix the position. Every day, as long as the sky was clear we would find an accurate position at dawn and dusk from the stars, and would find a reasonably accurate position from the sun at noon.

There were other ways to discover where we were, such as radio directional finders. Dotted around the globe are radio stations that pulse out long-range signals. We would tune in our radio directional finder to the radio signal and read off the compass bearing, then draw a line from the radio station outwards, knowing that we were somewhere on that line. Cross it with a sun sight, and presto, we had a position. Finally, even though the Pacific is huge, there are islands, large and small, mostly small, that we would encounter from time to time, to give us a land bearing. All of these things allowed us to progress fairly safely across the Pacific.

On a couple of occasions we encountered ships that made a point of altering course to come within a couple of miles of us. As they did so, they would start flashing the Aldis lamp, which sent out a light that was bright enough to see in the daylight. On seeing this, we would switch on the VHF ship-to-shore radio and hear the other ship calling us on Channel 16, the main contact channel. The conversation would be along the following lines:

'Calling black and white tanker, calling black and white tanker. Can you hear me? Over.'

The person calling sounded slightly excitable.

'This is the British ship *Horomya*. I can hear you loud and clear. Over.'

'*Horomya*, good morning. This is *Eastern Promise*. Where are you bound? Over.'

'*Eastern Promise*, this is *Horomya*. We are bound for Yokohama from Panama. Where are you bound? Over.'

'*Horomya*, this is *Eastern Promise*. We are bound for San Diego from Taiwan. We would like to check our position with you. What is your position? Over.'

The reality was that the *Eastern Promise* had absolutely no idea where she was. The navigation strategy had been to set off towards her destination and then waylay every ship she came across on the voyage to beg a position, which would then allow her to set a new course until she came across another ship. This was generally because no one on board was capable of navigating once the ship was out of sight of land. The captain would sometimes have a reasonable idea, but not always. While these ships went along the coast, everything was fine, as they could follow the landmarks in the day and the lighthouses at night. But deep sea voyages meant tackling celestial navigation and the mysteries of the sextant, which was a step too far for many crews. It must have been very frustrating when two of these lost and wandering ships came across each other, the blind meeting the blind, neither able to help, and both moving on to feel their way forward and hope they met a properly navigated ship before long.

I enjoyed the quiet days at sea. The morning watch was idle; apart from taking a couple of sun sights, I paced the deck from one bridge wing to another. Brian, the second mate, would come up at about 0930 to take a sun sight and potter in the chartroom for twenty minutes or so. The second mate is the officer responsible for navigation on a ship. We would chat for a while and then he would go. Sometimes the Old Man would make an appearance mid-morning, smoke his pipe for a bit, tell me a few tall tales and then disappear. The steward would bring coffee at 1015. There was generally no need for a lookout in the day; I would be the lookout. The watch sailor would be working around the bridge area, a bit of painting, cleaning, perhaps canvas sewing. Nothing too grubby, nothing too far away in case he was needed for bridge duties. The radar was turned off, there was limited noise, only the gentle shuddering of the ship as she was propelled through the water, and the background strumming of the thick wire stays as they vibrated in tune with the engines. If the crew was working on deck there would be the clatter of their work and the sound of their voices carrying up. If I leant over the bridge wing I would hear the hiss of the white wake as we cut through the sea and rocked gently along in the swell.

At night it was quieter still. Everyone was inside, there was only me and the lookout and the dark. If the moon was up it would shine its light on the rolling sea and show the white wake tipping back to fall along the hull. If the moon was down and there were no clouds, the stars showed as stark white lights against the black cloth of the sky, the brighter first-magnitude stars casting their reflections in the dark sea.

As we went further north and came closer to Japan, the air started to turn chill and the Old Man gave orders to change uniform from tropical whites to blues; I had bought a new set of blues in doeskin, the half-diamond gold stripe gleaming newly on the sleeve of the jacket. I admired myself when I put it on.

The east coast of Japan is one of the busiest seaways in the world, and the traffic began to pick up more and more the nearer we approached. We finally sighted the higher points of land of the main Japanese island of Honshu on the morning of the twenty-second day out from Panama. Several hours later, we closed on the coast to slip between Oshima Island and Nojimazaki Point, before swinging north-east and into the Uraga Channel, the entrance to Tokyo Bay. Down in the engine room, the engineers were gathered together on the plates in front of the oil burners, ready for whatever manoeuvre might be required. As we steamed up the Uraga Channel, we encountered ships coming and going in all directions, both large deep sea vessels and small coasters. All the coasters and the regular deep sea visitors were used to close quarters engagement, although I wasn't. It was nerve-racking stuff. I could feel myself age. I was pleased when the pilot came on board to take us to our waiting berth at Yokohama.

Everyone on board the *Horomya* was a bit sea-stretched. The land seemed strange to us, alien even. The sea was home, the sea was familiar. We were used to rolling on a long Pacific swell, not walking on solid ground. We took ten minutes to change our sea legs. The Panama

Canal is not a place that had allowed any time ashore and so Curaçao was the last time anyone had stepped off the ship, twenty-five days beforehand. We started to eye Yokohama covetously. It had a good reputation, one of the great Japanese seaports with a renowned crop of sailor's bars. I had been there twice before. We were due to be alongside for two days, discharging over half the cargo before going down the coast for further stops at Nagoya and Kobe.

Most of the crew had placed an order for hefty subscriptions of money from the Chief Steward. One British pound bought about 700 yen in those days, which had weakened from 850 to the pound since I was first there as a cadet, but was still good value for a decent run ashore. I resolved to be careful and avoid raucous behaviour. I didn't want to blot my copybook so early in my officer career.

I went ashore at the end of my eight-to-midnight watch, after four hours on deck supervising the discharge of cargo. I was in the company of Mike the fourth engineer, Porky's tormenter, and Mike's junior watch-keeper, the fifth engineer. I didn't particularly like either of them, nor they me, probably, but we were on a common watch so it made sense to stick together. Not that Yokohama had even the vaguest hint of menace.

The three of us camped down in the first bar we came to and guzzled Kirin beer until two o'clock, then moved further into the gut of the bar area to find a more animated place. The bars were all much the same: small, warm, too warm, low stools, smiling barmaid, a couple of twittering hostesses, a flat-eyed Japanese man in the corner, smoking and watching us. A mix of Japanese and Western music was being played, the lights were low, there were usually two or three other groups of people, mostly from ships, merry people, some singing along with the music. We ordered Kirin beer, with an occasional Suntory whisky chaser. As the evening wore on, Mike confided in me how he had cultivated an unreasonable hatred for Porky when he had first came on board, but that now he was ashamed and sorry for him after the crossing the Date Line episode. Every time he tried to make amends, though, he was rebuffed, Porky blanked him.

'I mean, what do I do, Simon? What can I do?' He slurred, he hung his head close to me.

'Aye, Fourth, what can you do?' said the fiver.

'I don't know, Mike,' I replied. 'Probably nothing. What's the problem anyway? You hate him, he hates you.' I smiled at the barmaid, she smiled back. She was gorgeous.

'No! No-oo-oh. No, no, no, no, no! It's not like that, I don't hate the fat, smelly bastard. I used to, but I don't now. I don't like him, uh-uh, but I don't hate him. Yet he treats me like I don't exist. Like an outcast. Like a leper. Why? Why is he like that?'

'Aye, Fourth. Can't understand the man,' agreed the fiver.

'Who cares anyway, Mike?' I said. The barmaid seemed to be raising her eyebrows at me. Was my luck in? I nodded back, slowly, suavely, mysteriously. I smiled. She smiled.

'I care! Because he's an ungrateful, fat, smelly, short-arsed bastard! I try to be friends and he bloody well ignores me! The guy stinks, he's got bad breath, he's got bugger-all personality, yet I try and be his friend and he won't have anything to do with me! Can you believe it? Fat bastard!' Mike was working himself into a state of true outrage at Porky's bad manners.

'Aye, Fourth, I can't believe it either.' The fifth engineer nodded.

I snorted. 'I can believe it, Mike. You humiliated him by dragging him down the deck bollock-naked, you shaved his head then stuffed grease up his arse. Of course he hates you. He's probably plotting to kill you.' The barmaid was coming towards me, smiling. I resolved to dump Mike and the fiver and enjoy the company of the barmaid. I looked at her, smiling back.

'You think so? You think so? He's goin' to kill me? The bastard! After all I've done! After all the effort I've made, and he wants to kill me!' He shook his head uncomprehendingly.

'Aye, Fourth,' said the fiver.

The barmaid plonked three more bottles of beer in front of me. 'Ah-so! Three thousan' yen, pliss!' She held out her hand. Romance flew, into the cash till.

I returned to the *Horomya* at four-thirty, dizzy but able to walk straight. I thought: 'Three hours' intense sleep should put me right.' It did, more or less.

After our stint on the Japanese coast we headed down to Singapore to load the ship again. We received our orders two days out: Nha Bè in the Saigon river, with a full cargo of jet fuel. The officers and crew cheered when this was announced. Vietnam was a war zone, so we would be in and out in less than two days although we would all qualify for the minimum war bonus of five days on double pay. Only the Old Man looked sombre.

When we reached Pulau Bukom, the oil refinery island off the southern coast of Singapore, the ship was put on a war footing. This didn't amount to much: sandbags were stacked around the bridge wings, the lifeboats were run in and out and checked over, the bridge was issued with helmets and flak-jackets for the watch-keepers, and that was that. We loaded our lethal cocktail for thirty-six hours, taking on board enough jet fuel for the South Vietnamese fighter planes to loop and swoop and fail to hit barn doors for a good fortnight.

Three days later we lay waiting at the mouth of the Saigon river, waiting for the river pilot to come on board. No one had their flak-jackets on. We had picked out our helmets, though, and would wear them when we went out on the bridge wings once the ship entered the river. This was late 1973. The Americans had signed a ceasefire with North Vietnam at the beginning of the year to allow the US troops to leave and finally get out of a long and ultimately fruitless war. President Johnson had sent troops into Vietnam in 1965, with high hopes and flags flying, to prevent the dominos falling. The domino effect theorised that if Vietnam fell to the communists then one by one the other countries of South-East Asia would also fall and the whole region would be lost to Western influence and control. Australia would also be threatened. America was rabidly anti-communist at the top. Once the war started in earnest, the US saturation-bombed the North, the strategy failed. US military superiority in the jungle couldn't defeat the Viet Cong. The Viet Cong were kings of the jungle, they could fight for a week on a bag of rice. The USSR and China funded the Cong from behind, fighting a proxy war. US public sympathy faltered, too many Americans were being killed. Outrages spooked them, the My Lai massacre shocked the country. College campuses exploded with protests. Everyone wanted the troops out. The USA lost nearly 60,000 men by the end, the North Vietnamese lost perhaps twenty times that number. President Nixon came to power and built up the South Vietnam forces as a prelude to leaving them to finish the war on their own. He agreed a ceasefire with North Vietnam leader Ho Chi Minh. The North Vietnamese ignored the ceasefire, it had no meaning for them. The South Vietnamese were now being pressed, the USA was getting out anyway.

We arrived in December with our 18,000-ton cargo of jet fuel to fill up the air force. We waited for the pilot outside the entrance of the brown river. He eventually came out on a fast launch, escorted by a fast gunboat. He was small man, wearing a gun, energetic, serious, full of Americanisms. He moved the pilot chair to the front of the bridge, sat with his feet up on the edge of the radar, smoking a cigar. The Old Man's face went tight at his lack of manners but he said nothing. We set off and entered the mouth of the Saigon river, the water was the colour of flour-thickened gravy. The trees and bush were cleared back for 500 yards from the river's edge, to stop Viet Cong sitting in the upper branches and lobbing grenades down the funnels of passing ships. The company had suffered several attacks on its ships over the past few years, one had been mined and sunk, others had been hit by rockets. We were all tense, there was no conversation, we snapped at each other down the ranks. The radio would periodically erupt in a blast of Vietnamese, the pilot would jump up and grab the handset and shout a staccato response, a machine-gun quick reply.

The river twisted and turned. There was no life on either side, just bleak ruined land for 500 yards then impenetrable jungle we couldn't see through. We nosed along at 8 knots, carving out a small bow wave that broke against the banks of the river behind us. Then there was a screaming from the radio, much louder this time. The pilot leapt from his chair. He shouted at the Old Man, 'They're attacking!'

A rocket whizzed overhead, high and fast, heading towards Nha Bè, heading towards where we were heading. Another rocket, lower this time, closer. Another. A roaring whoosh. More screaming from the radio. More screaming back from the pilot.

The pilot pointed: 'Look! They've hit the refinery!' Then he carried on screaming at the radio in Vietnamese.

We could see a dark plume rising into the air ahead of us, thick curds of arrow-straight black smoke, oil smoke.

The Old Man snatched the handset from the pilot. 'Tell me what's happening.'

The pilot brought himself under control.

'The Cong are attacking the refinery. They're attacking now. They're attacking with troops and rockets. We can't go there. We can't go on.' The pilot spoke fast but with conviction. He was on the edge of panic.

The Old Man said: 'Take us out.'

The pilot took control of himself. 'Yes, Captain.'

The pilot and the Old Man worked on the turning manoeuvre together. The pilot knew the right stretch of river bank to use for the turn, it was a few hundred yards ahead. As we approached, he steered the ship across to the left bank of the river, then went hard-a-starboard. As the ship swung towards the opposite bank, the engines were put on half astern to take off the speed, then back to dead slow ahead, then dead slow astern, then dead slow ahead. The rudder effect and the forward engine movements pushed the ship round to starboard, clockwise, the astern movements stopped us from ploughing into the bank, while the propeller, turning anti-clockwise when going astern, pushed the stern round and accelerated the swing. The ship was being manoeuvred to perform the tightest of turns. The bow nudged into the soft bank and we felt the swing halt. The engines were put dead slow astern, then slow astern. Nothing happened, just a juddering that ran through the hull. My breathing was laboured, the air felt as thick as treacle. It didn't take much imagination to think what the Viet Cong would do if they overran the Nha Bè refinery a few miles downriver and then came across a ship full of jet fuel stuck into the river bank. The Old Man walked round the pilot and over to the telegraph where I was standing and rang full astern twice, double full astern, as much as the engineers could give. The ship rumbled and shook, the engine laboured, the wire stays rattled. The *Horomya* shot out from the bank backwards, like a cork released.

The Old Man shouted: 'Stop engines! Half ahead! Hard-a-starboard!'

I shouted back from the telegraph: 'Stop engines! Half ahead!' And swung the handle.

The quartermaster shouted: 'Hard-a-starboard!' And wound the wheel round.

The Old Man said: 'Take her out, Pilot.'

The pilot replied, with a slight shame-face at being upstaged: 'OK, Captain.'

The Old Man was my hero. The pilot straightened the ship and we headed downriver and out into the safety of the South China Sea, the grisly fate of Nha Bè receding behind us.

I arrived home on a cold late February day and booked in my referral resit, giving myself another two months to absorb everything readable about meteorology. My parents quizzed me on my Far East trip, having received a telegram from the company a few weeks previously, which read: '*Disregard all press reports, all crew of* Horomya *alive and well.*' That caused them concern, having seen nothing in the newspapers or on television to give them reason to believe I was anything other than alive and well. My father contacted the company and the press agencies and found out about the Nha Bè attack and the escape of two British ships, one of which was the *Horomya*. I downplayed the episode, I didn't want them worrying about me.

My second visit to Ensign Street was altogether different from the first. I had to attend on the Tuesday afternoon for meteorology only, a two-hour exam. In my trip on the *Horomya* I had read the meteorology examination bible, *Meteorology for Mariners*, four times from cover to cover, as well as all the other books I had bought. I had managed to obtain twelve past exam papers and had memorised every question and answer. I went into the examination room feeling it would be difficult to fail, not impossible but difficult. I could always be ambushed by some completely new and previously unknown set of questions. I breezed the exam. When the results came through I didn't absorb the actual mark, I only knew that I had passed.

The relief was palpable. Three and a half years, plus study leave plus a follow-on trip as uncertificated third mate, and I had finally made it. My new certificate was eight inches wide by six inches tall, fixed into a hard folding case on which was embossed in gold lettering: Certificate of Competency as Second Mate (Foreign Going). I could legally sail as second officer of a British flag ship, although the protocol and expectation of most British shipping companies at the time was that officers served a rank below their certificate. With a British Second Mate's Certificate, I could obtain a Liberian or Panamanian First Mate's Certificate on simple application. A lot of people went through a full career at sea holding nothing higher than a Second Mate's Certificate.

I celebrated in the time-honoured way with a night on the town. I looked in on the London School of Maritime Studies for a celebration partner and found Roger, one of my old cadet colleagues from Plymouth. We started in Mayfair and worked our way through the West End. We drank recklessly, we told loud stories, we made a racket wherever we went, we were thrown out of several places, we charmed girls, we made and lost friends, we spent all our money. One morning, after an all-night session with Roger, I had to borrow the tube fare home from my brother Peter when he arrived at work the next day. I lurked outside his bank in Whitehall like a tramp, desperate not to miss him. He laughed when he saw me, and gave me a fiver. I went home and slept until lunchtime.

While I was on leave, I decided I had better learn to drive. I booked the first lesson and applied for my test, citing that I was a merchant seaman and had to get back to sea and so was available for any test at any test centre at any time. I applied on Monday and received a response on the Friday telling me that my test was arranged for the following Wednesday in Harrow. I had only taken two lessons. I didn't know how to drive. I went down to the driving school and booked ten lessons over the next three days. The driving school used me as a project for future boasting, determined I should pass. They cancelled lessons for other learners, my lessons often over-ran into someone else's. Sometimes there would be a second instructor in the back, shouting encouragement.

I breezed the test. I bought an ancient red Mini for £50. It was a heap. Peter and I roared around West London in my heap. On the second week, I drove it into the wall while pulling into the car park of the Coach and Horses in Ickenham. We laughed and went into the pub, my car was a heap anyway. I loved my new freedom, I could drive and I had money. My motorbike lay forgotten in the back of the garage.

Roger and I had wild nights out in the West End. We always drove, usually in two cars, often racing each other. The breathalyser had been introduced a few years earlier, but breath testing was still in its infancy and people weren't inhibited from drinking and driving. The culture of the day was to drive to pubs, drink and drive home again. If I was drunk at the end of the night, I used to drive home slowly, keeping a distance of two feet from the kerb, window open, concentrating as best I could. It was only when I had difficulty in walking after leaving the pub that I would generally leave the car behind and get a lift home. Late one night Roger and I had a race down the Mall from Buckingham Palace; I went the wrong way around Trafalgar Square after we shot through Admiralty Arch. Roger won, I bought the next round.

May arrived. The sea beckoned. I received a telegram: *Join S.S. Medora in Brest as third officer. Fly London to Brest Friday 10th May. Rail warrant and air ticket despatched today. Attend office for medical examination Monday 6th 10:00. Congrats on passing 2nd Mates. Rgds.*

Regards indeed. They were sending me to a supertanker, a 200,000-ton monster. A ship so big it could only go alongside in a handful of berths in the world. My intent to move to general cargo ships had become submerged in the euphoria of passing my Second Mate's Certificate. I resolved this would be my last trip on a tanker. I would hand in my notice to the captain before I signed off, to ensure there would be no going back.

In Brest, there was no one at the airport to meet me when I arrived late in the evening; I booked into a hotel near the port and had a good feed and a bottle of wine. I tracked down the ship's agent the next morning so he could pay.

The *Medora* was so large the bow was 1,000 feet from the bridge. It was dubbed a supertanker, or a VLCC; very large crude carrier. The ship was in dry dock having a complete overhaul and an Inert Gag (IG) system fitted. In the evening, I would go ashore with the other officers in a pack where we would wolf seafood and drink wine. The stay in dock, all two weeks of it, was instructive, but the work was near non-existent because of French union labour rules, which meant that we hung around doing little or nothing. The Chinese crew played mah-jong every night, a few went into penury. Brest itself was tame fare, I was itching to leave. The end of the month came and we received our payslips from England. I was outraged to find that all the subsistence pay I had been paid during my study period had been reclaimed now that I had passed, leaving me near broke. I questioned this with the Old Man, who told me it was hard luck and I should stop moaning. I fumed, I decided to dislike the Old Man for not making a stand for me, I became even more resolved to leave the company.

All the accommodation on the *Medora* was at the aft end, unlike the centre castle tankers I had served on up to now. The accommodation block was so high there was a lift running through it from the depths of the engine room to the bridge. There were two bicycles on board; the officer's had gears. I never used the bikes. There was automation galore, the loading and discharging was mostly done from a control room, no more running round the deck. Once we left Brest and set off down the Channel, the most disconcerting thing was the movement of the hull. As we stood on the bridge and looked forward, we could actually see the body of the ship bending in the middle as we went through the waves. It wasn't some optical illusion – we could actually see the forward part of the deck bending downwards. When I first saw this happening, I thought the ship was in peril. Once I became used to the movement, though, it became quite relaxing. Ships of this size couldn't be built too stiff, otherwise they would crack when they needed to bend.

We had no cargo at this stage, only a few tanks filled with water ballast to put of bit of weight into the ship and lower the centre of gravity; if this wasn't done the ship would stand too high in the water and become unstable. The draft, the depth of the vessel, when in ballast was about the same as an ordinary size deep sea ship. This meant that we had a reasonable amount of freedom to move about the ocean. It was a different story when the ship was fully laden; the draft would then be over sixty-five feet, which meant that we had to stay in the deep-water shipping lanes and could not move outside without going aground. This restriction produced a lot of heart-stopping moments when there was a crossing ship. If the ship was crossing port to starboard then she was the one to keep clear, if one was coming from starboard to port then it was for us to take the action. In either event, we couldn't manoeuvre. When we were to give way, we slowed right down; when the other ship was to give way, we sweated.

Everything was huge on the *Medora*: the anchors were the size of small houses, the links of the anchor cables were big enough to anchor smaller ships. The tanks were cavernous, cathedral-like. When I had stood at the bottom of one of them in dry-dock and looked up, the opening at deck level looked like a large star in the distant night sky. At the end of each watch, the bridge officer always had the job of doing rounds. This meant a walk around the ship to see everything was in order. A walk around the *Medora* was a long hike.

We were bound for Mina-al-Ahmadi in the Persian Gulf. The Suez Canal was still closed following the Egyptian blockade that had been set up after the 1967 Arab–Israeli war, and all shipping for the East went round the Cape of Good Hope, round the bottom of Africa. This was academic to the *Medora*, as we were too big to fit through the canal anyway.

We carried a squad of additional personnel on the first voyage round, to complete and test the fitting of the new IG system. IG was the latest in tanker wizardry and was founded on a simple principle: you can only have an explosion if there is oxygen to feed the ignition. No oxygen, no ignition, no explosion. Inert gas was pumped into the tanks when the cargo was discharged, rendering the air too mean to allow any ignition. When a crude oil carrier has finished discharging her cargo, she is in her most dangerous phase; the interior of the tanks full is of highly explosive air, one spark could ignite the whole lot.

As we steamed south toward the Cape, we were safe because we had just come out of dock and had tanks full of clean air. The IG team laboured away to fit the new system. Essentially, the inert gas was obtained from the fumes emanating from the boiler flue, which were then cleaned in a scrubber tower and manipulated to the right temperature and pressure before being pumped into the tanks. The IG team were on a deadline to have everything completed by the time we reached the Persian Gulf. They would have plenty of time for the work because the oil crisis was in full swing and ships were mostly steaming at half speed to conserve fuel, following the quadrupling of the oil price by the OPEC nations.

These additional IG staff should have made for a more lively ship. Most of them were seconded ship's engineers and so the officer's bar tended to be fuller than usual, and more lively. Forty-five days at sea is a long time. The only breaks from the ordinary routine were the helicopter drops at the Canary Islands and the Cape of Good Hope. The helicopters brought and removed people, fresh foods, replacement films, beer and mail; it was a fleeting burst of excitement that was over quickly. We then plodded on. Some officers liked serving on supertankers. These were the people who weren't interested in going ashore, who wanted to save money. For a shore hound like me, who at that stage regarded life at sea as an interesting way to travel between different and exciting parts of the world, it was like being in prison. I was a caged bird – I would have moulted if I'd had feathers. I sought relief in the bar, although found little. This new supertanker environment had small emphasis on enjoyment. I tried to invoke the camaraderie of the bar, which meant indulging in a good amount of drinking. The others humoured me but rarely joined in to the same extent. This was a new professional world and I began to be marked as a fool and an excessive drinker. The Old Man gave me a warning. I sulked in my cabin, my massive air-conditioned cabin, and drank cold beer and smoked too much and pined for small ship days on the *Horomya*. The food was poor, I disliked more people than I liked. I yearned for exotic parts of the world to explore. The exotic parts while on the *Medora* were destined to be Mina al Ahmadi and the Rotterdam oil terminal.

I found a kindred spirit in the fourth engineer, my parallel eight-to-twelve watch-keeper in the engine room. He was a diminutive Geordie who hated VLCCs as much as me. We used to meet after the midnight watch and sit in his cabin and drink beer and vent our dislike and vow to leave the company at the end of the voyage and never set foot on a tanker again. Sometimes we were still there when the twelve–to-four watch-keepers finished. The second mate and the third engineer would come in and have a beer with us, in our then incoherent state, and encourage us to go to bed. The second mate was eccentric, he wore a beret and liked to strut up and down the bridge during the afternoon watch singing bad arias, or badly singing arias perhaps, at the top of his voice. People said he had been on VLCCs too long; he had tankeritis. I found him pretentious and a bore.

I had my twenty-first birthday on board the *Medora* in the Persian Gulf. It was sad affair. The nutty second mate sang Happy Birthday to me at midnight in his best Caruso. The Geordie fourth gathered a few people after midnight: him, the chief engineer, a couple of fivers, the two deck cadets, Sparks. They all stayed for half an hour, after which it was just me and Geordie, bemoaning our fate in the usual way.

The next day, the Old Man came onto the bridge in the middle of the morning. I could see by his mannerisms that he wanted to strike up a conversation.

He said: 'Well, Third Mate, key to the door, eh?'

I said: 'Pardon, sir?'

'Key to the door! Key to the door!'

*The SS* Medora *at sea.*
*Used with the kind permission of www.fotoflite.com.*

I didn't know what he was talking about. 'I'm sorry, sir. I don't know what you're talking about.'

'Key to the door! Key to the door!' He parroted. 'You know! You know! Your twenty-first birthday.'

'Oh, yes.'

'That's your youth over with, Third Mate. Time to grow up. Old enough to vote now, you know.'

I thought: 'Silly old bugger, the voting age changed to eighteen five years ago.'

He walked back into the chart room, having given me my pep talk.

I muttered under my breath: 'Thanks for the bloody party.'

His head darted back round the door. 'Don't be so damned cheeky!'

The Persian Gulf in the summer was hot enough to roast meat outside. I clocked 110°F in the shade at eight o'clock one morning. In the full sun in the middle of the day it hurt to breathe, it felt as if I had stuck my head into an open furnace.

VLCCs take a long time to bring to berth. They have to creep along at sub-snailspace, otherwise the sheer momentum of the ship's mass becomes impossible to check and she will just plough on through everything in her path. So it took seven hours to moor the *Medora* in Mina-al-Ahmadi. I was on the fo'c'sle head with the crew, there was nowhere to hide from the sun, nowhere to escape the inferno. My pores opened and the sweat rushed out of me, snatched into evaporation as it hit the air. The chief mate used a mule train of stewards to ferry buckets of water to keep us alive, we drunk it down like crazed animals, slurping and gurgling before we poured the dregs over our heads and demanded more. There was no scrap of shade, just blinding sun and waves of heat bouncing off the steel, everything was too hot to touch. I wanted to leap over the side into the gulf waters. I could feel madness being cooked into me.

In the event, we didn't just travel between Rotterdam and the Persian Gulf but instead loaded at Mina for Singapore, with further orders to make round trips between Singapore and Halul Island, just inside the Gulf. The discharge port of Singapore had greater promise than the Rotterdam oil terminal. On arrival in Singapore we dropped the hook in the deep water anchorage and waited for three days. The agent arranged a fast launch into Singapore city and I went ashore after my watch to enjoy a brief respite and blow off some steam. As we were leaving we broke down: two days more in port. Then the IG system packed up: three days more. I whooped it up in Singapore every night, taking in the bars in Anson Road and the wild street market in Bugis Street. The fourth engineer came with me twice, but he was usually dragooned with the rest of the engineers into helping make the ship work again. I was quite happy going ashore on my own, making friends for the night, catching the launch to shore at half past midnight and getting back for breakfast. I slept in the afternoons.

We did three trips across the Indian Ocean betwixt our poles of Halul Island and Singapore. The eastern crossing from the Gulf was the more uncomfortable, the *Medora* had a deep and ponderous roll that caused things to break loose. Crashes and screams came from all around the ship; everything had to be lashed down. I kept tabs on the BBC World Service: Vietnam was hotting up and two company ships had been mined, no one killed but a lot of damage. All Merchant Navy officers received a massive pay rise in the middle of the year. The industry wanted more people at sea to address the crippling shortages, particularly of junior officers. We had the first decent party on board that night, to celebrate our newfound wealth.

On my third trip back across the Indian Ocean, we received a telegram saying that I would be relieved as we passed Ras Al Khaimah, Dubai; a launch would pick me up and deposit the relief third mate at the same time. I shouted with joy, the world's weight slipped from my shoulders. The handover would be quick, a handshake on deck as he stepped off the ladder and over the rails, then I in turn would go over the rails and down the ladder to the launch. I wrote out copious handover notes. I also wrote out my resignation and handed it to Old Man before dinner one evening with an inner sigh, knowing I would have to suffer a mighty and righteous lecture about thinking of the future, keeping on the straight and narrow and acting responsibly. He surprised me.

'Why are you leaving?' He looked at me quizzically.

'I feel I would like to gain experience in other types of vessel, sir,' I trotted out the guff I had written in the letter.

'Oh come on Third Mate. I wasn't born yesterday. Why are you leaving?'

I hesitated, then said: 'These ships aren't for me, Captain. I know it's the way of the future and one day all ships will be bigger and turn around quicker, but a life at sea doesn't have to be … this. At least, not just yet. I hate it.'

I waited.

He said: 'And where will you go?'

'General cargo. I want to serve on conventional general cargo ships while they're still around.'

He said nothing for a bit, and then, 'Good for you.'

I said nothing.

He continued, 'Sometimes I wonder what young man in his right mind would want to come on one of these things. It's all right for an old fellow like me, I've had my fill. I suppose it's OK for someone who wants to stay aboard and save some money.'

He shook his head, then continued. 'I spent the first fifteen years at sea with Andrew Weir Shipping, tramping the world in pre-war general cargo ships. We used to be away for up to two years. We'd be three, sometimes four weeks in port at a time. Aye, they were good days. They've all but disappeared.'

I never knew about his early life. I said: 'I never knew.'

He got up and returned with two cans of beer and cracked them open, passing one to me. 'No, you wouldn't. Cheers.'

We talked, I mostly listened. We drank, but my thirst was for the tales he told me.

I left the *Medora* in Rotterdam. The Old Man wished me good luck. I thanked him for all his advice. He had taken to coming up to the bridge on the night watch and telling me stories of his life as a young man in the 1940s and 1950s.

When I was back in London, the company asked me to come into the head office, where they endeavoured to change my mind. They told me that I was a 'company man', which made me want to leave even more. They told me I would enjoy speedy promotion if I stayed, which I didn't care about. They told me I ought to be loyal to the company that had trained me so diligently, I almost laughed. They eventually accepted I would be leaving, they told me to come back if I discovered that the world I was looking for was not what I expected it to be. I thanked them. I thought: 'I'll never be back.'

Roger was in town. We picked up where we had left off. I hired a car, a Morris Marina; I had pots of money after my imprisonment on the *Medora*. We alternated between visiting the smart pubs of Middlesex and Surrey, working our charms on girls when the occasions arose, then breezing into Soho and the West End for a full-steam blowout. We blew our money on drinks that we left, on food that we didn't eat, on girls who we didn't care about, in clubs where we stayed for twenty minutes before moving on elsewhere.

I made it plain to Roger that I was going to find a general cargo company to work for. He agreed to help. We breezed into shipping offices and asked for jobs. They all wanted us, two newly certificated officers, we were gold in the officer shortage of the mid-1970s. We wandered around Bevis Marks in the City and scoped plaques on doorways for names that promised adventure: Hector Whaling, Orient & India, Southern Seas Shipping. We went inside them and asked to see the personnel officer. He was always perplexed, then did his best to cling on to this sudden potential windfall. We were offered jobs everywhere we went. One afternoon, after a long session in a City bar plotting our strategy, we went into the offices of one well-known shipping company, I think it might have been Blue Star although I can't really remember. We were shown into the personnel officer's office, he had been out over lunchtime too. We spent twenty minutes waffling at each other, making claims and promises that no one could keep. The personnel man was keen to show us his ship staffing organisation system, he had invented it himself. On the wall was a large cork board, on which were the names of the several dozen ships in the fleet. Underneath each ship's name were pinned the names of the officers serving on board, with a coloured pin next to each name. He explained that a green pin denoted they had recently joined, a blue pin indicated they were mid-voyage, an orange pin showed that they were due to be relieved and a red pin indicated they were overdue a relief. There were a lot of red pins, which explained how happy he was that we had walked into his lair. He reeled off stories, lying through his teeth, of what a wonderful company it was to work for. As he did so, he gesticulated wildly at his board, his pride and joy. His hand slapped into the board and it came off the wall, crashing onto the floor, names and pins scattered everywhere. He let out a plaintive howl. We helped him hang the board up again. Half the names and most of the pins were on the floor. He grabbed a handful of names and started stuffing under them frantically under various ships, plonking in a coloured pin at the same time. He seemed on the edge of panic, talking to himself, stabbing pins randomly. Roger and I looked at each other and sloped off.

Eventually, I didn't sign for any of the London shipping companies. Instead I went north to Edinburgh, where I signed for an old established company of general cargo liners based in Leith. They had a good name, they had a fleet of conventional cargo ships, they were a traditional old-time shipping company, they ran a service between the UK and the Far East. It was perfect for me. The pay was lower than tankers but that would always be the case. Tankers paid the most, they needed to. The Leith company told me that I would receive my joining orders within ten days if I passed my medical. I would initially be assigned to one of their ships around the UK and European coast to familiarise myself with general cargo ships, then sent on the Far East run. I craved to be back at sea.

# 3

# *Slow Passage*

My first sight of the SS *Benalbanach* was in Antwerp. As I approached the wharf in a taxi, she was sitting high in the water; a thin line of dark smoke rising straight up into the clear blue sky from her funnel. The *Benalbanach* looked as if she could have been lifted from Somerset Maugham's ode to the Far East, *On a Chinese Screen.* Even though she had been built several years after the end of the Second World War, she had the old-fashioned clumpy look of a pre-war Eastern liner: straight funnel, accommodation castle with covered walkways that ran all the way around , high straight masts, wooden hatch covers with canvas tops, four derricks to each hatch. The superstructures were painted mostly white, the hull was grey, the funnel yellow, the decks, derricks and posts a sort of brown-orange. My stomach jumped as I walked up the gangway. I felt I was walking into a chapter of a book by Conrad, Somerset Maugham or Jack London.

My trip on the *Benalbanach* was intended to be a short one to introduce me to the world of general cargo ships. The Leith company ran a scheduled service of cargo liners to the Far East and back. The main Far East ports were Singapore, Penang, Djakarta, Bangkok, Manila, Keelung, Kaohsiung, Hong Kong and then north to the big Japanese ports of Yokohama, Nagoya and Kobe. In addition, there were a number of smaller places on the service, although these were not called into with the same regularity. The ships went out with industrial wares from the UK and Europe, discharged and then loaded to return with hatches full of raw materials, foodstuffs and light manufactured goods. There were two distinct parts to the trip. The first was the discharging and loading around Europe and the UK, the second was the trip out to the Far East and back. When the ship returned from the East, all the officers and crew paid off and were replaced with a crew who signed Home Trade articles and who then worked her round the coast and stayed on until she was ready to head east again, at which time the deep sea crew would return.

The *Benalbanach* was an ex-P&O ship that had been bought by the Leith company a few months beforehand. Most of the Leith ships carried Scots deck and engine room crew and either Scots or Chinese stewards, although the *Benalbanach* had an Indian crew and Goanese stewards who had been handed over with the ship by P&O. The officers were mostly Scots, from the Islands and the east of Scotland, plus me, an Englishman. The deep sea crew had already left and the home trade crew was in place. I signed on as an extra third mate, and my duty was to shadow the real third mate and learn the ropes. On my first day he gave me a tour of the decks and an explanation of how the ship worked, in particular the working gear, the derricks. Essentially, a derrick is a lifting mechanism, not unlike a crane. A long spar is fixed to the lower part of an upright post by a hinged mechanism that allows the derrick to pivot up and down and swing from side to side. A wire runs from a winch through cargo blocks at the heel and the head of the derrick, and there is a hook on the end of the wire to pick up cargo. Derricks are usually used in pairs to make the operation more efficient. In Antwerp, our derricks were all swung out over the water out of the way, because shore cranes were being used.

I found myself in a different world from my oil tanker days. The pace of work on a general cargo ship was much more relaxed, a contrast with the high stress and high-speed working of a tanker in port. We walked around the decks with a cargo plan, checking the right goods were being taken out and making sure the new cargo being loaded was stowed where it was intended to go. The shore gangs were at work, one gang for each hatch, hauling out cartons of general goods in cargo nets. When they finished discharging, the spaces would be swept out and inspected before the stevedores started loading crates of machinery.

Being used to tankers, I was expecting the three-watch system to prevail, but things were different. The second mate and the third mate split the cargo duties in port, while the mate didn't have a watch because he was responsible for all the cargo at all times and was therefore technically on duty throughout, even though in practice he had a leisurely time. In a port with twenty-four-hour working, the second and third mate worked twelve hours on, twelve off, although that didn't happen very often because not that many ports worked through the night on general cargo ships. And for those that did, our work was supervisory work, not the filthy graft I had been brought up with on tankers, where we would spend the watch running around the deck from one near crisis to another. It could be a bit grubby climbing up and down the hatches to check the cargo, but it wasn't difficult, it wasn't exhausting, it wasn't particularly stressful. It was practical, rather than technical.

Picture: we had to get a half-ton wooden crate into a space under the main deck and into one of the internal decks, the tween decks, where it would just fit with perhaps a few inches' clearance. The crate had to be lowered down the hatch and then somehow heaved horizontally into its home without damaging the crate, without damaging the other piles of cargo, without damaging the people involved in the operation. Once there, it had to be secured so that it didn't charge about when the ship started to roll. Cargo-handling work was a constant challenge of practical common sense.

After three days in Antwerp, the ship sailed for Amsterdam. I was told to report to the bridge and when I arrived I felt I was going back in time. The engine telegraph was a gleaming

*The SS* Benalbanach *arriving in port.*

brass chain-driven contraption. The handles had to be swung back and forward to make the bell ring, after which it would be left in the desired position: Slow Ahead, Half Ahead, Slow Astern, or whatever was required. This telegraph wouldn't have been out of place on a Mississippi river boat in the 1860s. The ship's wheel looked as if it had been lifted from some ancient tea clipper, big and wooden and unwieldy. The chart room was dim and cramped, the bridge itself was dim and cramped. The bridge party all squeezed in as we left port: the Old Man, the chief mate, me, the pilot, a cadet, the quartermaster, the standby quartermaster. The constricted space made us all irritable and snappy.

On arrival in Amsterdam, the agent came on board and told me that I was being transferred to another ship. The Leith company presumably thought that four days on the *Benalbanach* was enough for me to get the hang of things. I left, not having made many acquaintances and feeling disappointed that I hadn't stayed longer.

I flew out to Tokyo, taking a flight with the new British Airways, which had been recently formed from the welding together of BOAC and BEA. I was flying out to join the cargo passenger ship *Benlawers*. The rest of the people joining with me were Scots. The band consisted of a good-size complement of officers and an entire replacement crew. We rendezvoused at Kings Cross station, half of them turned up drunk on the night train from Edinburgh, where a coach was arranged to take us all to Heathrow. One of the able seamen had just been discharged from jail in the Midlands. He was a seasoned company man, and the Leith company took pity on him and decided to help him with a new start. Two other ABs had picked him up in a taxi from the prison gate as he was released; they had his discharge book and seaman's card with them. A handful failed to arrive. Several were acting in a menacing manner as they were herded on the plane at Heathrow. Two fireman/greasers started fighting in their seats. Once on the plane, one of the crew fell asleep in a stupor in the toilet and couldn't be roused, he had become wedged against the door and the cabin crew couldn't kick it open. They left him, although he came crashing out as we touched down to refuel in Moscow, shirtless, covered in vomit, creating a fuss because he couldn't get into his seat. We lost a sailor between Tokyo airport and Yokohama, where the *Benlawers* was berthed.

Some of the officers were long-term company men, a few were shipmates from earlier voyages and most had common acquaintances. I felt a bit of an outsider. In the getting-to-know-each-other conversations that took place, though, I found that my micro trip on the *Benalbanach* stood me in good stead. When we talked about our last ships I was able to say 'My last trip was on the *Albanach*'. I thus avoided the new boy label – quite unfairly of course because I was still brand new to this world.

The *Benlawers* was built in 1970 as one of the new breed of fast ships for the Far East run, designed to operate as general cargo liners while also being capable of carrying containers. The strategy didn't work, though; these hybrid liners were soon heavily outclassed by purpose-built container ships. This resulted in the new breed being sold off, unless they could be chartered out, as was the *Benlawers*. In their place, cheaper ancient ships like the *Benalbanach* were being acquired for the staple Far East liner service. The march of time was relentlessly hunting all these general cargo ships down.

The *Benlawers* was not on the regular UK to Far East liner run, having been chartered out to a South African company. She was a smart ship and carried cabins for twelve passengers. A lot of cargo ships had twelve passenger cabins to supplement the freight earnings with passenger income. Cargo passenger ships appealed to the adventurous traveller who wanted a more rugged experience than they would find on an ordinary passenger vessel. Under Department of Trade regulations, if a ship carried more than twelve passengers, she was designated a passenger ship and then had far more rigorous requirements on construction, lifeboats and safety procedures. Cargo passenger liners could just run as ordinary working cargo ships, although they were smartened up a bit on the inside to attract passengers in the first place and to prevent them from revolting once they were on board.

The *Benlawers* had a massive complement by the standards I was used to at the time. There were eighteen officers and twenty-eight crew. The deck officer complement was big enough for someone to get lost in the crowd. On top of the pyramid stood the captain, the Old Man, imperious and untouchable. Next came the chief officer, who was tasked with the general running of the ship under the captain. He was a sort of staff captain, the captain's mouthpiece, part organiser, part political officer. The chief officer/staff captain role was seen as the cushiest number on the ship. It seemed a bit of an emasculated position to me. Then there was the first officer, who kept the four–to-eight watch at sea and who was in charge of the cargo. The first officer wore two and a half stripes to the chief officer's three. After that there was the second officer, the third officer (me) and a fourth officer. The fourth officer kept the four-to-eight watch with the first officer. When the traffic was light and the Old Man was in bed, the first officer would decamp to the chartroom and carry out his cargo planning at leisure. At the bottom of the pile were three deck cadets, to carry out all the dirty tasks and to do the general drudgery. This structure was broadly replicated on the engineer officer side, although there were no engineer cadets on the *Benlawers*. There were then two electrical officers, who came under the engineering department although they liked to see themselves as independent, the radio officer, known as Sparks, who was independent, and the catering officer, otherwise known as the chief steward, who stood very much alone.

The *Benlawers* was a much more modern vessel in every way than the superannuated *Benalbanach*. I had a decent size cabin on the starboard side of the accommodation, below the boat deck and above the saloon deck. My cabin had its own shower and toilet, a novel experience, together with a small day area and a fridge. The other deck officers were also on the starboard side of the same deck, the engineers were on the port side and the chief engineer and chief officer were on the forward end. Above us was the passenger accommodation and the captain's suite, although there were no passengers at the time. Below us was the saloon deck, with the dining saloon, the bar, a pantry for late-night feasting, sundry officers and cadet's cabins that didn't fit on the main officer's deck, and the steward's accommodation.

The bar was the hub for the officers, as was the case on most ships. On a ship full of Scotsmen, it had a special atmosphere and resonance. Apart from the *Medora*, which had a special place in my mind in that I didn't recognise it as a proper ship, the *Benlawers* bar was the first one I had encountered at sea that had actually been built as a bar. On older ships, the bar was usually the converted smoke-room, or a couple of spare cabins knocked together. These conversions took place during the 1960s when ships' officers were allowed greater freedom of expression in their drinking. The *Benlawers* bar was built to be a bar, a place to drink. There were two fridges, mainly full of beer, one in use and one cooling down the back-up stocks. On the bulkhead behind, a parade of upside-down bottles stood on quarter-gill optics, there was a shelf of glasses caged behind roll bars, a music deck was screwed to the counter. The bulkhead was decorated with beer mats and photographs and various bank notes in different currencies. Four people could comfortably fit behind the bar, five more would sit in front on black faux-leather stools, several more drinkers could take up leaning and loafing positions. The lighting was muted, we rarely had any music playing, the ambient noise was the buzz of our conversation. On special occasions and celebrations, a steward would serve the drinks behind the bar, although for the majority of time it operated as an honesty bar, with a book in which drinks were marked down for each person. I was gratified to see that a lot of the officers had healthy drinking appetites, which came as a relief to me because I stood out on ships as someone who drank more than most. I could now run within the herd, undetected. There were generally people in the bar from eleven in the morning until five the following morning. It was never a lonely place.

My first bar visit of the day was at lunchtime after I finished the morning watch. I was usually there by quarter past twelve and stayed for half an hour until lunch. My next visit was from five in the afternoon until the dinner gong sounded at six-thirty and then back again from midnight until two or three in the morning. At lunchtime, the Old Man and the senior officers would be watering themselves. Before the evening meal there was a much bigger crowd, because all the day-workers had finished work. After midnight in the small hours, it would be me and the fourth engineer and whatever survivors there were from the earlier evening, usually Sparks, the electrical officer, some fivers, a cadet or two. The post-midnight conversations would follow the same ritual. The fourth engineer and I would be sober when we arrived and try to conduct a half-sensible conversation. Everyone else in the bar was usually lubricated. They looked at us inanely while we spoke, unable to contribute, occasionally bursting into laughter on remembering shared humour from earlier in the evening. Come two in the morning we were all in pretty much the same state and the talk flowed more freely.

In port it was different. A lot of ports only worked in the day. If cargo work started at seven in the morning and finished at nine at night, which was common, two of us would split the working day. These two would be chosen from me, the second mate and the fourth mate, which meant that the third person would always have the day off. An average stay in port was four days, although sometimes we would be in for much longer. When we were in port, the bar had a different ambiance in that it was the gathering place for people when they returned to the ship, usually very late, to exchange tales and carry on the party.

As we steamed around the East, our runs ashore generally went along the same lines. I would set off about seven in the evening in the company of two or three others. I didn't go off by myself as a rule, although I would if no one else wanted to go ashore. I found that a group of more than six constituted a mob, which meant that we spent our time arguing about where we were going to go, usually ending up staying at the first bar outside the dock gates. We would have readied ourselves with a few drinks in the *Benlawers* bar before leaving as we waited for the last person to get ready. 'Get ready' meant dressing in light slacks and a clean shirt. We were not creatures of fashion but neither were we slobs; we did not wear amusing tee shirts and we rarely wore jeans. We would discuss strategy in the first bar outside the dock gates, the strategy being to move to another bar further from the dock gates, although not too far. The evening progressed in that vein, from bar to bar, as we made our way across the town. We lingered in the bars that captured our interest. When we grew weary of our own voices and our courage was up, we headed for a livelier place where we could exercise our lubricated charms on whatever girls were there. Our successes and failures and the events that ensued in the lively place would constitute the conversation for the rest of the evening. Between midnight and one in the morning we became famished and so headed for a night-time street market where we could buy fried rice and steamed seafood and cold beer. We would arrive back at the ship between two and four and clatter noisily up the gangway. By that time, some of us were in a bad way and would bounce down the alleyways in search of our cabins. Those in a fit state would have the obligatory 'one for the road' and would meet other shore returnees in the bar to exchange stories. Not all runs ashore were like that, but most contained the same elements.

I settled into the ways of the general cargo ship. We carried cars in the upper tween decks from Japan to the other ports in the East, together with crated electrical goods in the holds. We took textiles and foodstuffs north to Japan, with transhipped wines and spirits from Europe. Sometimes we carried large deck cargo: cranes, engines, lorries, steel structures. We carried coffee and tea and cocoa, loaded from the quay and from barges. At the end of every day in port the officer on duty had to 'measure up'. This entailed taking a tape on a roll and measuring all the available cubic space left on the ship so the first mate could decide what could be put where the next day. During my duty periods, I walked the decks with a loading plan and a discharging plan. The discharging plan showed what cargo needed to be taken out from which hatch. We would argue when the stevedore gangs tried to take the wrong cargo, as they inevitably did from time to time. As the cargo was taken out, I would mark it off on the discharge plan. As cargo was loaded I would mark it on my loading plan then go into the ships office and colour it all in on the master plan.

The head stevedore would have non-stop questions:

'We now have 200 bags of jute, not 100. Where are the rest going to be stowed?'

'The cars are cancelled. We now have 20 pallets of electrical goods. Do they go in the same place or should they be broken down and put in the lock-ups?'

'Number 3 hatch is jammed.'

'The gang in Number 1 hatch are going to stop work. They say the sailors are laughing at them.'

'The snatch block is jamming on the aft derrick at Number 5. We need it changed.'

'This winch is not working properly. You must have it fixed.'

'The discharging is finished in Number 3 and the hold needs sweeping out before we can load. We don't have a sweeping gang. Can you get the crew to do it?'

'There's no labour tomorrow morning, but I can get a night gang tomorrow night. Do you want it?'

'We have to move the ship to another berth this afternoon.'

'The gang has dropped a case of wine. We need to count the damage.'

'One of the gang at Number 1 hatch has had an accident and cut his hand badly. You will need to do an accident report.'

And so on and so on. At first, each question baffled me and I had to ask the first mate what to do, but as the weeks past things fell more and more into shape and I could see the life for what it was: mostly common sense, improvisation and reading the plans. And a bit of knowledge and experience of course, which I was gaining fast.

✫   ✫   ✫

At sea, ships are moved by the motion of the waves, by the swell, although different types of ship move in different ways. There are two main points of force that affect a ship at sea: the centre of buoyancy, through which there is an upthrust that keeps the ship afloat, and the centre of gravity, the opposing downthrust. As the sea pushes against the side of the ship and causes her to heel over, the opposing forces of buoyancy and gravity lever her upright again. As the ship is righted, though, the momentum then causes her to heel over the other way. Thus the ongoing rolling motion is created.

For those on board, heavy rolling was at first amusing, then awkward, then inconvenient, then hateful, then a part of life. When the rolling started, there was always some good theatre when people were caught unprepared. The edges of the dining tables had one-inch wooden barriers that were raised, known as storm boards, to keep the plates from sliding off, and the tablecloths were wetted down to give more grip to the plates and dishes. Ropes were attached to the bottoms of the saloon chairs, and these were clipped to rings in the deck to keep them fast. Even so, a heavy roll could always produce a spectacular saloon event when a plate of food leapt the storm board and landed in someone's lap, or perhaps one of the chair clips would fail and the chair and its occupant would go barrelling across the saloon to crash into the bulkhead. Drinks slid around the bar, and there was a crashing and smashing from the galley as stacks of plates went over. In the cabins, anything not put away would move about and make a racket, or fall and break or both. There were howls of grief from all over the ship as people lost things. On the deck, every single thing needed to be secured, otherwise it would break loose and cause damage.

Life became more difficult, it required more attention, it needed the use of a hand to hold on. Eating, drinking, just standing up, all became a chore. Sleeping required us to wedge ourselves in our bunks with pillows and blankets to prevent being flung around. On severe occasions I would have to swaddle myself by taking an extra sheet and using it as a rope that went under the skinny mattress, tying myself down. On a couple of occasions, the motion was so violent I was flung right out the bunk, still lashed to my mattress. We all became tired and irritable, and longed for a change of course that would take the sea off the beam and cause the rolling to diminish.

A fully laden tanker, loaded right down to her marks, has a centre of buoyancy about one third up from the keel and a centre of gravity just below deck level. This results in a deep roll against a heavy broadside sea, causing the water to break over the side as the rails dip under the surface. Water boils down the deck, completely covering it in a foamy wash. The centre of buoyancy moves across the ship as she becomes more submerged – until the roll is checked, levering her upright, cascading the water out through the rails. A tanker's roll is usually predictable.

On a general cargo ship, the rolling motion is different to that of a tanker. The liquid cargo of a tanker is uniform, whereas on a cargo ship the centre of gravity varies according to what type of cargo is stowed where. If there is a lot of heavy deck cargo, the centre of gravity will be raised and will be closer to the centre of buoyancy, which means that there is then less force to make the ship come upright again after being pushed over by the sea. This manifests itself as a sloppy motion; the ship heels over and then hangs there, before reluctantly coming back. A loose roll like that is always unsettling, sometimes alarming; it feels as if the ship is not going to come upright again and will just flop over into the deep. If on the other hand, the weight of the cargo is mostly in the bottom of the ship, the roll becomes stiffer and the ship will snap upright violently after heeling, which can cause structural damage if left unchecked. The motion of a tanker can be relied upon, but the motion of a general cargo ship was different every time we left port, depending upon the cargo being carried and its distribution around the ship.

On the heels of motion at sea comes motion sickness, seasickness, *mal de mer*. We bipedal humans compute our movements by sound, sight, skin pressure and muscle activity, all of which is coordinated in the inner ear by the central nervous system. The inner ear receptor produces a set of balances and predictions that is transmitted to the brain. When this mechanism gets out of synch, because you are being moved about by external forces, because you try to walk in one direction while getting moved in another, or because the gravity keeping you on the ground is continually varying across your body, the brain becomes confused and it can no longer properly understand what's going on. This confusion of the brain and the resulting symptoms is motion sickness. People with highly developed senses tend to get more seasick than others. I was blessed with poor central nervous coordination in this regard and consequently never suffered. Other more sensitive souls would go through the seventh circle of hell. Seasickness causes nausea, sweating, dizziness, a general feeling of unwellness. It produces a pale and greasy pallor, a retention of liquid in the throat, drooling, dribbling, retching, vomiting. It makes the sufferer drowsy then sleepy, clumsy, then uncoordinated. It induces shortness of breath, suppressed panic and a feeling of foreboding. It can be a ghastly experience that generally lasts three or four days. People who are affected, even if they have spent a few years at sea, become accustomed to seasickness to the extent of developing an ability to function, but they never become completely immune. In the end you are either someone who got seasick or you aren't, it's that simple as that.

During the big rolling periods, the first sufferers would start to succumb after an hour or so. They would never be let off their duties, though, because shipboard life couldn't just cease. The only exception was when someone had an attack so extreme that it inhibited all normal motor reflex and ability to function, although that was extremely rare. This meant that during the rolling we always had several people moving around the ship in a zombielike state, barely able to contribute to the working of the ship, groaning, weeping, retching with dry rasps. Non-sufferers often took the occasion to wind up the unfortunates with elaborate commentary on greasy fried foods, or asking if they fancied a raw egg or a glass of scotch to settle their stomach. The afflicted would never see the funny side; the unafflicted found it unendingly hilarious.

The officers of the *Benlawers* were a mixed bag of personalities. I liked some of them, got on with most, disliked a couple. There were only two Englishmen on board – me and the second electrician. As an Englishman, I had assumed that I would get a bit of stick from time to time, although that was rarely the case. The real rivalry was between those from the Islands against those from southern Scotland. Most of the Islanders were from the Hebrides, with the biggest contingent from Skye. There were several from the Orkneys and a couple of Shetlanders, 'Sheltees'. There were also a few from the northern and north-western Highland coastal towns, who were treated as honorary Islanders, rather than Highlanders. The Islanders were slower in speech and manner than the southern Scots, who were predominantly from the eastern coastal towns, with a sizeable cadre from Edinburgh. Southerners were looked down on by the Islanders, who didn't even consider them real Scots. A couple of the Sheltees had maps of Scotland stuck to the bulkheads of their cabins with the English border moved north to a line penned in from Aberdeen to Bute, condemning the industrial Glasgow Edinburgh belt to a sort of quasi-English status. In turn, the southern Scots spoke of the Islanders as country bumpkins, *teuchters*, slow of mind and permanently behind the rest of Scotland. I kept a neutral line between the factions, although I generally found more common cause with the Islanders; I was demonstrably an outsider whenever I opened my English mouth, and this sat better with them. The Islanders regarded the southern Scots, particularly those from Edinburgh, as lording it over 'real' Scotland, inflicting self-interested laws while blaming the English for anything that ever went wrong, endlessly failing to address their own weaknesses and incompetence.

I got on with most of them well, though, both Islanders and southern Scots, and was pleased that I had come to work for a Scottish company. There were only two people who rubbed me up the wrong way. The first was Tam, the third engineer. He was from Glasgow, a west coast man serving on an east coast shipping line. It was out of the ordinary to find Glaswegians working on Leith-based ships; they usually favoured the Clyde shipping companies. Tam was a short square man in his late twenties with a ruined face, pockmarked and sagging from too much drink. He shaved sporadically, his uniform was always wrinkled, he was grubby. His driving interest was football, he was an ardent Glasgow Rangers football fan. He was not just ardent but fanatical, insanely fanatical. I had a passing interest in football, as I did with most sports, although I wasn't wedded to any club. I also had a very limited appreciation of just how obsessive and passionate football fans could be. One evening, I entered into a discussion about football with Tam. I was oblivious to the others around me looking uncomfortable, I was oblivious to Tam's increasingly stony expression and to the hostility clouding his face. I blathered on, airing my worthless opinions about the best football clubs in England, the best clubs in Europe, the best clubs in Scotland. I had no real knowledge, just information gained from hundreds of similar conversations on hundreds of different subjects. I was just yakking, and rather enjoying myself. Suddenly, I became aware of Ian the leci, standing behind Tam, waving his arms and mouthing, 'No! No! Stop talking about football!' I paused, I looked at Tam. He had put his drink down. He was glaring at me, his black eyes bright with menace.

He leaned towards me. 'Listen,' Tam said in a voice laced with impending violence. 'The best football team in the world is Glasgow Rangers. Rangers are the best team in the world. Not the best in Britain, not the best in Europe, they're the best team in the world. There's no other team anywhere that can compare with them. They're the best team in the world and that's all there is to say. Do you want to argue about it?'

The room went quiet. The air-conditioning hissed, the fridge seemed to be humming loudly. I looked back at him.

I said: 'Well, Tam, if you think they're the best in the world then that's fine, good for you. I can't agree or disagree.'

I started to comprehend the ugliness of the situation. I shifted my weight on my feet, trying to prepare myself as best I could to ward off an attack by a drink-fuelled madman from Glasgow. I wasn't relishing the prospect. I looked at Tam. Tam looked at me. We both tensed. I noted how solidly built he was, perhaps a bit of fat, but not much fat. Then the tension shrugged out of his shoulders, he tossed back his drink and stamped out of the bar, muttering. I learnt a lesson: be cautious about discussing football with Scotsmen.

Ian said: 'You were lucky there. He almost head-butted me the other day when I told him that Celtic were doing well in the league.'

The second person I had little time for was the Roddy, the fourth officer. He was a strange character, a long, gangling, clumsy man, a few months younger than me. He came from just north of Edinburgh. Roddy was uncompromising in his dislike of all things English. Sometimes his dislike boarded on hysteria. In all the years I sailed with Scots crews, he was the only person I found to be like this. Being a lone Englishman at sea among Scots, I was never so dense as to start an England-versus-Scotland discussion, and any joshing I received was always of a good nature. But with Roddy it was different, there was a real underlying unpleasantness, a bile that soured the air. In our normal day–to-day working we got on well enough. We were civil and talked to each other in a friendly manner. On occasions, though, Roddy would begin to change. He would seek out any opening in the conversation to bash the English, he would curse the bloody Sassenachs who had caused all the trouble in the world, how they robbed the Scots, how they should all be evicted from Scotland. When he noticed I was there he would rush to assure me that his remarks did not apply to me, just all real Sassenachs. I don't know what he viewed me as, presumably some sort of honorary Scot. I mostly ignored him. The others squirmed with embarrassment at his crassness and told him to shut up, to no avail. He was universally unpopular.

By and large, I liked the officers on that ship more than I had on others during my previous tanker life. I found the Islanders to be essentially better company than the southern Scots, I thought they were better people. They had a way of combining gentleness with fierceness that you don't see with those from the cities. It was easy to see why southern Scots regarded Highlanders and Islanders as slow, because they never reacted with the speed and panic that was expected of them and seemed to take longer to absorb what was going on. The ship could be sinking and Ian would have said: 'Aye, I suppose we had better be getting off then,' and he would then take another pull of his beer. Angus would have replied: 'Aye, we had best head for the lifeboats,' and slowly stubbed his cigarette out. They were not slow, though, nor stupid. They were men who considered what they did and said. They would not be rushed. They were decent men, with morals and principles. They would not let you down, they would never exclude you, they were not in the habit of deriding their fellows, and they would rarely mock. They had a deep underlying passion and loyalty for the things in life they thought were right and worth defending, and when they were roused they could be terrifying. It made me feel good to be with the Islanders, although being with them made me aware that the core of me was not as noble I wanted it to be.

Singapore was forever one of my favourite ports. I had lived in the city as a boy and I knew the feel of the place. I loved the succulent mossy taste as I breathed in the air, the screams of the wandering hawkers, the blasting rains in the afternoons, the close feel of over two million people crammed on an island only ten miles long and five miles wide. History indicates that Singapore Island was a fetid swamp off the toe of the Malay peninsula when it was founded by Stamford Raffles in 1819, although the populated history in fact stretches back to before the thirteenth century. Various parties have had a bite at the island over the centuries, including the Mongols, the Malay Sultanates, the Siamese and the Javanese, before the Dutch and British appeared over the horizon one day in all their modern finery. The name Singapore in Malay, Singapura, means Lion City although there were no lions around. There were tigers, though, reputedly still roaming on the island at the end of the nineteenth century. When Raffles arrived, Singapore was a backwater of little significance, either locally or internationally; there were less than a thousand Malays living there, together with a few Chinese traders. Raffles recognised the potential for a deep sea harbour at Keppel, and he could see the island rested at an important strategic location, both of which would help to weaken the Dutch stranglehold on that part of South East Asia. By various deals with the nearby Sultan of Johore, Raffles secured Singapore for the British in perpetuity. He built the harbour and turned Singapore into a free port, a tax-free trading environment. The traders rolled in, the Chinese arrived in hordes as workers, and the City State grew and grew. Singapore became a pivotal part of British Far Eastern strategy until independence was granted in 1959. In the mid-1970s, the place was booming, a capitalist business paradise. The population was 75 per cent Chinese, mostly the descendants of the workers who had been brought over in the previous century, even though the Malays were still recognised as the indigenous people. About 10 per cent were Indians, again brought in by the British in the nineteenth century.

This history, together with the cultural mix and the commercial drive, gave Singapore a unique frisson in the 1970s; excitement zapped through the air. The government was just beginning to crack the whip over its inhabitants to herd them into the tight civic discipline that now prevails, and a few civil liberty types were already starting to cry foul, although then it was still a free and fairly wide open place. Noisy markets peppered the streets day and night. At night in the city, the bars and clubs and restaurants were vibrant. On the fringes, the seamier side of nightlife bubbled away: the brothels, street whores and sex shows were always there.

The *Benlawers* would moor in Keppel Harbour, which was walking distance from Anson Road, the legendary street of sailor bars. The bar area was starting to wind down at that time, as the Singapore government began to map out its puritan phase, although a number of bars, including the famed Champagne Bar and the Ritz Bar, were still doing a roaring trade. The shifts for the Singapore dock gangs were either twenty-four or sixteen-hour working. This translated into two of the three junior deck officers doing a twelve-hour or eight-hour stretch while the third one had the whole day off. We would generally be in Singapore for four or five days. Our evenings ashore would usually start in Anson Road, perhaps half a dozen of us drinking ice-cold Tiger beer in the ice-cold air-conditioning, while the bar girls twittered around us, hustling for drinks and tips. The drinks we bought them were coloured water at twice the price of a beer, but the commercial wheel had to go round and we always bought.

Later, we would find ourselves in one of the dens off North Bridge Road or Victoria Street: dark, seedy, filthy, slightly dangerous. We would always insist that the beer bottles were opened in front of us. Later still, we would migrate to Bugis Street, the open air street market in the edge of the centre, famous for its transvestites, fights, seafood and wild reverie atmosphere. The clientele was mainly Europeans, largely seamen, some American and Australian servicemen on rest and recreation from nearby military antics. Bugis Street used to be packed with British servicemen every night, but Britain had formally handed over the defence of the island to the Singapore government in 1972 and all the troops went home, ending over 150 years of British military presence. In 1974 the Bugis Street market was still several years from being closed down. The strutting transvestites, known as Ki-Tis, the street kids hustling for games of noughts and crosses on small blackboards, the screaming fruit hawkers, the food sellers and the party atmosphere made it still the best late-night show in town. The Bugis Street toilets, a stinking block near the centre of the market, were internationally renowned as being the most disgusting to be found anywhere; many a drunk slipped over in the pitch dark inside and emerged sodden through from rolling in puddles of piss, smeared and caked with unimaginably foul pastes. Most people would avoid the toilet block and slip into the shadows to urinate directly into the monsoon drain.

If we were in the mood for a serious feed, we would go to Fatty Choys in nearby Albert Street. Fatty's didn't look very special, it looked uninviting: grimy, crowded and noisy, people sat on wobbly stools at mismatched wooden tables set on the pavement and the edge of the street. The place was lit by hissing naphtha lamps. Fatty and his team served the customers. The team was uniformly overweight, tired-looking, bored-looking, shabby, miserable, snappy. When we arrived, we would get a table wherever one was free. Sometimes we had to wait for a party to finish so we would sit on the edge of the monsoon drain, drinking beer until summoned. Once seated, we would gorge ourselves on bowls of steamed crab claws, duck roasted in soy sauce, braised chicken, noodles, stewed vegetables, slabs of fish, giant platters of fried rice, flushing it down with icy Anchor Pilsner in iced glasses. The food in Fatty Choys was as good as it was possible to be, it was food for the gods. Tourists in the Four Seasons Hotel, a few hundred yards away, paid five times more for food of a quality that Fatty wouldn't have dared serve to his guests.

Hong Kong was the main Far East port for the Leith company, and was regarded as the eastern home by most officers. But it was Singapore that held a special pull for me because I had lived and been to school there only five years previously when my father had been stationed at the Royal Air Force base at Seletar. His squadron flew Twin Pioneer aircraft into the Malayan jungle strips and he carried his pistol strapped to his hip in case they ran into trouble with the remnants of Chin Peng's communists insurgents who were still causing the odd stir of trouble in the remoter outposts.

On one free day while the others were splitting the cargo duties, I went to wander the streets of Katong on the east coast of the island, where I used to live, noting all the changes. We used to have the sea at the end of our road but the land had been reclaimed and was now choked with high-rise flats, relegating our seaside road to just another outer city street, hunched among other outer city streets. Mr Yan, the Chinese doctor who lived at the house next door, still lived there. He was sitting in a rattan chair reading a newspaper when I paused outside his chainlink fence. He didn't look up, so I walked on. I went on back to the city, to Anson Road, to drink in the bars, which is what I really liked to do.

I had always drunk too much. From the time I left home to go to sea at sixteen years old I liked to drink alcohol more than I should have done. I had drinking genes. My father was a big time drinker, he never stayed home at night, he went out every evening to the officer's mess or to the local pub. He came of age in the war when young men went off to die and partied in between, because that was the right thing to do. He was a young RAF officer who flew off to bomb Europe in a Wellington bomber, weaving through the flak, watching his friends caught in the searchlights, being shot down. Later in the war he transferred to Fighter Command and fought Germans in the summer skies over France in his Spitfire. What young man wouldn't have spent his time in wild drinking rushes between those bouts of death? After the war, he carried on the habit, as did all his generation. So when I went to sea, drinking was the most natural thing to slip into. The life at sea was a drinking environment, and it fitted me like a glove.

As a junior cadet I had worked on deck with the crew, mostly on ships plying their trade in the South China Sea. I squatted in the sun in a pair of shorts, chipping off the rust, scouring the metal, painting, the sun beating down on my back. I became stronger and more resilient. At the end of the day I would slump in the shade on the poop deck with the other cadets and we would drink down ice cold, ice cold cans of beer. I would spike the can with the opener that hung on a string around my neck, which was the fashion in the East at that time, and the amber fluid would slide down so sweetly, so beautifully. I could feel the beer fill my mouth then sluice in two icy channels down either side of my throat. After the first long swallow, I would light a Rothmans cigarette and pull the smoke deep into my lungs, then expel it with a sigh, then I would take another pull from my can. And I thought: 'This is so-oo good. It's so good to drink like this.'

As time went by, it wasn't just the oh-so-beautiful taste, it was also the ambiance, the drinking camaraderie, the drinking culture that I loved. I was getting enjoyment from every corner: I liked the taste, I liked the pleasure of taking the alcohol inside of me, I liked the loosening of life's grip as the effect of alcohol blunted my concerns, I liked the camaraderie of drinking with people who felt the same as me. I loved the whole drinking culture.

I loved the rituals; I observed them at all times. They were a fundamental part of the culture. The drinking world needs ritual to endure.

The first drink: no one took a sip from their glass or a swig from their can until everyone in the group was ready, and then we raised our glasses slightly to each other and said, 'Cheers' and we drank together.

The round: the first person, the one who arrived at the bar ahead of the rest, or had his hand in his pocket, or who had the lead of the conversation, would say: 'Beers all round?'

and we would say, 'Aye.' The round would then pass to someone else, and then to each of us in turn. It was rude to refuse, and it was near sacrilege to miss out your turn to buy the round.

The conversations: when we drank, we either told each other stories or we speculated about the future. That is how we communicated as men. There was rarely any philosophical debate, we did not talk of our feelings, we did not talk of our families or loved ones. We told each other stories, most of which involved drinking and girls, most entailed some wildness out of the ordinary that resulted in embarrassment or humiliation or violence or someone getting their just desserts. No one hogged the conversation, everyone in the circle was given a hearing to tell their own tale, and the rest of us listened respectfully, even if the tale was dog-dull. If stories weren't being told, we would speculate on where we were going next, when our next pay rise would be, who was leaving next, who might be joining. It was easy to fill a whole evening's conversation with idle and part-informed speculation.

The loyalty: no one would ever be left behind. If we were out on the lash in some dockland bar area and someone became too incapable to carry on, we would either carry him around with us to the next bar, or one of us would be charged with taking him safely back to the ship.

The humour: drinking would bring out the best in us whenever we were in a group, it would bring out the fun within. No matter how low someone was feeling, how tired, how undervalued, when we were together drinking in a group, the underlying sentiment was humour. It was used to lighten the load. Serious subjects were taboo within a drinking group. These only intervened occasionally between two people, very late on in the session, when both were very drunk. Then, and only then, it became acceptable for the pair to air grandiloquent bullshit of the higher calibre.

All of this was built into me when I signed on the *Benlawers*. Once on board, I found myself entering a drinking culture supreme. I was a rank amateur among all the Scots. I was like a child let into the sweetshop. All the officers drank, some constantly, most heavily. A few had prodigious capacities. I was a quick drinker. I drank at speed from the starting gun, I pushed the pace. Later in the evening I started to slow, and those who had refused a drink earlier in the evening began to overhaul me. I was a stayer, though, usually there to the end. As I drank more I talked less and less sense, although I kept at it until even I couldn't understand myself, at which point I became an enthusiastic nodder. On a typical drinking party that started at seven in the evening, I would be in the pole position for the first two to three hours, after which I would drop back in the pack and drink much slower. My incomprehensible phase arrived about eleven o'clock and would see me retreat to the periphery. At one o'clock or thereabouts, my second wind would arrive, like the relieving cavalry, and I would perk up, pick up, start drinking again, drive the pace again, take the second star to the right and continue straight on until morning.

In my drinking I mostly stayed with beer, which was usually bottled or canned lager. The Scots officers on the *Benlawers* would often switch to whisky later in the evening. I was not a whisky drinker, and whenever I tried I would be violently ill. I found I had quite a capacity for Japanese whisky, Suntory, but try getting a Scotsman to drink Japanese whisky – I made myself a figure of derision whenever I had a glass. Drinking wine in the mid-1970s was not a habit indulged in by men at sea. We drank beer or we drank spirits. I would occasionally go into a gin-and-tonic phase, and sometimes we would amuse ourselves by quaffing exotic cocktails, but mostly for most people it was beer.

I knew that I drank a lot, but I never considered myself a heavy drinker. No drinker ever does, until they look back. A thudding head and a general feeling of malaise in the morning was commonplace for me, although I was usually fine by midday. I had a few occasions of seeing dancing lights in the early part of the day, which puzzled me, then worried me, then I got used to their odd appearance so I stopped thinking about it. I never craved a drink, but I always missed drinking if I was not in on it.

There were several officers on board who appeared permanently the worse for wear. Tam looked blighted by drink, Ian looked ten years older than he was, Angus became addled easily, and he sometimes remained that way even when he had sobered up. I was aware that my drinking habits were on the march, although in those days I never thought it was time to start pulling on the reins. I was too young, I was too healthy, I was enjoying myself too much. I hadn't yet begun to properly stare into the abyss.

We arrived on the South African coast in February, at the height of the southern summer. Our first port of call was Durban in Natal province, the busiest port in the country; we were due to be there for two weeks loading steel. In the event, we anchored for three weeks in the roads, waiting for our berth. The anchorage was chock full, there were over fifty ships waiting to go alongside. A long anchorage spell in fine weather allowed us to ensure all the

*The SS* Benlawers *at sea.*

outstanding work was carried out. The crew and cadets spent their days smartly painting all the scruffy areas; the second mate laid out all his Admiralty charts and brought them up to date with the latest corrections, new lights and wrecks and amended depths and changing shoals. I was assigned two cadets for a week, and used them to strip out all the lifeboats, wash and paint the woodwork, oil the oars, change any worn or rotting rope-work, rig and air the sails. We changed most of the stores, the cadets ate the old barley sugar to the point of being sick, we changed the fresh water, we dumped the out-of-date pyrotechnics. I had both lifeboats run out down to the water, then wound back up again, greasing the wires as this was done. The winding in by hand was backbreaking, and I had to help the cadets. In the morning anchor watch from eight to twelve, there was little to do but idle. The Old Man was a stickler for uniform, so there was no chance of shedding my shirt to bronze myself on the bridge wing. I helped the second mate with some chart corrections, I corrected all the Admiralty Light Lists of the world. We checked the position to make sure we were not dragging anchor, although there was little point unless the wind was up, which it never was. At nights, I just paced the bridge and drank the brew of coffee and condensed milk made by the watchman. There were several other British ships in the anchorage and we would find a free channel on the VHF radio and exchange news. It was all the usual: where are you bound, where are you from, what beer do you have on board, where's a good place to go in Durban and so on. Sometimes they wanted Morse code practice, and I would drag one of the cadets onto the bridge to get out the Aldis lamp and engage. I was aware that a large number of ships in the anchorage would only have a watchman on the bridge while the officer was in the bar or in bed. Some would have no one up at all. Not us on the *Benlawers*, though, we kept full duties, fully uniformed, for the whole duration. The days dragged, time slowed. I lay on the monkey island atop the bridge in the afternoons and read, roasting myself under the African sun, falling asleep and waking up burnt. We drank cold beer when we weren't working and swapped tales and watched the time drag past.

When we finally went alongside in Durban, we were allocated a prime berth on the north side of the harbour, a short walking distance from the town. The southern side, along the Island View wharf, was known to be a bit dodgy at night; the black dockworkers, in those apartheid days, took the opportunity to rob and thrash any white sailor found returning alone to his ship in the dark. We stayed two weeks in Durban. The place was stark in its separation of blacks and whites. Being white, I was awarded the advantage, but it was alien to me and I found the rigid separation very disconcerting. My shipmates mostly felt the same, although we still made the most of the place, hypocrites that we were.

My last visit to Durban had been as a cadet when I was involved in a late-night drunken car crash as we were driven by a South African who fell asleep while we sped along West Street. It was with a sense of *déjà vu* that I hired a car, the intention being to use it to see the wide-open spaces of Africa. Once I had the car, though, I did little more than use it as a ferry to take us to and from the bars along Smith Street and West Street and to the Millionaire's Mile by North Beach. At the witching hour one night, following a hectic session in the Millionaire's Mile, a carload of us were heading for the Smugglers, a dark cave of a place, loud and vibrant and boozy. I lost control and spun the car and whacked into a shop window. The car was damaged but drivable, we were shaken but unhurt, glass was strewn across the pavement. It seemed best to back up and roar off, which we did. The next day the car hire company announced the insurance was invalid because we'd had a crash. We laughed. We asked the car hire rep what was the point of insurance if it became invalid when it was needed. He laughed back, but he had my credit card imprint. He said: 'Get a lawyer.' We hired a lawyer; he charged a lot, we lost anyway. It cost me half a month's pay. I was furious. The others sympathised; I didn't have to buy a drink for weeks, it was their way of chipping in.

Cargo work only took place only during the day and was easy. Cheap, compliant labour and lots of it meant that things went smoothly. The nights in Durban passed in a haze of partying. We enticed a host of nurses on board for a formal do one evening, dressing smartly for the occasion in half-and-halves, blue trousers and tropical uniform shirts. The event started in a controlled manner, all of us strutting and posing and eyeing up the girls and acting like gentlemen, while they posed and eyed us up in turn. As the evening progressed our standards slipped. Angus started slurring and leering, a group of engineers turned inwards and gathered in a clump to tell loud stories of debauchery to each other, we told inappropriate jokes to the girls. The nicer ones became repelled and left, those who stayed were as bad as any of us. I became hitched to a chubby marble-white girl called Bella. I asked her how she managed to stay so bleached in a sunny place like South Africa. She replied, unpleasantly: 'I hate the sun and why would I want to turn myself into a brown person anyway?' Bella became more offensive and more shrewish as the hours went by and I started to dislike her. But I fended off the other officers anyway, as they lurked nearby in predatory fashion waiting for me to slip, and kept her for myself, as men do if they have something that other men want.

We found a pair of stowaways on board after we left Durban. I was on the bridge wing at about one o'clock in the morning, it was a clear moonless night and traffic was light and we were about ten miles off the coast, near Port Edward. I sensed some movement behind me and looked round to see two burly figures in the gloom coming out from behind the funnel. I couldn't make out who they were and assumed that it was a couple of engineers checking something in the funnel housing. It niggled at me, though, only because normal manners meant the engineers would usually have come onto the bridge for a chat or just to say hello. I sent the watch sailor down to have a look around. He came back up after a few minutes to say that he had found two Africans scoffing food in the crew pantry. I told him to wake the bosun, the standby watch man and a couple of others, then find an empty cabin and lock them in with some food and drink until the morning. This was done; the stowaways complied with good humour and no resistance.

The next morning they were quizzed by the chief mate. As the discoverer, I was roused from my bunk to be in attendance. The two Africans were crestfallen when they found the ship was only bound for East London, just a day's run down the coast; they'd thought we were headed for some rich country where they would have a better life. They were young men, Zulus, broad and strong-looking although grubby and shabbily clothed, and they cringed when spoken to, as if we might start beating them. I suppose their dirty and unkempt appearance was because they had spent half a day in the funnel housing, although their cowed manner was most likely because of the apartheid regime of the day, which instilled wariness towards white authority. In the event we had them as our guests for three days because our berth in East London wasn't ready and we had to anchor in the roads until it was clear. The mate put the pair of them to work with the crew to earn their keep and they were content enough. The crew had no prejudice, which surprised and delighted the Africans. In the evening they would sit happily in the crew bar, being bought drinks and joining in the conversations. Perhaps they had a couple of days of the good life they craved after all. They looked defeated when removed by port officials after we docked. Several of the crew lined up to wave them off, and they turned at the bottom of the gangway to wave back, giving quick smiles before trudging off.

We tramped round the South African coast, from East London to Port Elizabeth, before arriving at Cape Town during the celebrations for the Van Riebeeck's Day, or Founder's Day. Jan Van Riebeeck was a Dutchman celebrated as the founder of Cape Town in 1652. He built a fort, and the Dutch retained control until eventually being hoofed out by the British in 1805. Cape Town people were engaged in eccentric antics to commemorate the anniversary. There was theatre and street parties, students were carrying the first underwater man up Table Mountain, a student submerged in a bath and breathing through a snorkel. We lay at anchor again for several days, seals and dolphins flopped in the water around the ship. We caught fat fish to barbecue. Cape Town was cooler than Durban, thick fog dropped on us in the night, the ringing of the ship's bells on the fo'c'sle travelled eerily through the wet air. We picked up half a dozen passengers, older retired types with time on their hands who wanted to visit a few off-beat places. They had their own bar up on the passenger deck, although a couple kept coming into the officers' bar to enhance their experience. We were civil enough but didn't want them there. Ashore in Cape Town, I made the obligatory trip on the cable car up Table Mountain with a couple of others, although we found it unenlightening and went back down to drink Castle Beer and eat monkey gland steaks. Like most people I thought that monkey gland steak involved monkey glands and was disappointed to find it was only a sort of barbecue sauce, which didn't have the same élan.

On leaving Cape Town, we set off north up the bleak south-west coast. The Admiralty Pilot No. 2 – Africa, Volume II – gave an appropriate description of the place: *Nothing is more uninviting that the appearance of the coast between Walvis Bay and the mouth of the Orange River … The whole of the country which extends from Cabo Negro to beyond Itshabo Island is a desert region and almost rainless … There is no landing place between Cabo Frio and Rocky Point; and the nearest known water holes are at least ten miles inland and very rare… Great caution is necessary when navigating in the vicinity.*

The northern part of South West Africa, now modern-day Namibia, is known as the Skeleton Coast, named after the hundreds of shipwrecks that littered the area after having struck offshore rocks in the fog. The name is also thought to have come from the whale skeletons that were scattered along the coast in the nineteenth century, when whaling was in full swing. We tracked up this notorious land, keeping well offshore, calling first at Luderitz for a day, to offload mining equipment. Luderitz had the feel of a frontier town, the place was fenced in to stop people walking into the diamond-rich areas in the Namib desert, where precious stones were said to lie on the desert floor. The government and the diamond mining companies were keen to protect the market price, and were rumoured to have issued shoot-on-sight instructions for anyone found inside the restricted zones. Luderitz was named after a German tobacco trader, Franz Luderitz. In 1882 he had bought the area from a local chief for £100 and 200 rifles. Further north, Walvis Bay was slightly larger, but still had the wood-built appearance of a place that had been put up a few years ago and could be returned to the Namib Desert next year. A spit of land protected the harbour, I could stand in Walvis Bay and see the endless sea to the west, then turn my head and see the desert rolling away to the east. This part of Africa had been known as German South West Africa, although it had been taken away from the Germans as a penance for losing the First World War and had since been run by a South African administration. A lot of the Germans were deported in 1918, although many more kept a low profile and remained. I went into a bar in town with Ian to escape the blistering heat and it was like going back a century. We squinted into the dark until our eyes became accustomed to the cool gloom. Bottles stood on crude wooden shelving behind a battered and stained bar-top, rough-looking men stood in a line along the bar drinking from bottles, spittoons lined the floor, mismatched tables and chairs were scattered around, a piano stood against one wall, the walls were splashed with whitewash. The customers stared at us with borderline hostility as we entered, then turned away. We ordered beer and sat at a table and talked quietly among ourselves. I felt as if I was in an old Western film and was about to be challenged by the local gunfighter.

We called briefly at Durban again before returning to the East, dropping off some transhipped cargo from Walvis Bay and picking up a full complement of passengers. The stewards were mightily pleased, anticipating big tips when they left. I leant over the rails and watched as the passengers filed up the gangway. They were universally ancient to my twenty-one-year-old eyes; the youngest of them must have been in their fifties.

We listened to the fall of Saigon on the BBC World Service as we crossed the Indian Ocean on a hot week in April, westbound for South Africa again with a full cargo from the Far East. I followed the news intensely, having had my escapade there fifteen months beforehand. I knew several people who were now sailing on the Singapore to Saigon run, carrying jet fuel to Nha Bè, as I had done. The BBC coverage was graphic, the event stood out as an iconic moment in history. The American administration under President Nixon had seen the writing on the wall and agreed a ceasefire with North Vietnam in January 1973, as a prelude to the USA getting out. The next two years saw the US forces disengage from South Vietnam and return home. South Vietnam was left to prepare itself for the final conflict. North Vietnam, under the leadership of Ho Chi Minh, largely ignored the ceasefire, they continued to harry and hassle the South. Eventually, in early 1975, there was a collapse of resistance from the South Vietnamese army; the towns of Hue and Da Nang fell in March, allowing the North Vietnamese war machine to roll south down the country and take everything in its path. Qui Nhon was captured after a brief fight, then Nha Trang, then Da Lat. Finally, Xuan Loc, the last line of defence before Saigon, fell in early April, and Saigon was left wide open. The place was in a panic, the roads to the airport were jammed, all flights out were booked, the army and police beat people back. North Vietnamese rockets destroyed the runway. The US embassy was besieged by people waving their passports, begging to be let in, US Marines held them back at gunpoint. The North Vietnamese entered the city at the end of April, US helicopters airlifted the last Americans off the roof of the US embassy and took them to the US Seventh Fleet waiting offshore in the South China Sea. It was a massive retreat of power; commentators speculated whether the dominoes would now start to fall to the communists all over the Far East: Laos, Cambodia, Thailand, Burma, Malaysia. Perhaps even the Philippines, perhaps even Indonesia. We were all Far East men, we talked about it nightly. We wondered whether China would use the occasion and the atmosphere to roll over the border into Hong Kong, crushing the tiny British garrison. Saigon fell and was renamed Ho Chi Minh City and all news of what was going on in the inside of Vietnam dried up. Rumours of horrors filled the airways: mass executions, city clearances, re-education programmes for all. It was an Orwellian nightmare to make you shiver.

The fall of Vietnam didn't affect our lives, apart from the boat people. The boat people were refugees fleeing the Vietnam regime, hundreds of souls crammed into small craft and heading out into the South China Sea, intent on being rescued by big ships and taken to a better world. Many merchant ships had orders to steam on by, some boat people adopted the tactic of opening the valves and starting to sink when a big ship was close, so they had to pick them up. Most ships did, but some still steamed on by. Our orders from Head Office were to avoid areas where we would be likely to encounter boat people, although if we did come across them we were to drop supplies and only stop to stop and pick them up if they were in obvious distress. We never came across any boat people while I was on the *Benlawers*.

We arrived in Durban after a second round trip of the Far East, and were told to go to the anchorage again for an estimated ten days. We also received notification that virtually the entire officer complement and crew were being relieved when we berthed. We celebrated with a massive party; for us the trip was over, a few days idling at anchor before we went alongside to hand over the ship for others to do the cargo work. The stewards were livid because passengers traditionally tipped when they left the ship and the current passenger crop was due to depart in Cape Town. This meant that the new stewards, who by that time would have been on board for two or three weeks, would get all the tips. The stewards slouched around the ship with wounded faces, sighing theatrically at every request, occasionally banging our food down in front of us in the dining saloon.

Our leaving party was arranged as a huge beano on Saturday. To accommodate the different watches, it would start at half past five in the afternoon, which would allow the twelve-to-four watch and the day-workers to kick it off. The evening meal would be a buffet served in the bar so that the party could carry on uninterrupted. After eight o'clock, the four-to-eight watch would arrive; after midnight, the eight-to-midnight watch would arrive, and so on, until things wound down in the early hours. I paced the bridge for my four-hour anchor watch from eight until midnight, clockwatching. The second mate arrived at ten past midnight, looking ill after having stayed up too late before hitting his bunk. I did a 30-second handover and vaulted down the steps to the bar. The whole crowd was there: the

Old Man, chief engineer, chief mate, first mate, fourth mate, cadets, Sparks and most of the engineers. They were all well-oiled and making a merry racket, the bins behind the bar were overflowing with empties. They hooted when I came in: 'Just in time to solve the crisis, Third Mate,' said the Old Man. I signalled for a beer and looked at him enquiringly.

'We need someone in sober authority to go and get the padlock key for the beer locker from the second steward, we're running out. No one wants to go and get it from him.'

The stewards had all been in a foul mood for the past few days over the loss of tips from the passengers, and no one wanted to wake up the senior second steward for the key in case he pretended he couldn't find it, or gave them a hard time. The second steward was very prickly, a pinched and angry little man who people didn't like to upset.

I said: 'Why hasn't someone just gone and said to him: "Give me the key for the beer locker"? That sounds simple enough to me.'

They all looked away, coughing and muttering and scratching their heads and mumbling that he was asleep. It apparently wasn't that simple. Someone muttered that they had knocked on his door several times but there was no answer. It was plain they were scared of the angry little second steward, and no one wanted to wake him up.

I looked at the chief mate. 'I'll tell you what. The second steward keeps the key to the beer locker hanging on the hook just inside his cabin. Let me have your master key and I'll quietly open his door and take the key. No fuss.'

'The chief engineer banged his glass on the bar and shouted: 'Brilliant! Give him the master key.'

I went down to the next deck and slowly slid the master key into the lock. I opened the door as quietly as I could. There was a pale yellow light inside coming from the overhead bunk light. I peered around the edge of the door. My jaw dropped on its hinges, I stared. The big beefy cabin steward was frozen in mid-stroke as he crouched in his hairy nakedness over the angry little second steward, who was on all fours, equally naked, his wizened bum offered upwards for the taking. Both their heads turned towards me, eyes wide like startled rabbits in the headlights, mouths hanging open, the dim bunk lamp causing a halo of light on the dark pelt that covered the cabin steward's back. No doubt his manhood was wilting fast. We stared at each other. Several seconds passed. I reached in and plucked the key from the hook.

I said: 'Carry on chaps,' then closed and locked the door.

I returned to the bar with a case of beer under each arm. Everyone cheered.

'No trouble getting the key, Third Mate?' said the Old Man.

'No Captain, he didn't say a word, he just stared at me.'

At breakfast the next day, the two stewards eyed me with terror as they served breakfast. I smiled at them. They didn't bang down my plate.

# 4

# Painted Iron

The trip home from Durban to London was a shambles. Virtually the whole ship's complement was leaving the *Benlawers* to fly home. The officers were to be put up in a hotel on the North Beach while the crew would be staying at an establishment in the outer suburbs. We went to the North Beach hotel first, leaving the crew behind on the coach to grumble at the unfairness of the segregation. Our flight home was scheduled for the following morning, and the agent impressed upon us that we would be picked up to go to the airport after breakfast. We gave our assurances that we would all be ready and waiting.

The coach arrived the next day. The crew were already on board and the militants among them were fuming, having whipped themselves into a righteous rage about what they called a 'maritime apartheid regime' being foisted on them. They moaned about their hotel, saying that they had been consigned to an out-of-the-way dump in the middle of nowhere with rotten food and no hot water while the officers stayed in the middle of town in the lap of luxury. We all kept our heads down, none of us wanted a big row before we set off and we were all feeling a bit delicate after a late night out in the bright lights of Durban, decadent *noblesse* that we were.

When a whole ship's complement was on the move, the responsibility for the logistics was usually given over to one of the mid-ranking officers, the second officer or perhaps the radio officer. The nominated person is then given all the tickets, vouchers and travel instructions and is expected to get the party from A to B, employing whatever tactics and subterfuges prove necessary. Our journey meant that we had to change in Johannesburg for the final leg to London. When we arrived at Durban airport, the senior officers, captain, chief officer, first officer, chief engineer and second engineer made it clear that they had no intention of getting involved in the shepherding of the masses. They went off in a group leaving the rest of us behind, telling the second mate they would meet us at the check-in desk. The second mate was given a large brown envelope by the agent. He hesitated for five seconds before passing it to me, saying: 'I think you'll be better than me at this,' then headed for the airport bar, followed by the other officers. I stood there alone among the crew, feeling betrayed. The crew milled around, muttering.

I shouted: 'Everyone over here, let's check who we've got.'

I heard someone say, in muted tones: 'You're not on the bloody ship now, you know, ordering us around.'

Someone else said: 'Yeah, that's right.'

I thought: 'Good grief.' I opened the envelope: an itinerary, tickets from Durban to Johannesburg on South African Airways, tickets from Johannesburg to London on British Airways, 500 South African Rand for incidental expenses, sundry telephone numbers in case of crisis. I signed for it all.

The bosun sidled up to me: 'There's two missing, Third Mate; Barton and McPhee; they're both in jail.'

'What did they do?' I asked.

The bosun shrugged: 'Dunno. Causing some sort of trouble. They're in court later today, apparently.'

I crossed off the names and gave their tickets back to the agent, telling him to go to the police station and sort it out, then put them on the first flight home when they were released.

I checked everyone else off, checked the tickets, checked the passports. As I called out each name, it was acknowledged by a grunt. Some didn't like to answer, to demonstrate their independence now that we had all signed off the ship. When this happened, I would say to the agent in a loud voice: 'Another one missing, take his ticket back,' which would raise a half-petulant, half-concerned shout of confirmation.

There was no one else missing. I marshalled the herd towards the check-in desks, sending a cadet to tell the officers to finish their heart-starters and join us. We stood in a ragged crocodile, me at the front, the senior officers behind, then the other officers and the rest of the crew, stretching back across the departure hall. A posse of porters stood alongside, guarding all the luggage. Over the course of a painful ninety minutes, the checking-in was completed. I felt sorry for anyone arriving for the Jo'burg flight and who had to join the back of our forty man convoy. The crew horsed around, swearing, leering at passing women. As each man checked in, I gave him back his passport although I kept the tickets, with the exception of the senior officers, who demanded all their paperwork to get them through to London, so they could detach themselves from the embarrassment of travelling with the main party.

I gathered the mob again to set off for passport control. A delegation from the crew came to see me. The elected speaker was the big hairy cabin steward, which I was pleased about. As the keeper of his secret, I would have the advantage in any argument.

He cleared his throat. 'Third Mate, the men want their tickets.'

I said: 'No. I've been given the responsibility and I'm holding on to the paperwork until we're ready to board the London flight at Jo'burg.'

'We're not kids!' shouted one, like a kid.

'You're not having the tickets and that's that. I'm holding onto them.'

'You're not on the ship now,' said another. 'You haven't got the authority.'

'I've got the tickets, though, and I'm keeping hold of them.'

The matter rumbled back and forth for several minutes until they finally accepted the lash and we all trooped off towards the immigration desk. The journey was as eventful as could be expected when a group of over forty men, mostly young men, are travelling together after several months away. Other travellers looked at our noisy, raucous, blaspheming band with dislike and contempt. I attracted particular glares of disapproval as soon as I was identified as being in charge of the pack. Airport staff hovered on the fringes, alert for any loss of control that would need them to intervene. The second mate stayed at a distance and smiled at me smugly. In return, I gave him a look of hatred for saddling me with the task. As soon as we had checked in at the transit desk and the boarding passes were issued for the London flight, I handed them all out, content that I had done my duty. Once on the British Airways plane I collapsed into my seat in relief.

After eight weeks' leave, I joined the SS *Benledi* in Hull one bleak Sunday morning. Hull is a nice place to those who are born and live there, I'm sure, but it was never a port that inspired me. On that Sunday in the early morning, the grey clouds matched the grey buildings, a thick yellow air hung over the place like a pall of sickness. I had arranged with Hertz that they would collect my hire car from the dock. I parked at the end of one of the long cargo sheds and sat in the drizzle waiting for the ship to berth. The company had given me a choice of a rail warrant or having the equivalent in cash expenses to make my own way, I chose the latter. I was staying with my parents who had moved to Oxfordshire, and the train journey would have been too fractured.

The ship represented a promotion for me in that I would be joining as second officer. The continuing officer shortage meant that many officers were often serving a rank up. Standard practice was that you had to have a First Mate's Certificate to serve as second mate, although that requirement had slackened with the shortage. I would be doing the coast voyage, discharging and then loading again for the Far East, before handing over to the deep sea crew. Hull was the first port, after which we would call at Newcastle, Grangemouth, then round the north of Scotland to Belfast, Birkenhead, Dublin, Swansea, then on to London, before finishing the loading in Southend. The estimated time on the coast was six weeks.

The *Benledi* eventually came sliding in through the morning gloom, a tug in attendance at either end. She had been launched in 1954, a six-hatch, three-castle steamship, four derricks to each hatch, trailing a drift of sooty black smoke as she neared. She looked orderly enough. This was now my third general cargo ship, even though the first trip had only lasted a few days, and I could acquit myself properly, which made acceptance by the other officers much easier.

I climbed the gangway and introduced myself to the second mate, who was leaving. He was keen to get home and gave me a swift handover, a tour of the decks, a tour of the bridge and a quick run-round of the accommodation. He had prepared the charts and drawn the

*The SS* Benledi *arriving in port.*

courses to Newcastle, then on to Grangemouth. The rest of the navigation had been left for me to sort out. The coastal crew and officers of the *Benledi* were again mostly Scots, and I noticed that many of them were older than the deep sea officers, and some looked less healthy. The Leith company had a reputation for treating its men well and inspiring loyalty. The coast trips were a good example; several of the crew were judged not fit enough for a deep sea voyage although they could cope adequately on the coast. The dockside shore cranes were generally used around Britain and Europe, and this meant the working stress in port was much less. The only time we used the ship's derricks was when we loaded from barges at anchorage, which was usually the case for dangerous cargoes when the port authorities wanted to keep us away from the population mass. We were due to take explosives on board in Southend and that would be carried out at anchor, well clear of populated areas. We also had a loading superintendent travelling with us who worked with the first mate to make us that the outbound cargo was loaded according to the loading plan produced by Head Office. This was different from the main deep sea voyages, when all the loading and discharging plans had to be worked out by the first mate personally.

The Old Man was most definitely an old man, on the cusp of retirement. He was small and wizened and quiet. I saw him on the bridge when the ship was entering or leaving port, but otherwise we rarely met. We had a short session together before we left Hull, so that I understood his requirements. He leant towards the cautious, wanting me to lay off courses that kept ten miles off any land and five miles clear of any underwater dangers. This wasn't practical in a lot of cases, although we agreed I would lay off the courses as safely as possible. The first mate, my immediate superior, was a man who liked to moan, incessantly. He had some sort of illness that required regular changes of his blood. It sounded very much as if he wasn't fit to work at all, although the company was content to give him coastal voyages. I found that he got on my nerves, though, with his unceasing monologues in which he exhaustively detailed all his maladies.

I found myself in a position that was a considerable shift up the ladder from my days as a cadet, which didn't seem that long ago. As cadet I had been the lowest of the low, I'd had to work like a beast, I was looked down upon by everyone and was constantly reminded that I was the lowest form of marine life. Now I was second officer at the age of twenty-two with a small queue of people further down the hill than me: the third officer, the fourth officer and three cadets. Up the hill and ahead of me were the captain, the chief officer and the first officer. Looking forward wasn't so much a hill, though, more an edifice.

The second mate has a comfortable position on board. At sea I had the twelve–to–four watch. From midday to four it was quiet, because the Old Man would make a quick appearance on the bridge after lunch and then go off for a snooze; from midnight to four the rest of the ship was asleep and there was only me and the lookout, alone in the dark. Apart from being a watch-keeper, my main role was the navigation, which included working out the courses to each port and drawing the lines in soft grey pencil on the Admiralty charts to show the route. I would work out the ETA each day at noon, together with the average speed for the day. I had a lot of autonomy, with only the Old Man changing my courses from time to time, which was expected but which some second mates took as a personal slight. I would try and always work three ports ahead, and by the time we left Hull I had laid off the courses as far as Belfast. I would usually spend an hour on the bridge in the morning after breakfast, updating routes and working out distances and steaming times. There were always sheaves of chart corrections to do, which I would try and deal with on anchor watches whenever I could.

We stayed in Hull for ten days, discharging our Far East cargo of light manufactured goods. There was little cargo for the East to load there, just some transhipments to be taken further round the coast. The hours were short and the dockers slack, cargo watches were dull. In our off-times, I went with some of the other officers to the few pubs and clubs that were near to the docks. They were universally grim, the buildings were broken and ragged and looked as if they had been bombed. Inside, they were peopled by those living on the desperate edge of society: blowsy ancient prostitutes, unemployed men not fit for employment, employed men shirking their employment, crooks, chancers, drunks, skivers, mendicants, liars, boasters. Everyone looked unhealthy, unwashed, uncaring, they all had bad teeth, stringy hair, fetid breath. Communication was exchanges of emphatic statement, punctuated by obscenities. They cackled at any hint of misfortune suffered by others. The dockland clubs were worse than the pubs. There were more prostitutes and crooks and less beggars and unemployed men, but the core of poor humanity remained the same. The drinks were more expensive in the clubs, and the entertainment value was sub-zero. Howling music punished our ears, tarty girls danced listlessly around their handbags on the tiny dance floor, shrieking at each other. Whores clawed at us as we passed, squawks of laughter rent the quiet passages between the blasting sound, the cold beer was warm, the clubs smelled, everything was cheap and cheaply done, the toilets had no towels or dryers although they offered a wide choice of condoms. I was glad to clear Hull for the twelve hour run to Newcastle. As we pulled into the channel I leant over the dodger and sucked in the fresh north wind that was cleansing the ship.

The run from Grangemouth in the Firth of Forth to Belfast took us along the rugged north coast of Scotland to Cape Wrath, the northernmost point on the Scottish mainland. We passed through the narrow Pentland Firth, the Orkney Islands to the north, John o'Groats to the south. It was one o'clock in the morning, bright oil flares from the offshore oilfields lit the sky and the Old Man made one of his rare bridge appearances as we went through the narrow pass. He didn't say much, just nodded in the backlit dark, muttering a few words of caution. I had taken the ship off autopilot and put a quartermaster on the wheel because the tide rips could be fierce; the Old Man seemed to approve. He stayed for twenty minutes then disappeared below. Coastal traffic was light although the tidal pulls were so strong that there was little room for error as we ploughed our 8,800 gross tons through the Firth. I felt my inner tightness unwind as we slid through the gap between the islands of Stroma and Swona and into clear water.

The next afternoon was clear and bright and breath-taking. We headed south with the Outer Hebrides to the west, their rocky coasts as remote as the moon, while to the east the mountains on the Isle of Skye clawed at the clouds, looking like some godless and magical land. On the final stretch we steamed past Islay, then went between the Mull of Kintyre and the grey-green shore of County Antrim, before swinging into Belfast Lough.

Belfast gave us trouble, or more accurately gave me trouble. We were taking crates of Irish liqueurs on board to be stowed in the lockers in Number 3 hatch. The lockers were already part-loaded with Scotch from Grangemouth. The Belfast loading gang wanted scotch, they believed it their right to break a case. They ask me if they could accidentally drop one. I said no. I put a cadet on guard. The dockers looked at me with hatred. They worked go-slow to the point of not working. I ignored them. After an hour, the foreman brushed past me and gave petition to the first mate. The first mate caved in. I thought he was a weakling.

He said to me: 'If we don't let them break a case of scotch we'll be here for days.'

I said nothing, I curled my lip in contempt. The foreman smirked at me. Two hours later the loading gang was too drunk to do any work at all, one vomited in the hold, one urinated in the hold. Two of them fought, half-heartedly. They smashed a case of liqueurs and cheered, then started drinking that. The gangs from Number 1 and 2 hatches climbed down and joined the party. I watched them all from the deck, leaning on the latch coaming. They saw me watching and started jeering and calling me a stupid English bastard. One came out of the hatch and staggered towards me, hurling insults. He said if I came ashore they would beat the shit out of me and that next time I had better give them a case of grog if they asked for it. I spat on the deck at his feet, he roared with rage at the insult and lunged towards me. He tripped over a lug protruding from the deck, piling face first into a ventilator cowl, a splash of red wiped across his face, he rolled back and lay there groaning and bleeding. I laughed and walked away. Fifteen minutes later, as I sat in the ship's office, the first mate came to see me; the chief officer and the Old Man were with him.

The first mate said: 'Did you punch one of the dockers? That's what they're saying.'

'No, I didn't punch anyone,' I replied. I explained what had happened.

'They're going crazy out there. There might be a walk-off.' The first mate looked at me accusingly.

I said: 'They're going crazy because they're all pissed.'

'Have they been at the whisky in the lockers?' demanded the chief mate.

I looked at the first mate accusingly. He reddened, he fidgeted, he blathered.

'I had to give them a case to smash otherwise they just weren't going to work. This is making me feel ill, I'm not well.' He held his stomach and groaned.

'They were hacked off with me because I told them earlier they couldn't have anything,' I said.

'Good God! What a balls-up!' the chief mate shouted. He paced up and down for a moment, thinking, then turned to the first mate.

'Go and see the foreman. Tell him the guy hurt himself because he was drunk on duty, but we won't report him if they get back to work now. Tell him he can have two bottles of scotch to give to the man who hurt himself as compensation and a case of scotch for himself if he gets all three gangs back to work now.'

He turned to me. 'You, Second Mate, learn some diplomacy. Now keep out of sight and off the deck until we leave port. The third mate and fourth mate can do all the cargo watches. And don't go ashore.'

'Yes choff,' I replied obediently. Thinking: 'Suits me.'

The Old Man nodded approvingly, then he and the chief officer trooped back up to the boat deck above the fray. I watched the first mate quell the seething mob with his bribes, then went into the accommodation and stayed there for the rest of the time we were in Belfast.

Our next port of call was Birkenhead docks, which were dreadful, a poster for 1970s decaying Britain. Everything in view was in a state of disintegration, it made Hull look grand. The place looked as if it had been blown up and badly reassembled. There was a single public house across from where the *Benledi* was berthed, which stood alone among a crumbled landscape, everything else around it had fallen down or been knocked down. It stood tall and grey and daunting, keeper of a thousand dockyard secrets.

The décor inside was gin-palace bright: part-dismembered chandeliers, chunky red-patterned wallpaper, scarred and peeling, a long straight bar the length of one wall, scattered tables, round and dark with mismatched stools, tinny music from an ancient juke box. The men were pinched, mean-faced and nasty, the sort who would cheer if they saw small boys fighting and hurting each other. They spoke gruffly in accents so thick they sounded as if they were choking on their own phlegm, their words were unkind, the course of their conversations was to attack anyone different to them. The women were worse, awful creatures, haggard, coarse, vile. One, recent from childbirth, with a crooked face, drunk, was amusing the men by pulling open her blouse and squirting milk at them from one breast, shrieking with laughter. They cheered and leered. Her daughter, sixteen perhaps, simple, stood by her, grinning lopsidedly. Other women stood in small groups, cawing, offering us sex as soon as we walked through the door. They would be on the ship later, stumbling up the gangway, bullying their way past the sailor on watch, down to the crew quarters, banging on the cabin doors looking for trade.

As we traversed those big old British ports, empire-built places that had seen such greatness, I felt I was witness to some final stand, the last guard had fallen away and all that was left was lone outposts of what had once been great, standing among the rubble of yesterday. Swing bridges, marvels of their day, rusted and immobile. Docks deserted and part-unusable, greening, rat-ridden, the waters so marvellously trapped by Victorian engineering genius now foul and polluted, toxic enough to kill you in minutes if you fell in. Idle cranes lined the wharfs like harsh judges. In a curious way, though, I loved these places, rotten as they were. They had the stamp of the past, the past I was following. I didn't want to serve on ships that called into twenty-four-hour floodlit container parks, eerily efficient, soulless, no gangs of dockers, just gantry cranes that didn't even look like cranes. I wanted the bleakness, the decay, the collapse, the ghosts of the past. When I walked along the dockside at Birkenhead, I felt a tingling in my groin and a heightening of my senses as the avatars of tea clipper crews wandered by unseen.

Swansea was equally rough; the fourth engineer made a joke about Welshmen and was thrown through a shop window. That incident apart, the people were kinder, though, welcoming us, buying us drinks, bidding us to return. The place didn't have the same menace as Birkenhead.

The King George docks in London were lively and bustling. The docks were not full, but there were still enough cargo ships in to give the proper character of a working port. We were there for ten days. On my first day off I took a train home to say hello to my parents. My father was nearly at the end of his RAF career, my mother was the same as I had always remembered. Of my two brothers, Peter worked in a bank in Whitehall, Anthony was still at school. Everything seemed a picture of normality against the background of my own strange life. Peter and I went out that evening and returned late. I entertained him with sea tales. I was back at the King George docks for duty at 0700 the next morning.

We had a few inter-ship parties while we were there, with a Clan Line ship just in from India, laden with spice and tea, and a Palm Line liner on its turnaround from the West African coast with a cargo of groundnuts, vegetable oils and timber. They were noisy boozy affairs, held in the bars of either the *Benledi* or the *Clan Macnair* or the *Ibadan Palm*. We kept among our rank groupings, I would socialise with the second and third mates, swapping tales, exchanging information. The three captains would do likewise; I would eavesdrop to see who was winning as each Old Man scaled for dominance.

The last call on the coast was Southend anchorage, where we spent three days loading explosives for Singapore. Clunky Thames barges moored alongside, and we hoisted the crates aboard with our derricks, stowing them securely in the tween decks of Number 3 hold. Once that was done and they were securely lashed, the ship's carpenter built a tough wooden cage around the whole area. The deep sea crew came aboard on the last day. They were mostly the same people who had left when we had joined, so the handover time was minimal. As navigator, I had drawn the courses down to Ushant, not bothering to go any further as I knew the deep sea second mate would always have his own routes all ready to draw.

✯    ✯    ✯

Four weeks later I was back in London, in the same King George docks, signing on the SS *Benreoch*. She was another long-serving general cargo liner, built in the early 1950s and a year away from being scrapped. I signed on as second mate for the deep sea voyage, Far East and back. The *Benreoch* had little modern equipment and few crew luxuries, but she was smart and in good order.

The Suez Canal had finally re-opened in the spring of that year after being closed since the six-day Arab-Israeli War in 1967. We arrived for our transit at the end of December, following a muted Christmas in the Mediterranean as we steamed past Malta. On the day, we had a decent feed, too much to drink and some general horsing around. I felt the cadets were let off lightly, but that was probably because I had always been made to sing at Christmas as a cadet and engage in antics that made me look ridiculous for the entertainment of the officers.

We took on a pilot at Port Said, at the northern end of the canal. Myriad traders swarmed on board to sell us worthless tat: brass figures of pharaohs and dancing girls, hopeless paintings, nudge-nudge phials of Spanish fly aphrodisiac, ancient pornography from my grandmother's era. Windy gully-gully men pulled chicks from our ears. I kept my cabin locked; some didn't and were looted by mendicants and others who trawled the decks. We loaded the Suez Canal searchlight on board and it was secured to the bow, to light the way through the water when night fell.

Suez Canal ships travel in convoys of about a dozen. There was some agriculture at the northern end of the canal, although that soon faded to reveal yellow sand stretching away at either side, broken by grassy scrub on the east. To the west, the Sinai Peninsula rolled into endless arid waste. There were scattered clumps of war-damaged buildings and occasional burnt-out vehicles strewn all the way down. The banks were blighted by barbed wire and tank traps and gun placements, aircraft of the Egyptian Air Force played overhead, troops, tanks, trucks and military hardware were in evidence everywhere. North of Ismailia, which was just under half-way down the Canal, there was a cut where northbound and southbound ships could pass each other, separated by an island of desert sand. As we looked across at the ships on the other side of the cut, they appeared to be steaming through the desert itself.

South of Ismailia, we reached the Bitter Lakes where we anchored and waited for several hours for the northbound convoy to pass us by. Fifteen ships had been trapped in the Bitter Lakes after the 1967 war when the canal was blocked: four were British, two West German, two American, two Polish and others from France, Bulgaria and Czechoslovakia. They became known as the Yellow Fleet because they were continually covered in sand blowing in from the surrounding desert. Once it became clear that they were going to be trapped in the lakes for some time, the Yellow Fleet formed associations, they pottered between each other in their lifeboats, played football matches, held parties and even organised their own Olympic Games. The only ships of the Yellow Fleet that could steam out of the canal under their own power when it re-opened in the spring of 1975 were the two Germans, all the others were towed away. The German ships were cheered by huge crowds when they arrived in Hamburg; it was a national triumph. One of them, the *Munsterlander*, had completed its voyage from Australia, a trip that had lasted over eight years. On the *Benreoch*, it took us fifteen hours to transit the twenty-two-mile canal, before finally being disgorged at Port Suez into the northern end of the Red Sea.

We steamed south into the Red Sea, taking care to avoid the mined areas. Navigation was difficult because most of the lighthouses and buoys had been out since the Arab–Israeli war and it was going to be a long time before they would all be working again. Shipping was moderate, the Red Sea was a funnel towards the canal. We overtook slower ships that had come out ahead of us in the convoy and were overtaken in turn by faster ones. Arab dhows littered the sea. We kept the radar on constantly. It was 1,300 miles from Port Suez to the southern end of the Red Sea, and it took us the best part of four days at our reined-back speed of 14 knots. We were all pleased to finally slip through the Bab-el-Mendab Strait and out into the Gulf of Aden.

Our destination ports on the Far East run were Singapore, Djakarta, Manila and Cebu in the Philippines, Pontianak in West Borneo, Rejang in Sarawak, Keelung in Taiwan, Naha in the Japanese Okinawa Islands, Hong Kong, then Pusan in South Korea. There would be a few additional loading ports, although we didn't know what these were yet, and we would receive further orders as the voyage progressed. A worm of excitement danced within me: in my mind, I was headed for the lands that Joseph Conrad himself had wandered, on the same type of ship doing the same job. Conrad had served in the British Merchant Navy on barques and clippers, on sailing ships that mostly ambled around the Far East and South Pacific. The *Benreoch* was an old ship when I served on her, although she had been launched sixty years after Conrad had signed off his last ship in 1894. Even so, Conrad would have easily recognised her as a general cargo steamer. Despite the *Benreoch* being sleeker, bigger and more sophisticated than the steamers that plied their trade before the First World War, she still had the same basic three-island layout, still worked in the same manner, picking up and dropping off the same sort of break-bulk cargoes, loaded into the decks using the ships gear by gangs of dock workers under the hot eastern sun. The Indian Ocean crossing was serene, but my mind was racing in anticipation.

We had four Chinese painters on board the *Benreoch*. Their sole job was to keep the ship looking smart. The Scots crew were unencumbered by painting duties and could spend their time keeping all the running and working gear in order. The demand on the crew was considerable. This was a five-hatch ship, with four derricks to a hatch, plus three other small derricks for stores and minor work, twenty-two in total. Each derrick had five blocks that the working wires ran through. All the wires had to be greased, and they had to be spliced if damaged or completely replaced. Each block needed to be stripped down to be oiled and greased, ensuring that the pulley wheels ran smoothly and the sides closed securely. The wooden hatch boards were covered with canvas and held down with wooden wedges, all of which had to be kept in good order, secure, seaworthy. The deck cargo of three trucks, a bulldozer, some large steel structures, were lashed down with steel wires wound tight with bottle-screws, which were checked and tightened daily. The lashings on the cargo below deck were also inspected regularly. The ventilator cowls for the holds were trimmed to the first mate's instructions, keeping the right air flow over the cargo. Mooring ropes were repaired, new wires were wound onto the winch drums, stays were coated with white lead, wooden upper decks were holystoned and the work went on. The Far East run was demanding on the ship's gear and everything had to be in tip-top order. But one thing the crew didn't have to do was paint. That job was for the Chinese painters.

Every day, day on day, the Chinese painters rose, and they painted, all day every day. The superstructure gleamed white, the decks and working gear were painted a creamy brown. Where there were tears of rust, they rubbed them clear, primed the bare steel and repainted. When the *Benreoch* arrived in port after a long fair weather sea passage, the ship looked as if it had just emerged from the shipyard. The painters' speciality, their *pièce de résistance*, was the wood painting of the bulkheads on the lower decks. When someone came aboard the *Benreoch*, they arrived at the top of the gangway at poop deck level, one level above the main deck, where they were confronted with the accommodation bulkhead – that's a wall to you landlubbers – which was made of timber. The bulkhead was panelled and studded, the wood was coarse-grained and there were wooden frames around the portholes and the doorways. There were occasional splits and seams, some scars and scuffs and paint smears and nail-holes, a few dry-looking and faded areas, as you would expect in any long wooden wall. It seemed remarkable at first view that a steel ship built in the twentieth century would have wooden bulkheads. The next deck up was the same, the same solid wooden bulkheads. It was only when you knocked against the bulkhead for the first time that you realised that it wasn't wood, it was steel. It was cunningly and artistically painted metal, not painted white as would be expected, but carefully and painstakingly painted to make it look more like wood than wood itself. No one on board the *Benreoch* tired of watching people come on board, doing a double-take, shaking their head, looking at it again, then poking and knocking on the bulkhead, shaking their head and smiling with realisation. The wooden bulkhead painting was done by the Chinese painters on every ship in the fleet, they were famous throughout the East. It gave the ships a special panache that made the crews proud.

The *Benreoch* had a good-size complement, nearly fifty souls. As was the case for the whole fleet, 90 per cent were from Scotland, mainly the Islands or the Edinburgh area. On my side of the business we had the captain, chief officer, first, second, third and fourth officers, plus three cadets. The third mate, Alex, resented me slightly, as he had been hoping to get bumped up to second mate. He looked for ways to put me down, although usually made a bad fist of it; he was a blowhard and I didn't pay him much heed. The Old Man was big and hard and known among the crew as Mac the Knife, for his habit of culling overtime claims. The chief officer, Mr Smythe, was a dandy, always pristine, always posing if there were any ladies within hailing distance. The first mate was English, from the north-west; he grew his hair down to his shoulders, and his favourite topic of conversation was his ancient MG, about which he could rattle on uninterrupted for hours. Two of the cadets were from the Shetland Islands, Sheltees, quiet, gentle, competent lads. The third cadet was from the Lowlands and was boastful and lazy. Then there was the fourth mate, who was a former company cadet who had failed his Second Mate's Certificate twice and was sailing as uncertificated fourth mate. He was known as Daze. Daze was laid back to such an extent that people said it was small wonder he failed. The real reason he kept failing was probably because he spent a large part of his spare time smoking marijuana. I smelt it on him strongly on Christmas evening, and there was more than a whiff on other occasions. Daze shared the four–to–eight watch with the first mate.

The engineers were a good crowd. I got on well with my opposite number, Bob the third engineer, who was a cheerful Geordie, as well as with Brian the electrical officer, a manic character who I sometimes thought was unhinged. The radio officer, Sparks, was a German. Well, he had a British passport although his mother was German and he had lived in Germany for most of his life after his parents' marriage had broken up. He spoke English with a comic accent, which brought us great amusement. He boasted that he had joined the British Merchant Navy to avoid being conscripted back home, and spent a lot of time crowing about the superiority of Germany over Britain, its glories, work ethic, business success and culture. The rest of us tended to retreat to the time-tested British method of arguing with a German by repeatedly crowding out his arguments with reminders of who had won the war. This always bounced off him, though, so we always ended up lowering the tone further by telling him to: 'Bugger off back to the Fatherland then!'

The deck crew were mostly Scottish Islanders, mainly from Lewis, Harris, Skye and the Shetlands. The bosun was from the Orkneys, and there were two ABs from Liverpool. They were all tough characters, they worked hard and were mostly decent men, although a couple had a mean streak. They drunk a lot and fought each other on occasions. I found them reliable sailors, grog and bad moods notwithstanding. The engine room hands, the firemen, were all from Edinburgh, as were the stewards, the cooks and the crew mess man. All in all, with a handful of exceptions, it was a good crowd. There were small tensions between the Islanders and the southern Scots, but nothing of great import.

We hit Singapore late one afternoon, our first port on the Far East run. The berth was waiting for us near Keppel, right on the city waterfront. We cleared customs and immigration at anchor, then picked up the hook and went alongside. The avenues of my life always seemed to lead me back to Singapore. I had gone to school there, it had virtually been my home port when I was a cadet on tankers, and now it was one of the main destinations for the Leith company. In early 1976 there was a hint of change in the air, heralding the transformation that would later destroy the ambiance and transform Singapore into an antiseptic and soulless city state. The changes were still some way distant, although the advance guard was already in evidence. Streets of Victorian and Edwardian buildings were being bulldozed and replaced by flats of glass and pressed concrete. Street shopping in cluttered shops along crowded pavements was under threat by the malls on the draughtsmen's boards. The Malay kampongs, carefully preserved jungle villages of wood and thatch, were becoming isolated curios among a sea of modern buildings, and their systematic destruction was getting closer. The street markets were being reported as being too disordered, the press was toadying to the government more and more. Citizens who didn't confirm to the new modernity were in danger of being labelled foolish or backward, or potentially dangerous. The Western decadence in the shape of the bars and the wild areas, such as Bugis Street, were coming under increasing focus.

My skewed viewpoint, of course, was from the bizarre angle of someone who would have preferred it if everything had remained unchanged since the turn of the century, but the headlong development rush made me sigh with sadness for a world passing away forever, too fast. But at that time, when we arrived in Keppel Harbour on the *Benreoch*, Singapore as it had been was still there: the Champagne Bar hauled us in, made us drink and dance and then spat us out so much the poorer. The Bugis Street market was still the best show in town. Serangoon was doing a roaring trade, drawing in those who were attracted by the hovering violence and seedy edge. The Thieves Market in Arab Street, off a mesh of streets along the grubbier end of Rochor Canal, remained the place to buy anything from surplus British military goods with War Department stamps to $1 waxed paper and bamboo umbrellas for sheltering against the afternoon downpours. Late at night, in the dark underbelly of North Bridge Road, dangerous-looking men beckoned, whispering the delights of sex shows in sordid upstairs rooms. I spent nights wandering the narrow alleys to the north of the city centre, watching the pantomime of Chinese street opera, striving to find joy in the screeching, failing to find anything but still loving the exoticism and mystery. I sometimes saw ancient Chinese ladies tottering on bound feet, or parties of rats pattering along the open monsoon drains, occasionally breaking cover into the street to forage. Sometimes I would go into one of the Chinese bars; they were in high rooms with big ceiling fans whooshing overhead, often on a corner, shuttered doors folded back to allow the inside to become part of the street. I remember the floors were mostly black-and-white tiles on which dark wood tables were scattered randomly. Very old men sat silently with tea and bowls of noodles. I would sit near the street drinking icy Anchor Pilsner beer and smoking Three Fives cigarettes, which I would buy singly from a tin for five cents each, and I would watch the life go by. I loved Singapore in the 1970s.

We stayed there for a week, unloading large crates of CKDs, cars-knocked-down, and other machinery from the UK, loading lighter manufactured goods for the homeward voyage. Keppel Harbour was the old part of the port, and we were only allocated a couple of shore cranes, which meant that we worked the ship partly under our own gear and partly under shore gear. The working day was twenty hours, with two to six in the morning being quiet. Between the three of us junior mates, me, Alex and Daze, we would work two watches: six in the morning until four in the afternoon and then four until two in the morning; one of us would have the day off. The shore gangs were skilled and well supervised, the duties for the officer of the watch were making sure the right cargo was taken, keeping the cargo plan updated and sorting out the problems that invariably arose.

After leaving Singapore, we headed for Tanjong Priok, the port for Djakarta, for a six-day stay. Djakarta is the capital and main port of the island of Java in Indonesia. Indonesia has the fourth-highest population in the world, Java is the most populated island in the world,

Djakarta is the most populated city in South-East Asia. Indonesia is an archipelago made up of 17,500 islands: lots of people, lots of islands ranging from tiny and uninhabited spots to the massiveness of Sumatra. Indonesia teems with romance and history – the Moluccas, once known as the Spice Islands, where nutmeg, mace, cloves and other spices were fought over for centuries; the Spice Wars in the seventeenth century killed off the whole indigenous population. Makassar: a centuries-old city port, melting pot of traders from all over Asia and beyond, of Arabs, Siamese, Portuguese, Malays, Indians, Chinese, Dutch, British, Javanese. Celebes: the strange-shaped island consisting of four long peninsulas, the home of the Bugis, the great traders, adventurers and mariners who spread their power to the Malaya peninsula and beyond. The Indonesian archipelago is breathtaking in its diversity, a place that has fascinated everyone who has visited. Djakarta was known as Batavia under Dutch domination, a period that lasted from 1602 until they finally ceded power in 1949. When the Dutch went home, the city reverted to a form of the ancient name of Jayawikarta. When I was there in the mid-1970s it was known as Djakarta, later dropping the D to become plain old Jakarta.

We were discharging more CKDs in Tanjong Priok, after which we were due to fill some of the tween deck space with plywood, rubber and timber. It was slow work with frequent delays, as we had to wait for trucks to arrive with each parcel of cargo. The agent warned us against going into central Djakarta, which was apparently too violent, particularly against Westerners who strayed into the wrong areas. The local street gangs all carried butterfly knives. Needle-pointed, these were as sharp as razors, and a practised hand could flick out the central blade from between the two enclosing handles in a fraction of a second to form a fearsome weapon. Gang members walked the streets of Djakarta with their shirts open to show the patchwork of knife scars across their torsos; badges of honour.

On the first night, Bob, Brian and I decided we should take heed of the agent's sage advice and restrict ourselves to having a drink in a couple of the local bars in the port area of Tanjong Priok. The bars were all clumped together in a strip in a badly-lit street outside the dock gates. They were shanty places, booming music, full of sailors, full of whores. We had been there for an hour, enjoying ourselves, keeping to ourselves, when a burly Polish man punched me in the face unexpectedly, for looking at him the wrong way, apparently. It dropped me to the ground like a stone, my head bounced on the concrete floor. The bar erupted in a mass brawl around me; a dozen of the *Benreoch*'s officers and crew felt obligated to avenge the assault. They slammed into the group of Poles. I lay dazed among cigarette ends; glasses and bottles and chairs crashed down around me, I could feel the warmth of blood on my cheek, I couldn't move. The situation was an uncanny repeat of what had happened to me in Makassar a few years previously, when a Dutchman had whacked me on the side of the head with a bottle for trying to take his girl, which I wasn't. I found myself reflecting that the way I was acting in Indonesian bars was all wrong, but I didn't know why. All I could see now from my supine position were ankles moving in slow motion, the room seemed to be becoming brighter and brighter, the sounds of battle were fading. I wondered if I was dying. The fight was short, the *Benreoch* won, the Poles were evicted. Several of our crew were bloodied, Bob's nose was bleeding, Brian's shirt was ripped. They heaved me off the floor but I had difficulty standing up. I fell down again. They picked me up bodily and sat me in a chair. Brian said I looked brain-damaged. The blood was sponged off my face and I had a bottle of beer and a smoke, which seemed to put me right. Later, we noticed that some of the losing Poles had sneaked back in again and were keeping a low profile at the other end of the bar. We left them alone, and after a while they sent over a round of drinks as a peace offering. We told ourselves we were pleased we hadn't gone into Djakarta itself, where we might have encountered more serious trouble. When I was back on board the *Benreoch* I tried to look up brain damage in the *Ship Captain's Medical Guide*, but I was too drunk to read it properly so I went to bed. In the morning I felt fine, albeit a bit hung over.

Pontianak and Rajang were windows into a different world. We called at Pontianak first, a dozen miles up the Kapuas river in West Borneo, almost exactly on the line of the equator. The word Pontianak translates from the local dialect as a ghostly type of vampire. The city was founded on the site where the founder, the local Sultan, apparently saw a ghost who told him where to build his palace. The native peoples are the Dayaks and the Malays, although there is now a huge Chinese population. The Dayaks were best known for their headhunting activities in earlier times. The idea behind Dayak headhunting was that if the hunter preserved and retained the head, which they did by cutting it open to remove the skull then boiling and stuffing it, the unfortunate victim would then act as their servant *post mortem*.

We tied up to big mooring buoys in the sluggish Kapuas river, which was thick and the colour of strong tea, to load rubber and tobacco from barges that moored alongside us. We heaved the cargo aboard in nets and stowed it carefully in the holds. In the first mate's cargo plan the tobacco was kept well separated from other cargoes to avoid taint. The wooden houses along the river edge with their tiled or tin roofs were mostly built up on pilings to keep them well off the ground and to guard against the regular flooding of the river. The whole area had a swampy feel. Canoes rowed round the ship, the occupants shouting up at us, trying to sell fruit and wooden carvings. We would lower ropes and pull items up for inspection, before carrying out the bartering process, mostly by gesticulation. The price agreed, we would insert notes into the lay of the rope and lower it back down again.

Further up the coast, we went deeper into this vast jungle island. We were headed eighty miles up the Rajang river, along a winding path of water, dark green jungle blocking either side. There were a few clumps of cultivated land, but it was mostly wild. As we wound our way up the river it was as if we were disappearing into a world remote from the twentieth century, a timeless land where the dark jungle crowded us ever closer from the banks, and monkeys whooped and flung themselves around the treeline as we thumped gently round a green bend, to see another green bend ahead. The water became thicker and browner as we moved upstream. When we came round the Kampong Banyok and neared the city of Sibu, the jungle fell away and we found ourselves in the company of other deep sea ships that had made the long journey inland.

Rajang is in Sarawak, which is now a province of Malaysia. The place has an interesting history. Sarawak was ruled for 100 years by the Brookes, a dynasty of Englishmen known as the White Rajahs. The first was Rajah James Brooke, who was presented with the province of

Sarawak for helping the Sultan of Brunei suppress rebellion. James and his successor White Rajahs, despite their obligatory post-colonial bashing, ruled with what was generally agreed to be a fair although firm hand. The widespread piracy in the region was crushed, as were a lot of the headhunting antics of the local tribes. The fast-expanding British commercial interests were grateful to Brooke for dealing with the piracy, while the liberal interests at home were pleased to see the back of headhunting. The last White Rajah, Charles Vyner Brooke, handed over his charge to the British after the Second World War, who then ruled it until independence in the 1960s.

Once the *Benreoch* was securely moored, we loaded more rubber, some timber and coffee and a few other raw goods; the shore gangs worked the derricks at a speed that was impossible to diminish. The whole pace of life slowed, it felt as torpid as the idle Rajang river itself, we all slowed with it. I spent a lot of time leaning on the rails and looking out at the quiet. Everything was so still, so unmoving, as if the whole world had lain down and gone to sleep.

We continued our wanderings north-west to Manila and Cebu, the two major deep sea ports in the Philippines. The Philippines comprises 7,000 islands and is the northern continuation of the shattered archipelago of the 17,500 islands that constitute Indonesia. I had always liked Manila, having been there several times as a cadet in my tanker days. It was blaring, gaudy and dangerous. Shameless corruption and exploitation ran through every corner of life, but no one could ever say it lacked excitement. Things had changed a lot since President Marcos had declared martial law in September 1972. His justification was to curb guerrilla insurgencies, although the reality was the curbing of the press, the crushing of civil liberties, the closure of Congress and the gaoling of the opposition. Wholesale graft and naked nepotism erupted. One of the dictates to keep the population in check was the disarming of ordinary citizens. The first time I had visited Manila, in pre-Marcos times, everyone seemed to be wearing a gun, it was like being in the Wild West. I felt undressed not having one. People walked down the street with guns in holsters, guns thrust into their belts, gun butts sticking out of their side pockets. Smart businessmen had pearl-handled executive handguns in shoulder holsters under their suit jackets. All the bars had had signs asking the patrons to hand in their firearms and other lethal weapons on arrival, saying that they could collect them on departure. All of this was now gone, and there was less noticeable menace in the air, even though the side streets were far from safe and the city still had one of the highest murder rates in the world. This was the beginning of 1976, before Manila hoisted itself onto the tourist trail. At that time, most travel companies remained nervous about sending clients to what they believed was their potential doom. There was no doom in the bar district of Ermita, it was booming, it was packed with merchant seaman, oil workers, gangsters, and United States army, navy, marines and air force personnel from the military bases nearby. The two main bar streets parallel to the waterfront, Mabini Street and M. H. del Pilar, were crammed with bars and cafés and hotbed hotels, booming music and bright light spilled outside, people milled along the pavements and into the streets among the clogged traffic. The air was thick with the scent of the urban East: wet mossy air, oils and spices, effluent,

*The SS* Benreoch.
*Used with the kind permission of www.fotoflite.com*

diesel fumes, the smell of packed humanity. Food stalls sold grim-looking items which we refused. Manila had a nasty reputation for food poisoning at the time, particularly from soiled seafood dredged from the toxic waters of Manila Bay. In the bars, we only drunk bottled beer, San Miguel usually, always making sure we saw the bottle being uncapped. Bar girls jostled us for trade, a procession of clumsy dancers strutted enthusiastically on the makeshift stages, flinging off their clothes flamboyantly. There were always fights. Most were short scuffles announced with grunts and thuds, which were usually broken up quickly. Others were prolonged tribalised brawls that dragged in a lot of participants: US Navy versus a German ship, US Marines versus US Air Force, British ship versus Dutch ship, and so on. The small fights made good theatre, although the bigger battles caused us to vacate the bar for a quieter venue, leaving the men to roar at each other and the girls to scream as the place was smashed up.

Back on the ship, half a dozen armed security guards lived on board for the duration of the stay in port. Manila was crime-ridden, the docks were gated although all sorts of miscreants tended to find their way in. Shipboard robbery was common and most of the robbers were armed, with knives at least. One guard was always stationed at the top of the gangway while the others were supposed to patrol the ship. They all wore blue uniforms with their names printed above the left breast, US army style. At seven o'clock in the evening the day shift were relieved by fresh people who worked until seven the following morning. There was a supervisor, although he always sloped off to find somewhere to sleep when it got dark, leaving his squad to guard us. This entailed them mostly hanging round the places where there was a good chance of hand-outs: the crew mess, the officer's bar and the galley. They punctuated their loafing with an occasional stroll around the decks. Most of the guards were women, and some would enhance their earnings by selling themselves. They did a busy trade as a lot of the crew considered them a good deal because they were less likely to be diseased than some of the Ermita bar girls, as well as providing the best possible cabin security. A few were attractive, or at least approaching attractiveness, although most had seen better days. Late at night, though, especially after a jaunt into Ermita, many people decided that even the grim ones were appealing, and the wheel of commerce would turn.

Cebu was Manila in miniature; many of the crew preferred it because the bars and associated pleasures were telescoped into a smaller area that was nearer the docks. Bob and I tried to find the famous Suzie's Blue Bar while we were there, but couldn't – we were told it had closed down a couple of years beforehand.

Borneo and Sarawak were slow, Manila and Cebu were wild, Keelung was electric. The atmosphere in Keelung twanged. Neon lights were everywhere, even during the day. We called in to load electrical goods, coincidentally. Keelung sits in the northern part of the island of Taiwan, off the coast of mainland China. The people of Taiwan called themselves the Republic of China. The people on the mainland called themselves the People's Republic of China. The two Chinas were separated by the Taiwan Strait, a 100-mile channel known by many Chinese as The Black Ditch. After the Communists under Mao Tse Tung won the Chinese civil war in 1949, the Nationalists under Generalissimo Chiang Kai Shek fled across the ditch and established the rival government. Since then the two Chinas have sniped at each other across the water, each claiming to be the true seat of Chinese power. The island existed on a semi-permanent war footing, the port of Keelung closed at night with submarine nets being drawn across the harbour. Keelung was a loud and vibrant city port, all noise and commerce and busy people, non-stop. Unlike most parts of the East, there was little deference to Western society, and few signs were in English. All road signs, shop names and advertising posters were resolutely written with Chinese characters.

As night fell, the neon signs dominated, a myriad of colours. The streets were a pageant of old China. Gnarled men squatted on wooden stools in white vests and baggy blue shorts, smoking. Old women slopped along in plastic slippers wearing style-free cotton print trousers and tops, squawking at the men unpleasantly as they passed. Hawkers fried mysterious food on street corners, calling in trade with strange cries. Open-fronted shops stayed open late into the evening. Small children wandered everywhere, dogs abounded.

I was ashore with Bob the Geordie, Brian and Daze. We wanted to eat something strange and then make contest with the local beer, which was called Taiwan Beer, imaginatively. Taiwan Beer was all we could buy, because beer was under government monopoly. It wasn't bad, in fact, having its roots in German lagers, the Germans having kick-started most of the Chinese breweries at the end of the nineteenth century. We had our strange meal in a throbbing restaurant that was half inside and half on the pavement. The clientele screeched at each other, screeched at the waiters, the waiters screeched back. One gave us menus, in

Chinese, and screeched at us. We made pantomime: I clucked and beat my arms as a chicken, Bob placed upward-pointing fingers at his temples and made a mooing sound. Brian pointed enthusiastically at some goo the party on the next table were wolfing down, Daze made drinking signs, then belched and wobbled his head as an inebriate. The Chinese patrons hooted: look at the stupid round-eyes. The waiter brought us Taiwan beer and glasses of brandy. No one particularly wanted the brandy, so we drank it quickly to get it out the way; mistake, more appeared. The food arrived, noodles, chicken, stewed vegetables, fried meats. Brian said we were eating dog, he barked at the other patrons and pointed at his plate, some looked offended. The meal was filling although not particularly good, and we only had a limited idea what we were eating. It cost us a wad of Taiwanese dollars.

Daze tried an elaborate mime to buy some weed to smoke. His target was a young hawker wearing a baseball hat and a tee-shirt with an amusing cartoon, which made Daze think he was the type of person who might have access to drugs. The hawker looked blank, although Daze drew a large crowd with his theatricals. The crowd started murmuring, a few shook their heads, hostility started to become etched across irked faces as they began to understand what he wanted.

Bob whispered to Daze: 'In Taiwan, they execute people by firing squad for drug offences.' Daze stopped looking laid-back, and the four of us walked away quickly. We finished the night near the waterfront in shady dives plucked from the Shanghai bund of 1920, behind the main streets, on dark streets, in the dark belly of the port where sailors go to play.

Naha on Okinawa Island was rigidly unfriendly. Japanese memories were fading about their bad behaviour in the 1940s, and the big American military presence on the island was becoming more and more resented. The locals certainly didn't seem to like us. Our Western appearance probably gave us honorary American status, although perhaps they just didn't like us. I had a walk around the town, people were civil enough in the shops but the civility never touched their eyes. The place was bleak, the ambiance was institutional, it was clean, over-clean, the citizens looked pressed, there was no jot of character, I never saw anyone smile. Bob and I were refused entry to a bar in the evening, for no reason. We walked in and the chatter stopped, the Japanese patrons looked at us with dislike. A man came from behind the bar, shaking his head and ushering us out. We were affronted and went stamping down the street to find a bar that would serve us. Our main discharge cargo was Johnnie Walker whisky from Grangemouth and liqueurs from Belfast. I felt the whole town could do with having a party with the Johnnie Walker and the liqueurs to lighten themselves up. We were all glad to get away from Naha.

Hong Kong was home from home for a lot of ship's officers who spent their time in the East, even though my spiritual home was more Singapore. At that time, Hong Kong was still over twenty years from being handed back to the Chinese – the People's Republic of China, that is, not the Republic of China. Hong Kong had maintained its position as a hard-edged capitalist colony, tolerated by mainland China even through the years of cool relations with Britain, the colonial master. The reason for the tolerance was because the port was a useful outlet for

Chinese goods, because it was a useful interface with the Western world and because China had a lot of investment there. The British ownership had evolved out of the opium wars and the gunboat diplomacy exercised by Britain in the mid-nineteenth century. It was all down to trade: Britain needed tea from China and China needed gold and silver from Britain. But the British found it easier and cheaper to give opium to the Chinese rather than precious metals, which caused protests, which in turn precipitated two conflicts that became known as the Opium Wars. The first Opium War lasted from 1839 until 1842 and the second from 1856 to 1860. At that time, the British Empire was years ahead in military supremacy and thrashed the Chinese, forcing them to cede Hong Kong island and later Kowloon, a small part of the mainland, to the British Empire by imperial grant. Eventually, Britain was granted a 99-year lease on a much larger chunk of the mainland, known as the New Territories. It was the New Territories that had to be handed back in 1997, although it had been agreed that China would repossess the rest of Hong Kong at the same time. In the meantime, however, the capitalist lights shone brightly and Hong Kong raged on as the biggest bazaar in the East.

We slid in through the West Lamma Channel and anchored in Victoria Harbour, before being taken to our mooring buoy. There was a buzz in Hong Kong like nowhere else. The harbour was alive with all manner of vessels: a mass of deep sea ships, small coasters, Chinese junks, small inshore boats, bumboats running supplies to all the ships. The green and white Star Ferries ran constantly between Hong Kong Island and the mainland. The modern ferries were still built in the same ancient two-deck style as they had been for decades. As soon as we had clearance, our Q flag was hauled down and a wave of boats came alongside: the agent's launch, the water barge, the stores boat with fresh food, the oil bunker barge, the first of many cargo lighters to take off our cargo, more boats carrying cleaners and maintenance men and unloading gangs. The ship became over-run. The chief engineer had ordered a gang of bilge cleaners; they slopped miserably on board, lowest of the low labourers who would squat down in the oily engine room bilges, below the floor plates, to clean them out. A lot of the bilge cleaners were believed to be heroin addicts. The cargo work started as if it were a race, the chief stevedore tried to overrule the first mate, waving orders he had received from the company office ashore on Hong Kong Island. They argued, the first mate was victorious although he had to give way on some working practices, which had probably been the stevedore's objective anyway. We had cargo lighters along both sides, our derricks worked at a furious pace. We all ran around for a couple of hours until things settled down. The watches were then divided up between me, Alex and Daze. We all had a cadet apiece to do any grubby work. The working hours were four gangs for the daylight hours and one working through most of the night.

The agent put on a shore launch to run to both Hong Kong Island and Kowloon. A timetable was attached to the gangway. The launch ran every two hours on the half-hour until half past eleven at night, starting again at six in the morning. I worked the first night and then had the next day and night free. After sleeping until midday, I caught the shore ferry to Kowloon side, then walked the length of Nathan Road to Mong Kok. I observed the casual cruelty to creatures in Mong Kok market, which caused distress to many visiting Westerners. Chickens were plucked alive by fat ladies sitting on stools who didn't pause in their chatter, fish were plucked from tanks and hacked up as they thrashed on the wooden block, ducks had their necks snapped on demand. I ambled around Kowloon before catching the Star Ferry across the harbour to Hong Kong side. The island itself had all the trappings of its imperial past. The grand Hong Kong and Shanghai Bank building was the prime edifice among many that were built to radiate power, along with the governor's residence, and Happy Valley racecourse. Looking back across the harbour, the grandiose Peninsula Hotel was visible across the harbour on Kowloon side. In the late afternoon I took the tram to the Peak, where the real kings of the island lived in their mansions. The Peak Tram is a funicular railway that has been running since 1888 and has seen little material change since then. The view from the Peak of Victoria Harbour and beyond would make a rushed man pause.

I had arranged to meet several people from the ship in Wanchai, the Hong Kong bar area. Wanchai was fast and bright, the pavements were packed, it was so crushed as to be impossible to take more than a few steps without have to move aside for someone. We met in the Ocean Bar in Lockhart Road. The others were all there and had been for some time: Brian, Bob, Daze, Mr Smythe the chief officer, the Sparks, a couple of fifth engineers. Mr Smythe was looking as suave as ever, although his forehead was crinkled quizzically and he rocked slightly in his desert boots. They were all roaring away at some tale Sparks was telling, jugs of beer stood on the bar. They saw me enter and I was greeted with hoots of derision: 'It's the culture vulture! Whoo-hoo!' If anyone went ashore for any other reason than to whoop it up in bars they were deemed to be a stuck-up intellectual and were roundly mocked, or they were denounced as being queer. I shelved my tales of Mong Kok's morality and the grandeur of the Peak for another time.

We stayed in Hong Kong for a week, moored to our buoy, small boats scuttling around us throughout the day. I liked to lean on the rails and watch the big passenger planes turning over the city to land at Kai Tak Airport, which jutted out into Kowloon Bay on reclaimed land. Kai Tak was renowned as one of the most dangerous international airports in the world. Surrounded by steep mountains and skyscrapers as it was, the approaching planes, not allowed to overfly Chinese territory, had to bank sharply within the mountains then drop quickly over the city, clearing buildings at a distance that allowed passengers to see inside the apartments.

We completed the cargo discharge and then spent a couple of days loading cartons of light manufactured goods in the upper tween decks. The supervisory work was easy; the cargo stowage was a matter of stacking the lower tiers on wooden planking laid as dunnage to keep the boxes off the steel decks and avoid any moisture damage. During my watch I kept a good eye on the working gear, making sure the shore gangs didn't abuse the derricks. Loading of light cargoes was carried out with two derricks paired together, one over the hold and one over the loading lighter. The derrick over the lighter would heave up the cargo in a net; when the net was above the deck, the second derrick would heave it across until it was positioned over the hold, then both derricks would slacken back their wires and lower the cargo down. This was known as a union purchase rig, which was fast and efficient, although it was easy to cause accidents and break running gear if the shore gangs working the winches were inexperienced and failed to coordinate with each other.

I had several more shore runs while we were there, to the floating restaurants at Aberdeen, to watch the early morning tai chi in the parks, to wander through the human tide. I ordered some clothing from Goh Kwok, the company recommended tailor. He measured me up slickly for six shirts: three tropical uniform and three civvies. The cost was the same as the price of one shirt from Marks & Spencer in England. The shirts were ready the next day; a runner brought them out to the ship on a morning bumboat, handing me a package neatly wrapped in brown paper tied with string.

One afternoon I explored the Walled City of Kowloon, the notorious crime district controlled by the 14K Triads. The place was in the early stages of being tamed by huge police raids, although at that time it was still ravaged by criminal activity. Humanity was packed close in the Walled City, the building was unregulated and blocks leant dangerously close together, sometimes it was hard to see the sky. The streets were filthy, there was a smell of stewed vegetables, dogs roamed, grubby children ran and yelled, young men loafed, old ones sat on their haunches and smoked. Some people looked at me with suspicion as I went past, some with dislike. I never felt menaced, although I still made sure I was out before the sun went down.

In the evenings, those of us not on duty would meet ashore. I preferred to go to the bars off Nathan Road in Kowloon, as did Bob. They were more relaxing and avoided the frantic hustle of Wanchai. The others mostly preferred Hong Kong side, which meant that in a spirit of compromise we would start in Kowloon and then hop on a Star Ferry to Hong Kong halfway through the evening. We usually missed the last boat back to the ship and would have to search the wharf area in the early hours, shouting at small craft until we could find someone we could pay to run us across the harbour.

Our last main discharge port was Pusan, the largest port in South Korea. Once we finished there we would have our additional loading ports confirmed, which were expected to be mostly in Japan, with a stop in Kaohsiung in Taiwan. We were all disappointed that Bangkok wasn't going to be included. It was late February and Pusan was cold, the temperature not far above freezing; we had changed uniform back from tropical whites into full blues a couple of days out. South Korea was starting to make its industrial drive to become second Asian hound after top dog Japan. The place was a mix of building site and bleakness. Outside the docks, squat men in short zipper jackets with their hands in their pockets lurked, and offered to take us for a good time involving food, drink, warmth and women. The men were dangerous-looking, they followed us down the street, making wilder and wilder claims. We went into small hot dockside bars and drank local Hite beer, sitting uncomfortably on small stools made for small people. The ambiance was charmless and the people in there were unattractive, thick of girth with mean and predatory eyes. We mostly stayed on the ship during our visit to Pusan and were pleased to finally break out into the Sea of Japan, to head for our main loading ports before the voyage home.

# 5

# An Interlude in the North East

The *Benreoch* slid into Dublin on a cool, wet morning towards the end of April, five months after we had sailed from London for the Far East. I was at my usual post on the poop deck, in charge of the aft mooring. We berthed in the docks on the north side of the River Liffey, where the river starts to widen into the Irish Sea. Everyone would be paying off the next day, when the coast crew arrived, although most would be returning for the next Far East run at the end of the coastal voyage. I would have liked to return myself, but I now had virtually all my sea time in to sit for my First Mate's Certificate, and just needed a few weeks. I didn't want to sign on for another full deep sea voyage. The cargo work wasn't going to start until the next morning, by which time the relief crew would be arriving. Our trip was effectively over. The duty deck officer and engineer stayed on board, together with the crew watch, although most of the ship's company went ashore in a huge mob in the early evening, sub-dividing into smaller groups outside the dock gate. I was with my usual companions: Geordie Bob, Brian, Daze, Sparks; we walked all the way to O'Connell Street, stopping to graze in most of the pubs we passed on the way. We made a point of drinking Guinness, which seemed the appropriate thing to do. Throughout the evening, we met and meshed with other *Benreoch* groups. The evening, being the final one, had a special resonance. The majority of officers would be returning, but not everyone, not me. These good friends would soon join the others I had left behind over the years. There was nothing unique in that, we all did the same. It was never sad, the last evening, it just had a sharper edge and we appreciated each other more, we even started to appreciate those among us we didn't really like.

The plan was that the deep sea officers and crew would all leave the ship in the late afternoon and take the evening ferry to Liverpool. The thought of this filled the senior officers with trepidation because they thought the crew would hit the bar on the seven-hour crossing, get drunk and start arguing with the officers. After arriving in Liverpool, the majority of the officers and crew would then take the same train north to Scotland, which sounded like a nightmare to me. At least I would be going south. A few officers were considering staying in Dublin overnight before leaving, to give the chaos a chance to clear. After my experience of having to shoulder the responsibility of moving the *Benlawers* crew from South Africa to London, I was anxious to avoid a repeat of this, so I kept myself occupied and distant until the point of departure.

When the coach arrived and it was time to go, I was relieved to see that the catering officer had drawn the short straw. He was standing at the bottom of the gangway, glumly holding the tickets while the raucous crew capered around him. In the end, it wasn't too bad. We officers had our own thrash at one end of the ferry bar, while the crew partied at the other. We were separated by ordinary passengers, although there was a bit of good-natured mingling from time to time. On occasions like this, we could usually rely on one of the sailors having a few drinks and then taking it upon himself to tell one of the officers what he thought of him, giving a loud mouthful along the lines of: 'Thank God that trip's over! You're the biggest bastard I've ever sailed with!' forgetting the fact that they would both be joining the same ship again in the near future. There was none of that on the ferry trip, though, and the crossing passed without incident. We reached Liverpool, and I left my shipmates with hearty farewells and promises that we would look each other up. Bob was taking the train across to Newcastle and prevailed on me to come with him for a night on the town I would never forget, but I knew that would prove a bad idea and made my excuses.

My mother looked at me blankly when I walked into the house. I had grown a beard and she didn't recognise me. I was both amused and offended.

I was due over eight weeks' leave after the trip on the *Benreoch*, but I wanted to squeeze in the last few weeks of my sea time quickly so I could apply for the September term at the School of Maritime Studies to sit for my First Mate's Certificate. I calculated that if I took my full eight weeks' leave before returning to sea, I would run the danger of not being back for the start of September, which would then mean that I would have to put college back until the January term. I asked the personnel department in Leith if I could just take two weeks' leave and then do a couple of months on the coast, which should give me my full qualifying time and get me home for most of the summer. If there was a delay for some reason and I ended up being stuck on the ship for a bit longer, then I should still make it back for September. Personnel said they would line me up in May for a coastal trip as second mate, signing on the first ship to return from the Far East.

In the meantime, I stayed at home with my parents, waiting for the call.

My father had just retired from a lifetime in the Royal Air Force to a sleepy village in Oxfordshire. I hired a car to get around. My elder brother Peter worked in the day, my younger brother Anthony was still at school. All my friends were at sea, I had no girlfriend; a long-term relationship for me was one that lasted beyond the night. In the daytime I found interesting places to visit in the local area: Rycote Chapel where the ghost of the Grey Lady was spotted on occasions, the hill above High Wycombe where Francis Dashwood of the Hellfire Club had his heart preserved in a stone urn, the Ashmolean Museum in Oxford, Blackwell's bookshop, the ruined abbey in Abingdon. In the evenings I went to pubs with

Peter and sometimes with my father; we drank pints of bitter and smoked and swapped stories. I developed a taste for Oxford and started going there several times a week. I made eccentric friends, and the girls I met liked my tales of the sea. There were a lot of good pubs in Oxford: the Lamb and Flag, the Bear, the Eagle and Child. Peter and I would go there on Friday and Saturday nights, drink at the Randolph Hotel, move on to the Eagle and Child, then eat Chinese food until late, before driving home, erratically. In the week I would go to late-night clubs in Oxford to drink, dance, strive to pick up girls, arriving home as the dawn broke. My parents asked me why I didn't stay in with them some nights. I tried doing so but that was so alien to me. I watched television but couldn't settle. I would twitch and fidget and eventually make an excuse to go out. Everything I did was to fill in time until I could get back to sea.

The call eventually came from Leith. They said they had something different for me, something special: fly to Norway where there was a laid-up ship in a deep water fjord, a tanker called the *Grey Hunter*. The company had bought two tankers, the *Grey Hunter* and the *Grey Fighter*, just before the oil crisis. Then the bottom fell out of the tanker charter market. They couldn't sell the ships, no one was buying; they couldn't scrap them because both were almost new and they would lose a fortune. The only choice was to mothball them until the market recovered. The deep-water fjords in Norway were doing a good trade in tanker storage; ours were anchored in Molde, a deep-water fjord on the west coast near Tromsø. The ships were looked after by a senior deck officer and two engineers, together with a cook plus three crew. The engineers made sure the ships remained safe and ready, the deck officer was in command, the three crew members carried out light general maintenance, and the cook fed everyone. My posting was to be for six weeks or thereabouts, and the purpose of me going there was to bring all the charts up to date on both ships. Chart corrections for the worldwide portfolio of Admiralty charts were issued constantly to show new light buoys, coastal changes, wrecks, recently discovered rocks, traffic routing and anything else that had altered. There were scores of changes each week. No corrections had been carried out on the *Grey Hunter* and *Grey Fighter* chart portfolios in the year they had been there, and the charts were becoming dangerously out of date. It sounded an easy job to me: six weeks at anchor while signed on the ship on foreign going articles, thereby picking up full sea time credit. I had vowed not to set foot on a tanker again, although this was different, it wasn't a working tanker. I was anticipating an easy, if dull, few weeks.

I flew from London to Oslo, then took an internal flight to Trondheim, after which I was driven the 150 miles to the Molde Fjord, where the ships were anchored. The drive along the fjord was spectacular, the rising hills brightly dressed in green pine against the blue-black waters of the fjord. Norway is a big country and the indented coastline is the longest in the world, although after leaving Trondheim we saw few people, or even signs of people. The total population of Norway was only five million souls, and not many of those lived along the Molde Fjord.

Of the three permanent officers, Gordon was the chief officer, he was in command. Jim was a second engineer, Pete was a third engineer. We didn't wear uniform and there was little formality. We all stayed on the *Grey Hunter*, which was kept powered. The sister ship, the *Grey Fighter*, was anchored next to us, although was closed right down and every morning someone would motor across in the lifeboat to check that all was in order.

I worked in the chart room from nine in the morning until five in the afternoon, laboriously inking in new lights, depths, rocks, warnings, land shifts and any other changes that had arrived from the Admiralty over the past twelve months. Like all second mates, I carried my own chart pens and made the corrections in black or magenta ink, striving to make the work look as close to the original print as possible, carefully writing the correction reference number on the bottom border of the chart.

Chart correcting was a task to get lost in. People might think it would be tedious and repetitive, but for me it was neither. I found it absorbing, even therapeutic. Charts were either the traditional imperial versions or were the new metric type. The metric charts were partially coloured – yellow land, sea shaded blue near the coast, lighthouses and light-buoys had a magenta tear-shape drawn over them – the heights and depths were in metres. The traditional charts, which were gradually being replaced although at that time were still the overwhelming majority, had the land coloured grey, the heights in feet and the depths in fathoms; the only colouration was the magenta tears that indicated lighthouses and light-buoys. The very old charts were a source of constant fascination to me, and I would always pause to study one when I saw on the bottom that it was first published in 1885 or some similar date. Long disused names were still in evidence: Siam, Cochin China, Tanganyika Territory and so forth. The style and detail on these old charts was far more elaborate than that of a modern utilitarian metric version. The oldest chart I came across was Vitoria to Santa Caterina in Brazil, first published in 1833; the only thing I needed to ink in on it was a new light buoy.

To me, chart correcting was a step back in time, and I would imagine the conversations of the day as the navigators had the freedom to name every island and headland and harbour. The captains and navigators found immortality in having 'Peter's Island' or 'Cook's Passage', dark experience was evident in 'No Bottom Sound' or 'Freezing Point', sycophancy abounded with many places called 'Victoria Harbour' and 'George Island'. Imagine Captain Arthur Phillip, in command of a fleet of ships bound for Australia, filled with convicts (there were more guards than convicts, actually) arriving in 1788 at the place that was later to become the city of Sydney, saying to the Secretary of State responsible for settlement: '*What shall we call this place, Lord Sydney?*' Still, Captain Phillip became the first Governor of Australia, which must have been reasonable recompense for not having the main city named after him.

At the end of the working day, we either sat in the ship's bar or took the motor lifeboat ashore to the nearby village of Vestnes and went to the local bar. Norway was hyper-expensive, so going ashore too often wasn't a realistic option. The company gave us subsidised beer, being alive to the important issues in life, but wouldn't do the same for cigarettes. A packet of cigarettes in Norway was three times the price in Britain. We smokers were forced into buying packets of Norwegian rolling tobacco so we could make our own, although I found it coarse and unpleasant stuff. There were several girls who came out to visit us regularly, seeing us as exotic seafarers who were different from the local lads. These were the tarty girls of the town – not that we minded of course, and we took every advantage of our minor celebrity status. The nicer local girls stayed away from the ships, although still tended to watch us with interest when we were ashore on our daily trips to buy fresh milk and to pick up the English newspapers that the company flew over for us. Once a week, one person would remain on board while the rest of us went ashore to Vestnes in the lifeboat with the cook to stock up on food, lugging everything back in a mule train. In our times ashore, we noted the young bucks of Vestnes staring at us with naked dislike, which we presumed was due to us being a distraction for the local girls.

One day, Gordon organised a party on the ship for the locals. He planned it in an effort to ensure that relations would remain cordial. Two dozen of them came out in a small group of boats, which they tied up to the bottom of the gangway. We were all on our best behaviour and the party went very well. When they arrived, we served cocktails and provided light snacks. Middle ground music played in the bar, and we all made maximum effort with our dress and our manners. Gordon conducted a tour of the ship and Jim took those interested in engines down the engine-room. Later, we had more drinks and laid on a cold buffet. The party was judged to be a great success and they all thanked us profusely as they left.

A fortnight later, we were invited to a function ashore, which was not such a success. The event was the Midsummer's Eve celebration, which was held each year on the beach to see through the shortest night of the year. Sunset was half an hour before midnight, and sunrise was half past three the next morning. In between these hours it became grey and dull although never actually got dark. The Norwegians dressed in traditional clothes, built a bonfire and sat around singing old Nordic songs and barbecuing delicacies. We British misinterpreted the sort of event we had been invited to, thinking it was a wild jamboree for young people. We arrived with a boatful of beer then proceeded to get drunk and make crass fools of ourselves, snarfing the food, singing inappropriate songs, arguing and scuffling among ourselves, having loud drinking competitions, grabbing hold of the girls and trying to get them to dance. We offended our hosts, and repulsed them with our antics. We had to lie low for the following week and did our best to avoid the looks of disgust that were thrown at us when we went ashore to shop.

We took a couple of trips to Molde town, six miles up the fiord. It was too far to take the lifeboat, so we would tie it up in Vestnes and then catch the ferry. Molde was a bigger place and made for an interesting day, even if it was still very expensive. On Sundays, I gave my chart correcting a rest, and went out fishing for dinner in the lifeboat with one of the sailors. We would motor round the headland then stop the engine and drift in the quiet while we bounced hooks off the bed of the fjord to catch cod. Sometimes they were the size of small otters and put up a battle as we pulled them splashing and thrashing out of the cold, clear water.

After a few weeks, I discovered Jim was as bald as an egg and wore a wig; he was only twenty-six. Apparently he'd had a childhood accident and all his hair had fallen out. The discovery was accidental. We were horsing around in the bar one evening and I grabbed him round the neck, he twisted away from my grip and his wig was left perched in the crook of my arm. The others went silent, I stood there holding the wig, I offered it back to Jim, he snatched it out for my hand and stomped off. I hooted with laughter. Gordon and Pete thought I knew he had a wig and had knocked it off him on purpose, which they said was cruel. I protested that I had no idea he was bald, but they didn't believe me. I thought the whole event was hilarious. Jim ignored me from then on.

Pete and I developed an unhealthy rivalry. It started harmlessly with us overdoing our efforts to win at table-tennis, darts, cards and the other activities we participated in to pass the time. We mocked and goaded each other at every opportunity. One night I spilt a glass of beer over his arm, accidentally, although he didn't believe me. At lunchtime the next day he threw a glass of beer over me and ran out the door. That night I crept into his cabin as he slept and heaved a bucket of water over him. He howled as I fled. Gordon told us to pack it in as things were getting out of hand. We were both relieved.

After six weeks, messages from Leith started to arrive, saying that I was an expensive extra and asking whether I had nearly finished my mission. They wanted me off and gave me a week to finish the task, after which I was told to take the next ferry to Bodø and then fly home. I left with regret and fond memories, and arrived back home during the longest heat-wave the country had experienced since records began. The green fields of England were all brown.

Having attended the Plymouth School of Navigation during my training as cadet and the London School of Maritime Studies for my Second Mate's Certificate, there was no logic in my decision to head to the North East and go to South Shields to study for my First Mate's Certificate. The majority of people tended to go to the same college from cadet all the way through to master. Well, when I say lack of logic, there was no academic logic, I was not seeking the greater intellectual prowess that South Shields might or might not have offered. There were other aspects that swayed me. First, I knew nearby Newcastle by reputation and occasional visit as a place where the Geordies enjoyed life, and second, I just itched to be somewhere different, to push my life forward. I had even thought of going to the School of Navigation in Hong Kong to study, but dismissed this as being a less forgiving environment to run out of money in, which I accepted was a distinct possibility.

I arrived in South Shields one afternoon in early September, a few days before the start of term, cruising down the main street in my bright red Ford Capri, vainly imagining that it was attracting admiring glances. I had spent a large chunk of my savings on the car after returning from Norway, although the inordinately high running costs and its propensity to break down at ever-decreasing intervals were causing me to become disillusioned. The Capri had been given a good airing throughout the summer of 1976, which had been the hottest on record, with six unbroken weeks of temperatures in the 90s. I had used the occasion to carry out a mini-tour of the kingdom, taking in Hampshire, Devon, Cornwall the Lake District and Scotland. I teamed up with a couple of former shipmates on the southern end of the tour; we stayed in seaside bed and breakfast joints and drank ourselves insensible every night. In the Lake District and Scotland, I wanted healthier themes, I went alone and visited castles. The Capri broke down in every region, but when it worked I loved it.

I had also taken a week in Bulgaria, which was enlightening even if I didn't enjoy it much. In a spirit of impetuousness, I had gone into a travel agent one day and asked them to book me somewhere off the beaten track for a week at a cost of up to £500, telling them that I wanted to leave as soon as possible. I ended up two days later behind the Iron Curtain in Sofia, regretting my lack of planning. Sofia was unremittingly grim. I walked the grey streets among miserable people. The city art gallery was full of tableaux of heroic workers thrashing capitalist running dogs like me, the museum had lots of photographs of my type being gunned down. My hotel was new, but it was as flimsily constructed as it would have been if built by impatient children. The restaurant only had pork on the menu for the whole week I was there, and the barmen were as slow as reptiles unless I bribed them. I went to the theatre one night to see *Swan Lake*, which was colourful, baffling, the theatre was baking hot, the kids in front of me made a bigger racket than the orchestra, my backside ached from the hard seat.

The only decent fun I had in Sofia was when I fell in with two girls who were trawling the hotels for someone to help them exchange currency, which was illegal. They said they were students, but their eyes and mannerisms gave them away as part-time prostitutes. I allowed myself to be talked into helping them, which involved me taking a bus across town and meeting a man in the cloakroom of a large hotel. I gave him a bundle of lev and he gave me US dollars in return. I stuffed the money down the front of my trousers then hopped on the bus again, feeling like Harry Palmer, to return to my handlers with the loot. We whooped it up in the hotel bar for a couple of hours and then took a taxi out of town to spend a large amount in a nearby hillside retreat for visiting Russians. I told my father about the experience when I returned home; he told me I was going insane.

When I arrived in South Shields I was still in funds and was due six months' paid study leave, which I believed should allow me to live in passable comfort as long as I could restrain myself. My opening impression of South Shields was a poor one; the place looked dented, the people looked injured. South Shields sits on the south side of the mouth of the River Tyne, opposite North Shields, ten miles upriver from Newcastle. It was a fishing port for several hundred years and became heavily industrialised with coal and shipbuilding during the eighteenth-century technological surge. The shipbuilding on the Tyne was declining fast when I arrived in 1976, the dock areas along Commercial Road and further south were decaying and were places best to avoid. South Shields has seen its share of troubles: the Romans marched through it, the Vikings sacked it, the Germans bombed it with Zeppelins in the First World War and bombed it again with Heinkels in the Second World War; parts of the town have struggled to recover. The colourful past is matched by colourful people: St Hilda the seventh century abbess came from the area, Richard Annand won the first Victoria Cross of the Great War, romantic author Catherine Cookson lived there. Saints, soldiers and sex – all of life's ingredients were in South Shields.

I booked into the Shipwrights Arms, a scruffy-looking pub near the water. I was intending to stay for a couple of days to get the lie of the land. The pub had an unpleasant smell, a cabbage-like staleness that made me feel queasy. I reasoned that I wouldn't be there long. On the first morning I went to Westoe in the upper part of town, where the School of Maritime Studies was situated, and called into the accommodation office to see what was available. They arranged for me to visit a few flats on their recommended list. I saw several although they turned out to be dispiriting bedsit hovels that I felt I would have only stayed in if forced to at gunpoint. In the evening I wandered the town and found the pubs and clubs dull and uninviting. As I returned to my cabbagey home, I briefly wondered whether I should hot-foot it south to London but realised that my employers had already paid for the course. I was marooned.

Two days in the Shipwrights Arms turned into five and I was desperate to find somewhere to live, but then it was the start of the course. I turned up to the registration process and met my fellow students. There were two dozen of us, mostly aged twenty-four or twenty-five; I was one of the youngest, having recently turned twenty- three. There were a handful of older men who had a lot of collective experience in failing the course. I noticed that there were more married men than singletons, and some were even on their first divorce. I still had to make progress to anything approaching a first serious relationship, which made me feel immature. The class polarised, from the grumbling non-smokers, who sighed theatrically every time someone lit up in the class and muttered that smoking in the college should be banned, to me and my fellow gaspers, who made their life such a misery. Smokers sat on the side of the class by the windows. I sat at the back with a couple of the habitual re-sit students and immediately regretted it. They were keen to talk over the lecturer and broadcast their spotty knowledge, and keener still to entice new members into their club.

My objectives were to enjoy myself in the fabled North East, stretch my money so as to keep myself in food and drink, go out and party as much as possible and pass my First Mate's Certificate. But by the end of the second college afternoon, the shades of doubt were already beginning to wash over me: I was living in a smelly dump of a pub that I couldn't afford over the longer term, the town appeared unrewarding, the company in my class looked uninspiring. The heat wave was over and it rained constantly. I went back to the accommodation office at the close of the day to get one of the bedsit hovels, but they were all gone.

At the start of the second week I took two days off, giving myself an express mission to find somewhere to live. I was half annoyed that there was apparently nowhere to stay in South Shields, and half relieved, because the thought of staying nearer Newcastle was more appealing. After a few false starts, I took a furnished flat in Ripon Street, Gateshead. This was a thirty-minute drive to the college although only ten minutes' walk to the Tyne Bridge and the bright lights of Newcastle. When I turned up at the college again, a late arrival had moved into my place at the back of the class, which was of no concern to me, so I sat at the front on my own with my tin ashtray and my books, and began the long suction of maritime knowledge.

The weeks dragged by. The classroom work was manageable, my attention span was strong, if occasionally blunted by the excesses of the previous night. I built relations with the sharper students who could explain the parts that went over my head. I avoided the dunces, not wanting to become contaminated. My weak subject was electronics. I addressed this by studying the syllabus to identify the easier areas that accounted for 60 per cent of the marks. I resolved to learn them all by heart, reasoning that I should be able pick up the remaining 5 per cent I needed from luck and from whatever underlying knowledge that I did possess. In meteorology I had a head start, partly because I had read all the books from cover to cover several times for my Second Mate's referral exam, and partly because I had started dating Janet, the meteorology lecturer. Janet was pretty and youngish, five years older than me, probably doomed to disappointment in life. She had too much hope in other people, as evidenced by her curious interest in pursuing me after a chance meeting in town one evening. I wasn't sure what it was she thought she saw, but I didn't pay it that much heed and took advantage of the situation. We made a pair around the college for a month before she came to her senses, to the amusement of the rest of the class and to the abject loss of her own credibility. The other subjects flowed past and I flowed with them, the work was much the same as I had done for Second Mate's, albeit stepped up a few notches with some new items stirred into the pot. I felt confident I would pass, perhaps not immediately but certainly on a re-sit or, if I was lucky, a referral.

At the end of the college day I would repair to my flat in Ripon Street, cook myself whatever was in the fridge and then head out for the evening. I started treating myself badly: I rarely slept more than six hours a night, never restorative sleep, just the slumber induced by alcohol. I shaved every three days, I showered at weekends, I smoked in bed, I washed my clothes sporadically, I never cleaned the flat, my sink was full of revolting dishes that I never washed, I couldn't cook, I ate trashy meals. After a few weeks, I started to feel badly nourished and decided to start eating properly. I telephoned my mother and asked for some recipes and guidance on how to produce a stew and a roast meal. Stews became my mainstay because I could simply put whatever meat and vegetables I possessed into a pot on a low oven before I went out in the morning and then eat the whole mess when I returned in the evening. Sometimes the result was good, on occasions it was not fit for dogs. I poisoned myself twice, once so badly with some ancient pork chops that I rolled round the floor in pain, hunched and retching, thinking I was going to die. In the evenings I rarely stayed in my flat. I didn't have a television, just a record player, although I did buy a small snooker table to amuse myself.

On the weekends in the daytime I would visit Gateshead art gallery and stare at Dennis Barrass's *Blue Lion*, sometimes for an hour or more. I felt I had things in common with the blue lion, although I wasn't quite sure what. For the very best, I would visit the Newcastle art gallery where there was an exhibition of Ambrose McEvoy paintings, which I would hog. The women he painted were so hauntingly beautiful and cultured and decent they made me ache to meet someone so fine, but they were all so far removed from my own experience of the opposite sex they might just as well have been from another planet. Every Sunday morning I would go down to the quayside market along the north bank of the Tyne, just down from the bridge, where I would spend hours wandering through the junk, good and bad, and mend myself from the night before with bacon rolls. Newcastle itself was a marvellous place: I loved it. The city was bright, noisy, happy. The inhabitants were so cheerful they were like a different species to the dour crowds in most other North East cities. I had no favourite haunt, just a raft of places I would wander round. I became a sort of irregular regular to a string of pubs in Gateshead and Newcastle and made different groups of friends. To my ears, the Geordies spoke with amusing accents, and in turn I was gently mocked for the way I spoke. Sometimes strangers would provoke me into speaking so they could snigger. The girls loved my south-eastern accent as much as I lived their north-eastern one. We would both exaggerate: I would inject artificial poshness into my speech, '*I sa-ay, anyone faw another tipple?* and they would throw in a lot more of the '*whey-aye-man, whey-aye-man*' than they really needed to. I met a striking Geordie lass called Rose who lived near St James Park. Rose was so tough she even frightened the hard men from Benwell and Scotswood. She was tremendous fun, though; she drunk Newcastle Brown out of the bottle, chain-smoked, spouted obscenities, game for anything, frightened of nothing. I stopped seeing her when her boyfriend was released from prison, where he had been incarcerated for several months after causing grievous bodily harm to a West Ham football fan. I was never lonely in Newcastle, I made friends as I went along. Fridays and Saturdays were always extensive and challenging and I would come back to my flat at three o'clock in the morning, with empty pockets and feeling punished.

My funds diminished as Christmas approached, I sold my Ford Capri and bought a cheap heap from a man on the quayside market one Sunday morning, a mouldy Ford Escort held together with patches of fibreglass. The Escort let me down periodically, always at the most inconvenient time. It was stolen twice, but the police found it twice, always before the time expired for the insurance company to pay out. I grew to hate it as it returned to haunt me, with its flat battery and flat tyres and dented doors and inexcusable starting manners.

My money ran out completely at the end of January. I was totally broke and in debt, the next study leave payment would be my last and would barely pay off my credit card. I was ill from poor eating and too much drinking, my flat was icy cold because I couldn't afford to heat it, it was dirty and cluttered because I didn't clean it. I had a supply of cheap dried food and tinned food, but it was all so unappetising I couldn't bear to go near the cupboard until I was starving. I had become an increasingly erratic attendee in class.

Finally, I did same as I had done in London. I abandoned the course and planned to work in the library by myself, I planned to sit the exam early. The others thought I was foolish, the serial failure crowd said they looked forward to seeing me next year. I sold everything I had – my records, books, my snooker table. I sold my heap of a car for a disappointing price to a man on the quay. I had one last consuming weekend in Newcastle, said goodbye to all my friends, then handed the keys to my flat back to the agent and took a train home.

Back in libraryland I worked from when it opened at nine o'clock in the morning until they emptied me out at seven o'clock in the evening. I worked through ten years of examination papers, I read my notes, I studied the syllabus for traps. I booked the exam. I passed orals, I passed communications, I nearly passed the writtens, picking up a referral in navigation for a narrow fail. Game over. I was good at navigation and knew I was nearly there.

I did all the navigation papers again, worked through every examination I could find, I called the lecturers in South Shields and asked them to post me more, post me anything and everything they could find. I studied for sixteen hours a day and re-sat the navigation exam five weeks later. I passed. I had a First Mate's Certificate. I called my employers. They congratulated me. I told them I was too broke to exist and begged for a ship. They said they had nothing but would organise the first coast trip that became available. My orders came through a few days later: join the *Bencruachan* in Hull. I cheered like a madman.

It was a relief to get back on board a ship that went to sea again. What with paid leave, study leave and a stint on the *Grey Hunter*, which never left the anchorage, it had been nearly eleven months since I had actually been to sea. The *Bencruachan* was a relatively new vessel of a similar vintage as the *Benlawers*. She was just over 12,000 tons gross, and was sleek and poised with twin funnels and twin hatches, built in 1968 at the Scotstoun shipyard on the Clyde. The hatches were the automatic McGregor type, hydraulically operated by a button in the control panel on the deck; the hatch covers folded back neatly in the well, each one pulling the other behind. This was a far cry from the wooden hatch boards of the *Benalbanach*, the *Benledi* and the *Benreoch*. The bridge was roomy, the superstructure of the accommodation block was set more towards the aft end, the officers' cabins all had their own bathrooms, the bar was purpose-built, rather than a converted cabin. The *Bencruachan* was famous for having been badly damaged in a freak wave incident off the South African coast a few years previously, the deck machinery and deck cargo all ripped away and her back almost broken. She was one of the last general cargo steam ships built for the British Merchant Navy, the SS *Bencruachan*. All the ships built afterwards had diesel engines and would have the prefix MV, for Motor Vessel. MV *Bencruachan* wouldn't have had the same panache.

I joined her in Hull. I used my rail warrant to travel, not having the money to hire a car. I needed to work, I needed decent food. I had both on the *Bencruachan*. I was back in my cosseted world of silver service, three-course lunches, four-course dinners, a steward to fill my fridge with beer, order, discipline, structure: my life was arranged for me. I could drink without paying, running up a bar tab that would be deducted from my salary at the end of the month. The duty free bond was closed because we were in UK waters, but I bought cheap cigarettes from the chief steward who had a hidden stash of his own for the coast men. In port I walked the decks and climbed up and down the hatches, measuring the cargo spaces, setting guard on the valuables, bribing the dockers when the need arose, keeping the ship working. I was a valuable addition: many of the coast crowd were old or unfit, or just hopeless. I was young and strong and experienced, and this was now my fourth general cargo ship. I was second mate with a shiny new First Mate's Certificate on its way. I had joined with my examination pass papers because my new certificate hadn't yet been issued.

I didn't go ashore in any of the ports until we reached Swansea, apart from a few occasions to stretch my legs with a walk around the dock area. Hull, Sunderland, Leith, Belfast, Liverpool, they all slid by, and I worked most of the hours in most of the ports. I needed to recover my financial position, not aggravate it further. The third and fourth mate had a whale of a time, being free in every port we berthed. They couldn't believe their luck. They wanted to buy me drinks in return, so I used their bar tabs for the most part, which kept my spending to the minimum. The first mate was also delighted with the arrangements, because they resulted in him having a top qualified man on deck for all the cargo watches. Occasionally, after the pubs closed, rough-looking women would come up the gangway and try and charm and bully their way into the officers' bar. That was usually fine by me; I bought them drinks on the tabs of the third mate and fourth mate, who in turn would be pleased because it lessened the guilt they felt about me doing all the work. The rough women were usually in pairs for protection, sometimes in groups.

One evening in Liverpool, after we had been there a week, I let eight girls on board for a party in the bar. It was a Saturday night, the shore gangs had finished early and virtually everyone else had gone ashore. I felt lonely and bored. I was leaning against the bulkhead at the top of the gangway, smoking, when they appeared from round the side of one of the cargo sheds, all noise and shrillness and short, tight skirts. They were in various stages of life, the younger ones were my age, the older ones in their middle forties. A couple were pretty, most were adequate, two were grotesque. They wore cheap clothes that were easy to shed, lots of make-up, high boots; they had all been drinking. They had common characteristics: they looked dangerous, defensive, challenging, ravaged by life but not yet defeated. When they laughed, their laughter was brittle, like stones swirled in a metal pan. They reached the foot of the gangway and called up to me in their guttural scouse accents. I waved them all aboard, they clattered up excitedly and I herded them into the bar and bought them all drinks, courtesy of the third and fourth mates. I encouraged them to tell me stories of their adventures in earning a living in Liverpool dockland. They started tentatively, almost shyly, feeling their way with me. I fed them more grog, they loosened up, they started competing with each other, their tales became ever more outrageous. They told me whoring tales, they compared the cocksmanship of Arabs and Greeks, of Chinese from Hong Kong and black men from the Caribbean. They complained of the cheapness of the North Africans, they respected the intentness of the Germans, they feared the violence of the Dutch, they loved the charm of the French. We drank more, I turned up the music and danced with them all. They offered me sex for nothing, I thanked them and declined. I concocted a story that I was recovering from a bad dose of gonorrhoea, so as not to hurt their feelings. A couple wanted to prowl the ship for custom, but I told them they couldn't, I told them there was no one on board but me, the duty engineer and an old watchman, and they had to either stay in the bar or get off the ship. They stayed. Our party racked up the tempo. They asked me if they could smoke marijuana and I said yes, no problem. They lit up joints and passed them round. I tried a hit, it was good stuff. They told me it was Jamaican and I nodded appreciatively. We discussed the merits of different types of grass. One brought out tabs of speed, and they passed them among themselves like Smarties. I organised games of charades, giving them hard tasks that were funny for the rest of us to watch: Gone with the Wind; Call of the Wild; Goodbye Mr Chips, Son of Frankenstein. They screamed and whooped, they were like children again. One of them, a beefy half-Jamaican girl, burst into tears, fell on the floor, shoulders heaving. Her name was Roberta (*'but it's not me real name'*).

I knelt down and said: 'What's wrong, Roberta?'

She said: 'I'm so happy.'

Her friend said: 'She's all right. She's had a bad time from her old man, that's all.'

I opened a bottle of Captain Morgan rum, and shouted, 'Who wants to play pirates?' to deflect Roberta's maudlin mood from spreading. We drank it all, like competitors, swigging from the bottle, saying; '*Arr-rrrr*,' in our best pirate voices.

People started to arrive back from their night ashore. The first group was the second engineer and the leci and the Sparks, then came the third mate and the fourth mate and the cadets, then a group of junior engineers. They all gaped when they walked in. They looked and me and made frantic hand signals and mouthed: 'Who are they? What's going on?'

I shouted: 'Come on! Join the party!'

They joined in, hesitantly at first, then with enthusiasm. Someone dimmed the lights, which was kind to us all. Everyone danced, we all sang. It was a great party. At two in the morning, with eight drunken whores and a dozen drunken officers, everything was still going strong, the first mate sidled up to me, grinning inanely, a women hanging off him. He flopped his drunken arm round me.

He said: 'When you joined, everyone was saying you were a real piss-head, Simon, but who cares if you are, this really is something else.'

I felt wounded, as if I had been stabbed. I was sober in a flash and my mood dropped away. I didn't want that reputation. I left and went to bed.

The next morning I was leaning on Number 3 hatch coaming, watching the shore gang load suitcases of personal effects into one of the lockers. I had placed a cadet on guard to discourage any pilferage, but I was mindful that he looked dreadfully hung over, and I didn't

*The SS Bencruachan.*
*Used with the kind permission of www.fotoflite.com.*

want him falling asleep. He was pacing up and down in the tween deck to keep himself awake, glancing up at me from time to time, waiting for me to disappear, no doubt so he could slump down on one of the pallets. Between unloading each sling of effects, the shore gang would gather into a cluster to hold a conference, occasionally looking up at me and pointing as if to illustrate some point. I could see something was afoot. Eventually, the shop steward came to see me. We looked at each other with expressions that neither of us liked.

'My members are upset because you're having them watched, Second Mate,' he huffed; 'they don't think you trust them.'

I replied:' Of course I trust them. I'm not watching them, I'm watching the cargo. The shippers are concerned about damage, and I have to make sure that I record any of the personal effects that are already damaged, otherwise they might blame your members.'

He said: 'Why have you put a cadet down there as well? That means there are two of you watching us.'

I nodded. 'Ah, that's different. The cadet is tallying the cases, which is what the insurers require. That's nothing to do with the shippers, or us. The insurers insist on having the cases counted in and counted out.'

He shook his head. 'Tallying is a union job, not a crew job. We've got our own tally men; you should use them.'

'I know you've got your own tally men; but your tally men work on the deck, not in the hold. I've no objection to you having a tally man as well. This is our own separate tally.'

'Don't you trust our tally man then?' he bristled.

'Of course I do. It's the insurers; you know what they're like. They need a separate recorded tally done by the ship.'

We batted this sort of nonsense back and forward for a while, each playing the part that was expected of us. The shop steward adopted the persona of 'mildly outraged' while I took the role of 'earnestly concerned'. He finally accepted the situation and went back to his members to report, after telling me that he would be arranging for a union tally man to be stationed on deck for the next shift. Although pleased at first, I then started to think that I had won the argument too easily and wondered if he was playing a long game. The accepted protocol was that if one side gave ground in one dispute then the other side would be expected to give way in the next. We were due to load cases of spirits in the afternoon, and I wondered whether his tally question was in fact an opening strike, a feint to gain an advantage and an expectation of victory in the next argument. I began to suspect that the next dispute would arrive after lunch and would be about claiming a compensation case of gin because of the grave danger of handling glass bottles. I pondered on this, wondering whether to extend the fictitious insurance requirements to the loading of the spirits, or to give in and let the gang have a few bottles. If I refused to let them have anything, the gang might adopt the tactic of accidentally dropping a whole sling-load down the hatch from deck height, which would then allow them to pocket a few surviving bottles during the resulting clean-up. The best plan might be to neutralise the problem by agreeing to give them a few bottles once the loading was complete, thus guaranteeing they would work at double speed so they could get at it. This would avoid delay, avoid disruption and avoid breakages.

I was mulling over my counter-attack when I noticed the Old Man coming down the port side ladder from the accommodation and starting to walk along the deck towards me. At the same time, I saw the chief mate coming down the starboard side ladder, which I assumed was a pre-planned pincer movement to outflank me and cut off any escape. I stayed where I was, waiting for them, thinking: 'Cowards, it doesn't need two of you.' They arrived and stood either side of me. The Old Man made a few inane remarks about the cargo loading. The presence of the captain and the chief officer at the top of the hatch, looking down with me, a grand total of nine gold stripes, unsettled the loading gang even further. The shop steward was glaring at me venomously, thinking I had betrayed whatever agreement or protocol he felt had been reached. The cadet saw them and started parading like a guardsman. The Old Man cleared his throat: 'Bit of a party last night, Second Mate?'

'Yes, so I believe, sir.' I was non-committal.

'What do you mean, so I believe?' said the chief mate. 'You bloody well organised it!'

'I was there choff,' I said, 'but it was more a case of it organising itself.'

'Bollocks!' he retorted. 'The ship was full of tarts, and you invited them on board!'

I kept silent.

The Old Man said: 'What about the fight?'

This was news to me. 'What fight?'

The Old Man explained. Apparently, after I'd left there was a brawl over one of the prettier girls between a fifth engineer and the radio officer. Glasses were broken, blood was drawn, a chair was broken.

I said: 'That must have been after I left. I didn't stay late. I had to be up early for cargo watch.'

'So who was in charge when you left?' asked the chief mate, seeking another victim.

'Well, when I left, the first mate and the second engineer were there. They would have been the senior officers, so you'll have to ask them.'

I felt a margin of guilt about shifting the blame upstream to more senior shoulders, but not much. They could fend for themselves better than me. The Old Man and chief mate looked at each other, defeated.

'You shouldn't have let those women on board in the first place,' snarled the chief mate.

'I'll make sure I ban all women from the ship from now on, choff,' I replied, knowing full well that he had a lady friend who travelled along the coast and stayed overnight from time to time.

He glared at me for a few seconds, wondering how to rescind this, then he and the Old Man turned away and trudged back to the accommodation ladders. I smirked to myself, pleased with my petty victory.

After a few weeks on the *Bencruachan*, my health and bank balance repaired. I had a brief leave then received orders to join the *Benstac* in Bilbao. The *Benstac* was tramping. Ships either have regular runs as liners, or they sign a long-term charter, or they tramp around on short-term charters. Most of the Leith company ships were regular liners on the Far

East run, but times for conventional shipping were becoming difficult. Although the world economies were out of the oil recession that had lasted from late 1973 until mid-1975, the oil price surge had led shipping companies to seek greater efficiencies, which in turn led to new generation engines being developed that were more fuel-efficient. Steam ships were no longer being built, and diesel engine motor vessels held sway. In the ongoing quest for cost savings, containerisation took a leap forward, because this allowed the loading and discharging process to be carried out ashore and saved expensive port time for the ships.

The *Benstac* had been built on the Clyde, and the Leith owners had taken delivery in 1968. She was a modern general cargo passenger liner of her day, not dissimilar to the *Bencruachan*, although smaller. I felt she was prettier and had better lines. She had five hatches, four forward and one aft of the accommodation, four derricks to each hatch. She had a single funnel, 8,327 gross tonnage, 530 feet long and could crack along at 21 knots if need be, although was generally restricted to 15 knots on grounds of fuel efficiency. As a cargo passenger ship, she could carry twelve passengers without having to undergo the greater safety requirements of a full passenger ship.

She carried a big crew, as did all the company ships. As usual, the officers were almost all Scots from Edinburgh and the East coast, with some from the Islands. The crew were mostly from Shetland, Orkney, Skye, Lewis and Harris, with a couple of Englishmen. The stewards and the painters were Hong Kong Chinese. There were no passengers during my time aboard. The second mate's cabin was miserably small, the most cramped accommodation I had been assigned since I was a cadet. The third mate's cabin was marginally bigger than mine, although I thought it would create too much ill-feeling at outset if I demanded we change. I had been anticipating a high standard when I walked up the gangway, but my hopes were dashed. I had a sink in one corner, with a shower room and toilets down the alleyway. By contrast, the first mate's cabin next door was huge – a three-room suite with dayroom, bedroom and shower/toilet. On the deck above, the chief officer had an even more palatial residence, having assigned himself one of the better passenger cabins. I seethed with envy as I unpacked in my hutch and stowed my gear away.

The officer's bar was decent, big and light, with plenty of room at and behind the bar. There were tables to sit around and play cards, there was a table tennis table at the far end, and a pull-down screen on the bulkhead for us to show films. The crew had their own bar on the lower deck, which looked battered and threatening at first glance but wasn't too bad on the few occasions I went in. On the bridge, the equipment was good: two Raymark 16 radars, a Decca Navigator, Sperry gyro automatic steering, a big separate chartroom; it was a wide, uncluttered bridge with good-size windows and small outside bridge wings.

I joined in Bilbao, in northern Spain, with a few others. The charter was due to end when the *Benstac* completed unloading the last part of the cargo, and the owners were scouring the shipping world for a new charter party. Pending something being agreed, we had received a LEFO telegram. LEFO stood for 'Land's End For Orders' and meant that we would crawl along and lurk at the entrance of the Channel until something turned up. After stowing my gear in my box of a cabin, I went up to the bridge in search of the second mate to receive my handover. There was a grimy young lad in the chartroom, scrabbling on the deck for some papers he had just dropped.

I said: 'Oi! Have you seen the second mate?'

She stood up: 'I *am* the second mate,' with some indignation in her tone.

It was Happy Linda, the only female deck officer in the Leith company and one of the few female officers in the whole British Merchant Navy. I knew of her but we had never met. Happy Linda's reputation was of someone who never smiled, never engaged in conversation beyond what was strictly necessary for the job, never drank or came in the bar, never went ashore. She was single and had no boyfriend as far as anyone knew. Many people had tried to have sex with her but no one had succeeded. She was consequently branded a lesbian. I had a cordial twenty-minute handover on the bridge before going out on deck; the charts all seemed in good order and the courses were laid off for the next port of Antwerp, in line with expected protocol. The chronometers were functioning correctly and the radars, steering gear, gyro compasses and Decca were all in order and were all familiar to me. We went down to walk the decks, and she showed me the remaining cargo that was still to be discharged in Bilbao. We looked at the cargo gear – the derricks and hatches were all pretty straightforward – then we went forward onto the fo'c'sle head and aft to the poop deck. Happy Linda explained the idiosyncrasies of the ship, such as the way to open the hatches if the hydraulics jammed and how to free the port anchor brake, which had a habit of sticking. She took me into the ship's office and showed me the cargo plan, the port books, the hatch keys, the safety torches. We did a brief inspection of the medical locker, which was orderly, although I checked the seals on the morphine and counted the stocks of codeine, tetracycline and penicillin anyway, which I could tell was annoying her because of her repetitive sharp sighs. We walked the crew quarters, and she showed me the petty officer's cabins – the bosun and the storekeeper– then the AB's cabins, the engine room hands' and where the Chinese lived. The passenger accommodation was empty apart from the biggest and best cabin, which had been commandeered by the chief officer. There was a very smart passenger bar which was used for functions whenever shore dignitaries were invited on board, which the Old Man was apparently fond of doing. Happy Linda had moved her cases into the hospital to allow me to move into the second mate's cabin. She was staying on board until the next morning, and would then be taken to the airport. As we walked around, I did my best to arrest her robotic manner by calling on my charm, such as it was. I fantasised how my stock in the company would rise if I were the one who managed to bed Happy Linda. I might as well have saved my breath, though; all attempts at conversation bounced off her like marbles thrown at a wall.

She curtailed the handover by saying: 'That's it. Any questions?'

I said: 'It all sounds fairly straightforward to me.'

She said: 'Good.' Then turned on her heel and walked away. I never saw her again.

We left Bilbao and headed north-north-east for Ushant, the island off the coast of Brittany, after which we would alter course and slowly steam due north for Land's End. We would then find a patch of water out of the main shipping lanes and drift until we received a Marconigram to do otherwise. There was plenty of speculation as to where we might end up next. Everyone was hoping for a decent charter to the USA or South Africa, although my preference was the Far East or Australia. As we approached Ushant, I was on the bridge with the captain. He had the nickname 'Dancing Jack' because of the way he would seize any opportunity to show off his ballroom skills; he was well-known for it within the company. Dancing Jack liked to organise shipboard parties whenever possible, inviting ladies from the British embassy or from any prominent British businesses that were in town. Failing that, he would order the agent to organise a social event on the ship, for export and promotional purposes, he said. His real motive was to get himself on the dance floor, the cool cat that he was.

It was mid-afternoon and traffic was light for the vicinity when the radio officer appeared, clutching a telegram which he thrust on the Old Man. I looked at Sparks from behind the Old Man's back, raising my eyebrows in an enquiring manner. He affected to ignore me, making the most of his role as keeper of the secrets. The Old Man said: 'Hmmm. What do you think, Sparks?'

Sparks replied, 'Interesting, Captain. Very interesting. I never would have thought it.'

'Nor me, nor me.' The Old Man nodded his head and studied the telegram again.

They were goading me, trying to get a rise. It worked. I pretended to appear completely uninterested, although it was difficult because I knew they had the ship's orders. I walked out on the bridge wing to take a bearing of a crossing tanker, making sure it was going to cross safely ahead and not on a collision course. I studied the tanker with unnecessary intentness through my binoculars. I felt Dancing Jack standing beside me. He handed me the telegram with a smile and said: 'We're on with the Greeks; Antwerp then Sweden for the Red Sea.'

Antwerp is the biggest port in Belgium and one of the biggest in Europe. The main port complex is sixty miles up the River Scheldt. We took a week to load several thousand tons of bagged cement, filling most of the hold spaces. The dock area is massive and ancient, the main complex originally established by Napoleon Bonaparte in 1811, although it has been extended and modernised several times since. Monitoring the stowing of bagged cement was a dull job for the deck officers. The bags were carefully stacked on wooden dunnage to raise them off the metal decks, and similar wooden protection was laid against the bulkheads. It was important to avoid the bags coming into contact with steel otherwise any subsequent condensation would cause the cement to harden. The gangs worked through the night. The twenty-four-hour day was split between three eight-hour shifts shared by me, the third mate and the fourth mate. In practice, we rolled forward four hours a day, which meant that one of us had a twelve-hour stretch every day, but this allowed us to vary the work hours and we all had a chance to get ashore both in daytime and at night. I had been to Antwerp before and I liked the place, preferring it to the other major Netherlands ports, Amsterdam and Rotterdam. I wandered the historic old town in my time off and drank in the dockland bars at night. The bars were far from the tourist quarter, they were dark and they had a tenseness in the air and it seemed dangerous to let my guard down. A group of us were speaking to a couple of girls one evening, and one of them told us not to look at the man at the bar because he was a well-known gangster. She said he had killed people. We looked at him anyway and he seemed ordinary enough, although there were a couple of large men nearby, standing still, who looked as if they were on duty. One of the ABs jumped ship in Antwerp before we left, but he was an unpopular and lazy man and so no one was particularly concerned.

We went through the Kiel Canal on the way to Karlshamn in Sweden. The Kiel Canal is the busiest artificial waterway in the world and connects the Baltic Sea to the North Sea, cutting through the northern German state of Schleswig Holstein. It was called the Kaiser Wilhelm Canal until the end of the Second World War, but the post-war desire to remove Germanisms caused it to be renamed. This was the same sort of sentiment that had caused the German Shepherd dog to be renamed the Alsatian after the First World War, a name that stuck for sixty years until canine enthusiasts finally wrestled the old name back. We slid past Brunnsbüttel at the western end of the canal late at night, to begin the transit of its sixty-mile length. During the midnight-to-four watch, my watch, we glided along with Teutonic efficiency through an avenue of orange sodium lighting, the pilot murmuring commands to the quartermaster. The Kiel Canal is mostly large enough for two ships to pass, although there are wider stretches and large cuts from time to time to make sure that there would be no difficulties for ships of broader beam. We entered the lower Baltic Sea very early the next morning, passing the grey form of the U-Boat U-995 mounted high on the bank at Laboe as a poignant memorial of other times at sea.

Karlshamn was memorable; we spent ten days there loading timber on deck. The July weather was bright and the nights were short. Karlshamn itself was a dull town, which I thought was true of so much of Sweden. Everyone said that Swedes had a good life with high living standards, although to go with that they seemed to slavishly accept whatever was dished out by their politicians without a murmur. It seemed to me they had limited public entertainment: almost no nightlife, heavy income tax, sky-high prices and hefty tax surcharges on anything vaguely connected with enjoyment. Most Swedes stayed in when they weren't working, and those who ventured out managed to look both self-satisfied and miserable at the same time.

Dancing Jack got straight onto the agent as soon as we arrived and asked him to drum up a party. I was in the Old Man's cabin with him at the time, searching through the deck log books for the past few months, trying to find out the occasions when the Sperry gyro had started malfunctioning. The steering had failed as we were coming into Karlshamn, and we'd had to connect the old wooden wheel up on the monkey island. The Sperry failure was a repeat of earlier problems, and the Sperry engineer had cabled to ask us to supply details of past occurrences. I was sitting at the Old Man's desk, leafing through the logs to compile a schedule of gyro faults, and was able to eavesdrop on the conversation.

Old man: 'Right. Let's organise a party, then.'

Agent: 'Err. What do you mean, Captain?'

Old man: 'I mean, I want you to arrange for some guests to visit this ship tomorrow night. We'll supply the drink, some snacks and the music. You supply the guests, about a dozen, all girls, decent-looking ones too. We like to fly the flag, you know.'

Agent: 'Err, Captain. I don't usually do this. Who would I ask?'

Old man: 'It's your bloody town, man, use your initiative. Some nurses, they're usually good value. Perhaps teachers, maybe some girls from the telephone exchange. You decide.

Get them here tomorrow night at seven-thirty. Actually, thinking on it, organise a couple of men as well, and you'd better come yourself with a few friends. Wouldn't want them thinking we were a load of perverts trying to get at the girls, eh? Don't let me down. Right, let's move on. Now, where's that manifest that's giving us all the problems?'

I sneaked a glance. The agent was looking stricken at having been ordered to pimp his citizens.

We ended up having a run of parties in Karlshamn. The first hour of the first one was a bit strained, then it improved to become better than our highest hopes. The agent arrived, looking nervous with some cronies in tow: the harbourmaster, the pilot, the chief customs officer and the fire chief. We were all up in the passenger bar, and one of the Chinese stewards was serving. All the officers were smartly dressed in half-and-halves: uniform blues trousers, tropical white short-sleeve shirts with epaulettes of rank. We glad-handed the guests, they grabbed drinks. We toasted their wonderful town and wonderful country. They thanked us for the invitation and toasted our ship. The officers' eyes slid to the doorway, waiting for the girls to arrive. The girls arrived, ten of them, stereotypical Swedes as if plucked from a magazine: tall, blonde, blue-eyed, classically beautiful, rather cool and distant. We zeroed in like flies to jam. The agent had done a general round-up of the females in Karlshamn who were free. There were a couple of teachers, three from the port authority, the pilot's daughter and friend, and a clutch of others. We officers smarmed, we charmed, we competed, we passed round plates of snacks and bowls of peanuts. Dancing Jack took one off to dance. Two went to dance with each other, although a pair of junior engineers immediately cut in with them. We fed the rest beer and gin, we told jokes, trying to loosen them up. Slowly everyone began to unwind. The music became louder and faster and less appropriate. Someone put on a punk rock cassette. Punk rock had started in Britain the previous year with The Clash, The Stranglers, the Sex Pistols, The Damned. It hadn't really hit Sweden in a big way, and in distant Karlshamn it was still just a curse in the newspapers. The girls were impressed. We all looked nonchalant, acting as if we lived in the world of punk every day. Dancing Jack complained about the music being too loud, the chief mate opened the doors to the boat deck, and the party spread out. Dancing Jack was happy to dance on deck out of the immediate din. More bottles were opened. Slow music came on and we grabbed girls and slow danced. We were pictured in the local newspaper a day later, in what passed for the society page, grinning at the camera in groups.

The next party night we were besieged, thirty visitors, mostly girls but a good mob of men who had heard about the first event. More people arrived as the night went on. The third party took place when we had been there a week: we had 100 guests, we were the best show in town. Several of the younger officers made good friends with the local girls. A girl called Anika took a shine to me, and me to her to some extent. She was the daughter of one of the town bigwigs. She showed us all round Karlshamn, which didn't take long; it was a small place, clean and pristine, it mostly existed for the timber trade. There were two pubs, dull flat places. No wonder our parties were so popular. Anika was pretty in a very Scandinavian way – tall, blonde, blue eyes. She spoke fluent English. She flattered, although her eyes wandered; I liked her but I didn't trust her. The day before we left, she said she wanted to come to

England to see me. I made appropriate noises of encouragement, although I thought 'Not a chance', shallow beast that I was.

Loading our timber on deck was straightforward. The timber was graded and the dockers were expert and organised We built ten-foot high blocks that covered the decks, and when we'd finished a shore gang took a whole day to securely lash everything down with wires and bottle screws. Karlshamn was a good stay, and when we sailed out for the Red Sea half the town was on the quay to wave us off. We were a full ship, chock-full, cement below decks, timber above. The charterers must have been slapping themselves on the back.

In the Suez Canal, the ship was arrested, pulled out of the southbound convoy halfway through and told to anchor in the Great Bitter Lake. The Old Man quizzed the Egyptian pilot, who shrugged as if this sort of thing happened all the time. After a couple of hours a launch came out, carrying a brigade of officials in various uniforms: customs, immigration, police, sundry canal officials and a few other men in suits. The Old Man went down to his cabin to await the delegation.

The Greek charterers hadn't paid the canal dues. We became a ship of shame. Our official log book was confiscated, along with our certificate of registry. We were then taken on through the canal to the southern end and exiled to a lonely part of the anchorage. Armed guards came on board in case we tried to make a run for it. The *Benstac* lay there like a great steel leper, while other ships rushed by quickly. We had no doubt the fees would be paid, otherwise the Leith owners would pay and repossess the ship and its cargo; it was just a matter of how long we would sit there. After two days the money was found, all the canal dues were paid, our papers were returned and we set off again, south into the Red Sea.

We had three discharge ports: Aqaba, Jeddah and Yenbo. The Red Sea is cigar-shaped and over 1,300 miles long. At the northern end it divides into two fingers, two smaller gulfs. The one to the west is the Gulf of Suez leading to the Suez Canal, the one to the east is the Gulf of Aqaba. At the top end of the eastern gulf, the Jordanian port of Aqaba confronts the Israeli port of Eilat across the narrow stretch of water. On leaving the canal, we steamed south-west for sixteen hours until we reached the bottom of the Gulf of Suez, then turned sharply and headed north-east for Aqaba up the other gulf. We didn't go alongside in Aqaba, but stayed at a deep water anchorage, discharging our timber into barges. Aqaba itself looked dusty and defeated. Across the other side of the gulf, Israelis water-skied in front of luxury hotels.

Our cement was for the Saudi ports of Jeddah and Yenbo, the major consignment being for Yenbo. We stayed on the Saudi coast for weeks, cooking at 110°F in the shade. The shore gangs doing the discharge were mostly Egyptians and Yemeni migrant workers, with some Sudanese. They all moved in slow motion, slumping down in the shade as each net of cement was heaved off the ship, dragging themselves to their feet again when the empty net returned. The bar on the ship was closed and the bond was sealed, to conform to Saudi attitudes on alcohol. We all received a stern warning from the Old Man on the perils of secreting stashes of booze. None of us did – no one wanted a spell in a Saudi jail. In my time off, I walked around the old part of Jeddah and visited the gold souk. Some of the officers I went ashore with bought gold puzzle rings and other gold trinkets for wives and girlfriends. I had neither, so bought nothing. The third mate and I were invited to dinner with an English family one evening. The food was good but the evening was strained because their fourteen year-old daughter had dangerous eyes and kept trying to make suggestive contact with both of us. We had the sense to avoid her looks – she was a firework waiting to let herself off – and we constrained ourselves to polite conversation with the parents. We went water-skiing with them the next day, and had a picnic on the shores of the Red Sea. The daughter sulked all day, thank God, because we'd ignored her.

In Yenbo, there was a Norwegian in charge of the cement unloading. He lived alone on a barge in the harbour and seemed partly mad. He hated Yenbo, he hated his job, he hated the Saudis, he hated the Egyptians, he hated the Yemenis, he hated the Somalis. He said someone kept shitting outside the door of his barge at night to goad him. I said it sounded as if they hated him, but he didn't laugh. He told me he was being paid a fortune and he was going to buy a pub in England when he finished his twelve month tour. The Norwegian took us on a tour of Yenbo although there wasn't much to see. He showed us a hostel for migrant workers where Lawrence of Arabia had stayed, reputedly. He showed us the dirty modern hospital where people helped themselves to pills from a counter on which there were plates of them left for grabs. He showed us the new Yenbo highway, a deserted three-lane road which went three miles out into the desert and ended at a roundabout. One day he took us snorkelling in the Red Sea and we swam in warm clear water among bursts of bright fish. That was the best day in all our time on the Saudi coast.

As we were roasting in the relentless summer heat, everyone began to get tetchy. Arguments flared up over the smallest thing. We argued with each other about which of the bad films we'd already seen we would show ourselves again. The first mate argued with the chief mate about whether the cargo plan should be pinned to the bulkhead or pinned to the table. The chief engineer argued with the second engineer about which of the junior engineers should be on watches and which should be on day work. We all argued with the chief steward. We told him the food was awful and his choice of menus was inappropriate. He punished us by having the cook make Diamond Stew, thick and beefy, for our 110-degree lunch, followed by steamed pudding. We howled with rage. We grew to hate the country more and more. Three Korean workers raped and killed a Saudi woman. Two were beheaded, but the authorities couldn't find the third so they took 500 other Korean workers and gave them a lashing in public. In the streets and around the docks, fat Yenbo flies as big as fingernails roved in thick clouds. Cats, mangy and diseased, picked their way along the dusty roads. Gangs of idle dogs lay in the sun, goats were everywhere. Rats, big and black, ran around day and night, night and day, without fear. We watched a man beat a donkey, we saw a dead camel by the roadside covered in insects. The Taiwanese ship next to us was arrested when the religious police found signs of some of the crew drinking. Its unloading was cancelled and the ship was taken to the other end of the harbour until a monstrous fine was paid. No mail arrived, and the married men grew despondent. The days dragged. The ship ran out of toothpaste, and we cleaned our teeth with salt.

# 6

# Indian Ocean

The next charter for the *Benstac* offered more promise: loading in Scandinavia and a scattering of European ports for New Zealand. Most people on board applied to stay on for the trip. I was in the vanguard. After our long roasting in the Red Sea, we arrived at Gothenburg with our tongues hanging out, but the place was profoundly disappointing. Most of the big city ports of Europe have had character impressed into them: bombed into them or bombarded into them or enforced by siege in one of the many wars that have bedevilled Europe over the past 200 years. This has led grand city ports like Hamburg and Bremen, Antwerp and Rotterdam, London and Liverpool, to grow a mix of architecture and character: the old town and the industrial areas and newer city centres and the ruined parts that no one knows what to do with. Cities that have escaped such external remodelling end up like Gothenburg: uniform, organised, clean, sterile, striving for perfection. When the Swedish laws of restraint and control are grafted onto such a place, the result is a city so utterly soulless that even a maniac would find it difficult to get excited. Our intent to have a wild time in Gothenburg broke against the crushing dullness of the city, and we ended up staying on the ship for the most part, creating our own ambiance.

There was a partial change of crew in Gothenburg, replacing those who didn't want to stay on for the New Zealand voyage, followed by a fairly hectic run towards the Mediterranean, stopping to load finished goods, electricals and agricultural machinery. In northern Europe, we called at Oslo, Hamburg, Antwerp and Rotterdam, then steamed south to Lisbon and Genoa. We didn't stay long in any of the ports – two or three days at most – and by the time we arrived in Genoa we were feeling the effects of a busy trip.

Hamburg was renowned for its undiluted hedonism. The Reeperbahn was the wide street in the St Pauli red light district holding top spot out of all the European ports for a wicked no-holds-barred night out. There were numerous sex shows held in dimly lit auditoriums off the main streets, the crowd were a mix of baying fools and those who squirmed with drunken embarrassment. We were in the first category; we visited a show that was hilarious, the man looked determined, pumping away with mechanical German efficiency, the women looked bored to death. We were asked to cease our explosions of laughter or leave. Bars screened hard-core pornographic films against a blank wall while customers drank and talked and mostly ignored them. Bars littered the streets that led off the Reeperbahn: the Grosse Freiheit, the Talstrasse, the Davidstrasse. The people who thronged the area were mostly men, mostly young, predominantly foreign, usually in small packs. Drunkenness was the expected state by the late evening, fights were commonplace. It was a place of excitement for young men, a place for them to boast about having been to.

For the most part, we loaded machinery and manufactured goods in northern Europe, and liqueurs and fine foodstuffs in the southern European ports, with some raw goods from both. This broke down into a wide sweep of cargo: drums of chemicals, medical supplies, tinned fish, wood veneers, cheeses, furniture, drums of zinc dust, copper oxide, reels of wire, cartons of nylon, crates of machinery, soya oil, rolls of paper, crates of typewriters. Then there was a lot of deck cargo: big machinery and plant, several containers. I went ashore in most ports. Lisbon stands in my mind as having the most enormous hills – I always seemed to be walking uphill, both when I left the ship and when I returned. The small shops that burrowed under the city gave it a unique character. Genoa remained one of my favourite places in the Mediterranean: on the one hand it was a filthy, corrupt, seedy sink of a place, while on the other it shrieked colour and passion, noise and wine. Genoa had all life's ingredients.

On the way to our last two loading ports, Lisbon and Genoa, we encountered a fierce storm while crossing the Bay of Biscay. The barometer had been dropping for a couple of days and the forecast was predicting a big blow. The Bay of Biscay is the big indent of sea between France and Spain, and is renowned for severe weather, having taken down hundreds of ships over the centuries. As summer ends, deep depressions roll in from the west, pushing the Atlantic waters into giant swells, whipping the tops of the seas into foam, lashing them with rain, striving to push ships onto the rocky shores or drive them under the surface of the sea itself.

We entered the bay with a force 8 gale blasting into us, increasing to storm force 10 as we cleared Ushant rocks. We were not deep in the water, luckily, because we were loaded with lighter cargo that was mostly space-hungry and which had filled up much of the holds without sinking the hull too low. Even so, the seas tore across the decks when we rolled into the swell as we steamed south-south-west towards Cape Finisterre on the northern corner of Spain. Visibility was down to less than two miles, the radar picture was fouled by clutter for three miles due to the high seas being picked up by the scanner. The Bay of Biscay is a busy shipping lane, with most northbound traffic taking the shortest route from Cape Finisterre to Ushant Island at the gateway to the English Channel. On the radars we could see echoes of ships coming towards us, although we would lose these once they entered the radar clutter, at which time we would strain our eyes into the darkness outside, until they appeared out of the gloom, often sliding past closer than we would prefer. At three in the morning there was a grating sound coming from the main deck. I switched on the floodlights and saw that the deck cargo was starting to shift. We were carrying two combine harvesters, a road roller, an excavator, a giant pea picker and several forklift trucks. I called the chief mate, who called the Old Man, and together we surveyed the developing crisis. The Old Man stayed on the bridge while the chief mate and I put on our wet weather gear and went below, picking up the bosun and several ABs on the way. We all climbed down onto the main deck, seawater sluiced our legs up to the knees, the wind yanked at our clothes. The two combine harvesters had broken free of their wire lashings and were sliding back and forth with each roll of the ship, smashing against the hatch coamings, breaking themselves to bits. We were less concerned about the combine harvesters, as they were relatively lightweight and would eventually either become wedged or disintegrate. We were more concerned about the possibility of the huge road roller or the excavator or the forklift trucks breaking loose; these were all heavy and solid, and could do far more serious damage to the ship. The captain pulled the ship round to the east, to put the wind and seas behind us although he couldn't hold the course for long otherwise we would run the danger of getting too close to the shore. Every twenty minutes he would flash at us with the Aldis lamp, and we would take cover, crouching under the forecastle, while the *Benstac* was hove round to head back out into the voice of the storm. Waves smashed over us, the wind howled with a deep whooping as we pitched and rolled. Once we had made some distance out to sea, the Old Man brought the ship round to put the storm astern again, and we clawed our way back out on deck to carry on with the work. Over the next two hours we went round all the deck cargo, tightening up the big bottle screws to pull the securing wires taut, and then putting on more and more to hold them down. We became drenched, tired, cut and bleeding from falls. The cargo was mostly secured by five o'clock, although one of the harvesters was still clattering around; it was too dangerous to tackle so we pitched in pile upon pile of wooden dunnage to clog up the area. By six, we had the last harvester under control and lashed to the deck again, not that it was going to be fit to do much harvesting when we unloaded it. We all went back up to the bridge for hot tea and congratulations. No one was injured and the ship had been secured, I went to my cabin and passed out like a dead man.

When I went up on the bridge the next morning, the wind was groaning through the stays and the sea was white and still breaking over the ship, although the teeth of the storm were drawn; it just looked more shocking in the light of day. The deck was a shambles of damaged cargo, debris and broken railings. We radioed ahead for a dockyard gang to come on board when we arrived in Lisbon, to patch up things as best they could.

Dancing Jack had left the ship in Gothenburg, to my disappointment. He had been replaced by a far less engaging Old Man, who was known as Big Dennis. Big Dennis was a mean man from Edinburgh, tall, cadaverous, unsmiling and unrepentantly disapproving of most things in life. He disliked most people, I think he probably disliked and disapproved of himself for the life he found himself in. He would have been better as a brimstone preacher or a hanging judge. He certainly took an instant dislike to me, which remained constant with the exception of the occasions when he allowed his dislike to change to naked hatred.

To Big Dennis, my standard of navigation, which I was proud of, never rose above barely adequate. He used to pore over the charts, searching my courses for a change he could pointedly make. If he found something, he would blow his breath out in a bark and shake his head, then call me over for a lecture on my inadequacies. If he couldn't find anything, he would mutter and mutter before going off, looking annoyed. Sometimes, for his greater satisfaction he would make an alteration just to show who was master. If I had laid off the course to pass eight miles off an island he would change it to six miles; if I had laid it to six miles he would change it to eight miles. As this developed, I found that it caused Big Dennis the most pain if I acted in a loud and outrageously cheery manner whenever he had anything miserable to communicate to me.

He would say to me, in his low, disapproving, doom-laden voice: 'Second Mate, you've laid off the course unnecessarily far from Bird Island. Seven miles! What were you thinking of, man? We haven't got fuel to waste! I've changed it to five miles. Think, next time! Think!' He would shake his head in pity at my oafishness.

I would jump about and reply: 'Crikey, Captain! That's super! Super! Five miles! Gosh! Wow! Five miles! I would never have thought of going so close! Five miles? Five miles? Wow! Gosh! Shall I call you when we get close? I can't wait to get there! Wow! Super!'

I could tell he hated it. I would see him grinding his teeth while I capered about. It gave me a lot of pleasure in a small-minded way.

There were three deck cadets on the *Benstac*: Ross from the Shetlands, who composed poetry and spoke so quietly I could hardly hear him. Ross also played the bagpipes. The second was Ferdie, who was from Musselburgh, a few miles east of Edinburgh. Ferdie was an unlikeable aggressive eighteen-year-old, who spent his time trying to outmanoeuvre the other two. The third was Mark, who was from Lancashire, skinny with a pointed face and long hair, passive, lazy. None of them was a natural worker, and all would rather spend energy plotting the best way to avoid spending energy. I had Ross on watch with me a lot of the time, who I marginally preferred to the other two. His prattling on about seeing poetry in life's every event grated on my nerves, though, and I would send him off to do meaningless tasks whenever that happened, just to get him away from me.

Then there was the chief mate, a hugely unpopular man known as the Flounder. Until we reached Gothenburg we had five mates: chief mate, first mate, second mate, third mate and fourth mate, which was the usual convention for the Leith ships. However, this charter was leanly pitched, and it was decided that there was no need for such numbers so the first mate and fourth mate were discharged, leaving the chief mate to take the four-to-eight watch as well as dealing with the cargo and running the crew. The Flounder was incensed. He felt it was his rightful prize to carry out chief officer duties only, a staff captain to dish out orders, telling everyone else how to do their job. To suddenly find that he had serious work to undertake was mortifying.

To me, things couldn't have worked out better. I vacated my squalid little box and moved into the first mate's palace next door, where I had a day room, a double bunk bedroom and a shower. It was heaven on board. Once he had calmed down, the Flounder started to chat me up about promotion and the importance of ensuring that I had a good understanding of cargo work. His pitch was transparent, and I could spot it coming over the horizon. His plan was to offload the major part of his duties, the cargo work, onto my shoulders. I felt I had enough to do in coping with the navigation and did my best to swerve out of the way, but he was a wily man and I ended up with a lot of the work being dumped on me. It later emerged that this was mostly courtesy of Big Dennis, who didn't like to miss an opportunity to do me down. He felt that as I was occupying the first mate's cabin I should do some of the work. I tried to act in kind by passing a lot of the navigation down the line to the third mate, but the Old Man took pleasure in vetoing that. The Flounder was also a bitter man because at the age of forty-six he had not yet achieved command. In the Leith company, assuming no continuing run of exam failures, a deck officer would take his master's at age twenty-seven or thereabouts, meaning that he would be promoted to first mate shortly afterwards. He could expect to serve four years as first mate and then gain promotion to chief mate. A particularly good officer might gain his command at thirty-six, and the average was nearer forty. Most would be promoted to captain before their mid-forties. The Flounder had been passed over again and again. He was disliked at sea, and he was disliked in Head Office. After we left Genoa for the Suez Canal, he told me that he had sent in his letter of resignation to Leith and was going to work for the Iranian state shipping line; they had offered him a position where he would serve one trip as chief officer and then be given a command.

During the handover at four o'clock in the morning, he would rail at the way he had been treated. 'I've been working for this bloody company since I was a cadet, since I was sixteen. Thirty bloody years! Can you believe that? Thirty years of experience! I should have had my own command ten years ago. Bastards!'

'That's a shame, chief off.'

'A shame? It's bloody criminal, that's what it is!'

'Aye, it doesn't sound fair,' I sympathised.

'It's not fair! It's not bloody fair! See Big Dennis? I was senior deck apprentice when he was a snot-nosed first tripper! And he was crap then! But now look at what's happened, he's been Old Man for five years and I'm still stuck as chief mate! Bastards! I'm leaving this outfit! I'm off!'

'Don't blame you, chief off.'

I was desperate to get away and sink a couple of cold beers with the third engineer before turning in. I knew from developing experience that the Flounder's rant could go on for some time.

'I'd better do my rounds, chief off. I thought I heard some creaking from the main deck, up near Number 3 hatch by the sound of it. We don't want that deck cargo coming loose again.'

'Oh, right. Aye, right, you had better go up and see.'

And I would make my escape. I didn't regard the Flounder as having thirty years of experience, I saw him as having ten years of experience followed by another twenty years doing the same thing while he waited for his due. That's what he didn't understand; that's why he would never be promoted to Old Man with the Leith company.

The third mate and I got on well. The second mate and third mate have to work closely together, and it's always better if the relationship is good. On the *Benreoch* things hadn't been harmonious between me and the third mate, and that had often been awkward. On the *Benstac*, the third mate was Charlie, who was from North Yorkshire. He was dry and calm and very bright and good company. In the mornings we would carry out our sun sights, chatting as we ploughed through the longwinded calculations in our pavlovian manner. At noon, we would stand together until we were sure the sun had reached its zenith, then capture the latitude for the day. During the long haul down to New Zealand he would often stay long after he handed over the watch to me at midnight, and we would drink coffee and lean on the dodger, gazing out into the darkness under a star-studded black velvet sky, the balmy Indian Ocean breeze on our faces, seeing the world and its ways with clarity and talking of great things.

The other character on board was Tom, who was a favourite of most people. Tom was an ugly grey cat with a broken back. Someone had stepped on him a couple of years previously. He scuttled along with a crab-like gait, dragging his injured rear end behind him. Tom spent most of his time in the crew's mess, although sometimes ventured up into the sun. When we arrived in port the crew would hide him away so that he wouldn't be impounded by the health and immigration officials. I didn't particularly warm to him myself, but most people took time to greet Tom whenever they came across him, picking him up so that his useless withered back legs hung down like two soggy socks; they stroked him, nuzzling his ugly great face.

Our passage from the Suez Canal to Auckland, our first port of call in New Zealand, was twenty- three days. After leaving the Gulf of Aden, we were out of sight of land for most of that voyage. We crossed the Indian Ocean keeping south of the Chagos Islands, and didn't sight land until we closed on Cape Leeuwin on the south-west coast of Australia. Merchant ships did not have satellite navigation in 1978. Satellites had first been put in orbit by the Americans as navigational aids for US Navy submarines in the 1960s, but it was decades before the use spread beyond the military. On the *Benstac* we used celestial navigation, as did all merchant ships. Where the sky was overcast and we couldn't take any sights we were reduced to dead reckoning. DR was pretty easily understood and didn't require any great navigational instinct. DR entailed using the last location where we were certain we had known the ship's position – let's say this was ten hours ago – and then taking our speed at 14 knots, which meant that we should have travelled 140 nautical miles from that last position; we put a mark on the chart 140 miles onwards along the course we were steering, and presto, that was our DR position. Of course, the reality was that our true position would rarely if ever coincide with our DR position because of the effect of the wind and the current. We would either be behind or ahead, or north of the line or south of the line. We would never know exactly where we were until the sky cleared, at which time whoever was on watch would rush out with a sextant and snap the sun to get an indication of our actual position.

By these arcane methods, we worked our way across the Indian Ocean. Sometimes we would go a few days without any sights because of overcast weather, but generally speaking there were enough breaks in the cloud for us to make our way. There was a lot of ritual to plotting the course by the sun and stars. The Flounder, on the four–to-eight watch, would take the morning and evening star sights and fix the position quite accurately, marking the chart with a precise eight-armed cross to represent a star. The third mate, Charlie, on the eight-to-twelve watch, would take the first sun sight at nine o'clock or thereabouts and run the line up to noon to make allowance for the speed of the ship. I would surface at nine-thirty and take a second sun sight. Charlie and I would then take the noon sight together. Noon was when the sun was due north or due south, which resulted in a position line that was an east–west line of latitude. I would look through the telescope of my sextant at the sun, scope shades flipped on to avoid grilling my eyeballs, measure the angle by 'bouncing' the sun on the horizon in the sextant viewfinder, then count the seconds as one-and-two-and-three as I walked back into the chartroom to read off the exact time from the chronometer. I would then carry out the calculation to the precise second the sight was taken.

The day's run was worked out from midday to midday. This would give us the speed we had achieved over the last twenty-four hours. I would then work out the distance we still had to travel, and calculate the estimated time of arrival at the next port. The ETA would change as we went along, depending on the speed we achieved. We didn't use calculators, because the ones then available were simple machines that weren't capable of carrying out the complex mathematical calculations which underpins navigation. The art of navigation rests on spherical trigonometry, which is mystical mumbo-jumbo to most people. We used our Norie's logarithmic tables to look everything up and build these into a series of formulae. When I had first started trying to do these calculations as a cadet, I thought I would be dead of old age before I understood what was going on, but it eventually clicked into place, as things do, and then became second nature to me each morning.

There were few hazards in the ocean crossing. The Chagos Archipelago was one, the vast British Indian Ocean Territory of atolls and reefs, riddled with shoals and a place to avoid. Some of the islands were inhabited. The most populated was Diego Garcia, which was leased by Britain to the USA as a military base, a stopover for planes to refuel and ships to replenish. The native inhabitants had been evicted by the British in the 1960s and sent to India, and have been arguing with the British government ever since about self-determination, compensation, the return of Diego Garcia, the eviction of the Americans and a host of other gripes. From time to time they won a small victory, but the British flag continued to fly as we steamed past the place. We used our radio directional finder to take a couple of radio sights as we passed the islands, although none of us liked DF lines. We preferred celestial sights to give us our positioning, stick-in-the-muds that we were.

Passing other ships was a rare event. I only saw five between the Gulf of Aden and south-west Australia; the other watches saw about the same. It wasn't a major shipping route and the ships that travelled it would spread out quite a bit over the thousands of miles of the voyage. Against all logic, sighting another ship in mid-ocean warranted special attention because many watch-keepers would think the sea was empty and would pay scant attention to keeping a lookout. It was always good to come within a couple of miles, though, to see another ship and wave to the other officer on the bridge. It made me feel we weren't alone on the planet. If we passed at night we would call them up on the VHF, or they would call us, and we would have a general chat. Of course there were the inevitable lost waifs and strays who had no idea where they were and would head in our direction as soon we came into view and beg us to give them a position.

South of the Chagos, we crept up on one Japanese ship that was on the same course. We were faster by about half a knot. It took nearly two days to overtake her from when she first appeared on the horizon ahead, then another two before she dipped below the horizon line astern of us. We felt we had lost an old friend.

After we rounded Cape Leeuwin and headed east across the Australian Bight, we started to see more shipping. I amused myself by writing messages in bottles and throwing them over the side, hoping one would wash up on the coast of Australia and give someone a thrill. The Bass Strait, between Tasmania and the mainland of Australia, was busier with traffic, giving us our first taste of seeing more than a couple of ships at a time since we had left the Gulf of Aden.

The twice-weekly event on the *Benstac* that everyone looked forward to was film night. We had an allowance of two boxes of films a month through the service supplied by Walport Films, an entertainment company that has been supplying films for sailors since the 1950s. The boxes were big, heavy metal chests, each containing three films. The films were on large reels about eighteen inches in diameter, three reels to the average film. We had an ancient projector through which the first reel of the film was threaded; the projector was coupled to a single speaker. We would pin up a sheet at the far end of the bar as a screen and sit back to enjoy the show. When compared to the quality of entertainment available in a night at a big city cinema, our film night was a sorry spectacle. The film juddered and jumped and rattled as it went through the projector, the speaker crackled and spluttered and was often out of synch with the film itself. The screen swayed with the movement of the ship so that the image on it became a strangely angular shape, and dipped in and out of focus. The film would break or jam and burn from time to time, necessitating a break for restoration. Every forty minutes or so, the reel would end and there would be a five-minute break while the next one was made ready. The audience was generally rowdy and people shuffled back and forward to the bar to get beer; a fog of smoke hung over the screen. The films themselves were a mixed bag, more bad than good. Occasionally we would receive what we regarded as a corker, which was something less than four years old with a recognisable star, but for the most part the films were weak fare, often foreign, badly dubbed. Some of them were older than the oldest man on board. There were times when the film was so bad we started to jeer and throw things at the screen, although there was never an occasion when the screening was halted. We always saw them through to the end.

We had picked up two new boxes in Suez, so had a film showing every four days on the voyage out to New Zealand. The officers had two showings: the first at 1630 for the eight–to–twelve watch, the twelve-to-four watch and any day-workers who had finished early, and the second at 2030 for the four-to-eight watch and anyone who hadn't made the first showing.

*The SS* Benstac *alongside port.*

The earlier showing was generally raucous; the later one had the Old Man, chief engineer and other senior officers, and so more decorum was shown. The crew had their film nights in between ours. On the trip to New Zealand, the films were the usual standard: the stand-out one was *The New Centurions* with George C. Scott; we watched it twice. The dud was a screamingly bad Italian comedy musical that made us gnash our teeth with rage at wasting our lives watching something so dreadful.

On a deserted sea, the *Benstac* was in the middle of the circular blue plate of water; an empty horizon ran 360 degrees around us. Any speck that appeared on the horizon in any direction became the focal point of interest. On calm days, the ocean was turned aside from the bow as the *Benstac* cleaved through it like a plough through soft, willing earth, the surface of the water folded back to reveal the underbelly of the sea, displaying its insides; it was like looking into a clean wound. The sea was a deep emerald green as we left the Gulf of Aden, gradually changing to a light then dark blue as we steamed south into deeper waters. The further south we went, the fewer ships we saw. And there were less pollutants: the odd brown smears of oil became more occasional, there was no shipboard detritus, just the occasion limb of a tree, long since pushed out from the land, fast becoming waterlogged.

When there were no specks to contemplate, our other neighbours became more apparent. Flying fish skipped across the surface like stones skimmed across a lake, occasionally flitting against the water, drawing small splashes, appearing to bounce along until they finally dipped below again, down to where they belonged.

A few days after we crossed the equator, albatrosses started to appear. There were never many, perhaps two or three at a time. They hung in the air with their great wings, wheeling and dipping in the wake then soaring up again. There are many different species of albatross; over twenty, the best known probably being the Wandering Albatross and the Sooty Albatross, although albatross experts squabble about the way in which they are divided up into genus and species. The birds following us appeared to be the Wandering Albatross, *Diomedea exulans*, the biggest of them all, with a wingspan approaching twelve feet. I watched them for many hours and they never seemed to power themselves with their wings, they just swooped and soared, angling their wings with little apparent effort. Albatrosses are loyal to the grave, and can be relied upon to stay with their mate for life: like angel fish actually, unlike humans.

We saw whales on several occasions. Near the equator we passed close by to two blue whales, surfacing and blowing, then rolling back under the sea. The blue whale is a member of the baleen group and the largest creature on earth, 100 feet in length and weighing 200 tons. The name baleen comes from the plates that hang down from the front of the mouth, which are used to strain out the water after the whale has mouthed a shoal of krill, the massed crustaceans on which they dine. We slowly overtook the blue whales one afternoon; I estimated they were travelling at about 12 knots. Every ten minutes or so they would surface, blast an enormous spout of water straight up in the air from their blowholes, pause for a few seconds to take in more air, then dive down again, their big tail flukes flipping up as they went under. As we steamed up to the last position where they had dived, they stayed under for longer and when they finally resurfaced they were out on the beam, a lot further away.

Nearer Australia, we encountered humpback whales. These were smaller than the blue whales, although still massive. The humpbacks had a knobbly, ridged appearance, a sleeker shape than the rectangle of the blue, with big pectoral fins that were almost like wings. The humpback sightings were entertaining; several whales were together in small energetic groups, rolling over as they surfaced, sometimes leaping right out into the air and landing in a spray of white water.

The dolphin, every sailor's favourite, was a regular attendee. They leapt and rolled and charged sleekly through the waters. Dolphins were never shy to come right up to the ship. They particularly liked to ride the bow wave, three or four at a time in the immediate wash alongside the bow, keeping in time with the speed of the ship, nuzzling up and down from time to time, jockeying for the best position in the fairground ride they had encountered.

At night we couldn't see creatures, but we could see where the creatures were. Bioluminescence is the light emitted by marine micro-organisms. It manifested itself as a green and white shimmering light as the wash from the bow rushed down the side of the ship. Sometimes the whole wash was alive with light, sometimes it was just a dull paleness in the night with scattered bright sparkles, as if we were steaming through a field of diamonds, tossing them aside as we passed. On occasions, the bioluminescence was so intense it lit up the whole side of the hull, which in turn reflected back into the sea, making us appear as a ghostly ship on some spectral mission as we tore through the dark. On moonless nights when the skies were clear, the stars studded the universe from horizon to horizon. The brightness of the stars made the blackness of the night more intense, made it blacker than black. The very brightest first-magnitude stars, Sirius, Canopus, Rigel, would fling their reflections down into the inky sea. Then it became a magical journey: alone on the bridge wing in the warm tropical night, I heard the wind sing through the stays like an Aeolian harp, and I felt anointed by my good fortune.

☆   ☆   ☆

On sun-drenched balmy days, after I had finished handing over the afternoon watch to the chief mate, I would sometimes go below to my cabin to get a book, then come back up to stretch out on the monkey island wearing only a pair of shorts, and grill myself in the afternoon rays. It was my habit to have three or four books on the go at any one time, and the one I selected would fit in with my mood of the moment. Monkey island reading needed to be casual, because of the gusts of wind that would tug at the pages if I wasn't gripping them firmly enough, and because I would often find my eyes drifting off to follow the passing sea. There were a lot of John Creasy books on board, which charted the instantly forgettable adventures of The Toff and The Baron. They were great time-passers and I could read one in ninety minutes.

A couple of days after I started my sun routine, the fourth engineer's wife, Tessa, started to appear after I had sprawled myself out. I would nod and make polite chat and she would spread her towel out on the deck to lie alarmingly close to me, face down, legs akimbo. She would reach behind her and unclip her bikini top, her micro briefs covering very little. She was an elfish woman, wild and bored at the same time. In shipboard terms, Tessa was as dangerous a person as it was possible to be. I would strive to concentrate on my book, staring at the same page for several minutes, my eyes not grasping the words as my mind raced between trepidation and bad thoughts. From time to time she would give a low purr. After a few days she started to position herself to lie so close that her legs brushed against mine. I lay there as tense as a man about to be hanged. Then she asked me to oil her back, which I did, obediently, my breath catching thickly in my throat. She moaned gently as I rubbed in the liquid. I stopped my visits to the monkey island after that day. I was aware of my own baseness and didn't want to become dragged into the cardinal sin of cavorting with another man's wife at sea, which could create unimaginable problems. Tessa kept up her sly pursuit, though, often looking at me quizzically and invitingly from across the bar. I made a point of having a chaperone at all times when I was around her. Others could see the game she was playing and leered at me when she wasn't there, asking me 'So, what's she like?' My denials brought snorts of disbelief. The poor fourth engineer went about his life obliviously, as such men do.

We had a memorable scare story half way across the Indian Ocean. Most days, particularly if the ship was moving about, one of the cadets would be sent down the hatches to check if there had been any movement in the cargo. There were different blocks of cargo everywhere: bags and bales were mostly freestanding, although the majority of the cargo was lashed with wires and ropes and nets to stop it shifting; some was blocked in with timber barricades. As the ship pitched and rolled and vibrated, the lashings could work themselves loose and it was therefore good practice to walk among the cargo to see if there was any shift. One morning,

I was up on the bridge working out sun sights with Charlie, when Ross the cadet walked into the chartroom. He was ashen-faced.

'What's up with you?' said Charlie. 'You look as if you've seen a ghost.'

'I've seen something worse,' he replied.

Charlie and I looked at each other.

I said: 'What's the problem, Ross?'

He said: 'There's a dead body in Number 3 hatch.'

We scoffed.

'Aye, there is. I've seen it, just twenty minutes ago.'

'Have you told the chief officer?'

'Aye, I have, but he said he was busy and that you would go and have a look, Second Mate.'

I thought: 'Lazy bastard.'

Ross and I went down to the ship's office. I picked up a second torch, then he led the way to the entrance to Number 3 hatch. He opened the door, then stood back and looked down and shuffled his feet.

'What's wrong?' I asked.

'I don't want to go down there,' he replied.

'Oh, come on. Stop being so soft. I'm not looking forward to it either.'

'No. You don't understand. I can't go down. It'll make me go mad. There's a body down there, a leg's sticking out of one of the crates: someone's been murdered. His ghost is going to be there and he'll be after us.'

'For crying out loud, Ross, there's no ghost that's going to get you.'

But Ross was shaking. His Island soul carried too many unnerving tales, he was petrified. I couldn't get him to come down the hatch with me.

'All right, I'll go on my own. Just describe exactly where this body is.'

'You can't go on your own! It'll get you!'

'Just tell me.'

Ross described the location, which was in the lower tween deck on the starboard side. There was a row of crates stowed together, and the one at the end had been damaged. According to Ross, there was a body hanging out of it. I clambered down into the dark hatch, the torch hung round my neck on a lanyard and the beam danced around as I climbed down the ladder. I reached the upper tween deck, located the hatchway to the lower tween deck and continued my descent. The lower tween deck was much darker; the only light was the weak yellow beam of my torch. The crates were plain to see; we had picked them up in Genoa and I remembered them being swung on board. I walked down the line to the end, the air was full of shrieks and creaks and cracks of cargo trying to work its way loose as the ship swayed. I shone my torch on a naked leg protruding from the end crate, my heart jumped into my mouth. I stopped. I studied the leg as it gleamed in the torchlight, building myself up to make a full inspection of the cadaver. The leg was very smooth – a woman's leg, I thought. I moved forward, stepping round some trays of rat poison. I bent down and shone my torch into the broken crate; a row of tailor's dummies sat in mute companionship, apart from the one that had toppled sideways, its leg poking out through the gap.

I arrived back at main deck level and raised my head slowly through the opening. The door to the main deck was partially open and I could see Ross standing there. I waited until he turned away then quickly swarmed up the last few feet of ladder. I stood inside the doorway, waiting until he turned back in my direction again. When did, I slammed the heavy steel door open and burst out of the hatch entrance holding the dummy in front of me screaming, 'Urrggg-ggahhhhhh!' at the top of my voice. I then flung the dummy at him. He shrieked, the blood dropped from his face and he fell over on the deck in terror, the dummy flailing on top of his body. I nearly wet myself with laughter.

After we left the Red Sea, the Flounder announced that it fell to me to invent navigational amusements to keep the ship's company engaged with the voyage in a meaningful way. I spent a couple of hours drawing up two broadly accurate maps of the eastern hemisphere on the plain white back of a couple of cancelled charts. At the top left was the Red Sea, and at the bottom right was New Zealand. I pinned one on the bulkhead in the crew's mess and one in the officer's bar. In each map there was a pin with a flag, and every day I would place the pin to show the ship's position at noon. Next to it on the map I would write our latitude and longitude, our speed over the past twenty-four hours, the estimated time of next landfall and the ETA for Auckland. This created huge interest, and people would crowd round as I did my daily updates. Encouraged by this, I started adding to the information, scribbling down the weather forecast, the names of the ships we had passed over the past twenty- four hours, the birds and sea creatures we had sighted. Towards the end, I was adding news headlines from the BBC World Service. I marked all the ports we would be visiting in New Zealand; I wrote in the distances and times between them, their populations and any other information I could coin. It became the most important ritual of the day. The whole ship's company was captivated, and I was scolded if my daily updates were too thin.

Next, I started a clock raffle for the time the pilot stepped on board, one New Zealand dollar per entry. This entailed drawing a large circle on another cancelled chart and dividing it into sixty segments, numbered clockwise from 1 to 60. Each segment represented a minute, and people would pledge a dollar into the kitty and write their name in their chosen minute. If the pilot for Auckland, our first port, stepped on the *Benstac* at, say, 0652, then the person who had written their name in segment number 52 would win the whole NZ$60 kitty. I hawked the clock around with me as I went to do my chart updates. All the segments sold out in three days. It was so popular that I drew up another for the exact time that 'Finished with Engines' would be rung on the ship's telegraph after we completed mooring.

Crossing the equator went without incident; there was no crossing-the-line ceremony because there was no one to induct into the Kingdom of Neptune. There were no first trippers – even the deck boy had crossed the line before. We had a mild party in the sun anyway, dressed foolishly although without embarrassment in fish-like garb, with crowns and tridents. Plenty of water was thrown around.

The radio officer, Charlie the third mate and the third engineer formed an entertainment committee and organised a host of competitions, all with money or beer as prizes. A table-tennis championship: I reached the semi-finals, only to be thrashed by one of the engine-room firemen. A cribbage competition where I was confident of doing well but was bombed out in the first stage by the second engineer - by luck, not skill, I maintained. A quiz night that was an awful failure; everyone got drunk and started cheating and abusing the quizmaster who went off in a huff. An evening on the boat deck with a barbecue where the steward burnt sausages for us in a contraption built by the junior engineers out of engine-room plating and half an oil drum, while we played deck quoits under the floodlights. A darts tournament, officers versus the crew, the crew pounding us. A fancy dress party, I turned up for the party still in uniform, to be roundly derided for my forgetfulness, and I ended up with a rolled-up chart on my head, as a dunce. Film nights were given an extra spin with ice cream and wafers served between reels.

Looked at in isolation, all these were little things of no apparent importance, but collectively they were important to us. They brought us together and put a brake on the arguments that would have otherwise arisen, the nasty squabbles that divide men when they live together in close confinement. They made the days go by with meaning, they made the long voyage sweeter.

We arrived in Auckland like a caravan cresting the dunes of Al-Hasa oasis. We needed the fuel afforded by a relaxing stay. The European ports had been hard work and quick turnaround, and few of the crew had managed a decent run ashore. The whole ship's company were keen to stretch their legs over the next few weeks. The *Benstac* was due to be in Auckland for a fortnight, and the cargo berths were right in front of the town; we only had to go down the gangway, along the wharf and there we were, in the city centre. There was a buzz of excitement running through the ship as we berthed. New Zealand had a great reputation among British seafarers; the people spoke English, they had the same essential values, they liked the British, the girls were friendly, the pubs were good, everything was close to the ship. The dock workers, wharfies as they were known in New Zealand, didn't work nights. All the ingredients for a good stay.

Once the ship was cleared by customs and immigration, the arrival activities got under way. The agent arrived with bags of mail, a fresh-water barge pulled alongside to replenish our tanks, a bunker barge tied up astern for the engineers to take on fuel, the bosun had the ABs swing the derricks over to the water-side of the ship so the shore cranes weren't impeded. The agent provided the New Zealand dollars that had been ordered; off duty officers and crew alike queued up outside the chief steward's cabin to collect theirs. I collected the clock raffle money and paid out the prizes to the lucky winners. One was Tessa, who gave me an appreciative kiss that lasted too long, the other winner was an AB who shook my hand, thankfully. The Old Man was given several books of gate passes to allow us to bring guests on board. He gave four of them me with instructions that they be used sparingly. In turn, I gave one to the chief officer and one to the chief engineer, and then signed every pass of the third book and gave it to the bosun. I kept the last book for myself.

We mates had a strategy meeting in the ship's office. It became clear that the Flounder was going to do nothing but potter around in the morning then go ashore and play golf in the afternoon, and a lot of the responsibility for the cargo work was going to be foisted on me; there was no first mate and I was the next best thing. This seemed worrying to me at first, but then it became more attractive as I thought the matter through. The cargo planning was actually all going to be done by a supercargo, someone who was hired by the charterers to oversee the discharging and loading. The ship's officers would just have to make sure the supercargo's plans were executed properly. Once it became clear there was a supercargo, I accepted the Flounder's idea of being the officer in charge of cargo, on the basis that it would immediately place me in a supervisory capacity, which meant that Charlie would have to do most of the deck watches. It was immaterial to the Flounder, although Charlie started to grumble once he saw what had happened. I walked around with a hugely self-satisfied smile on my face, knowing the situation wouldn't last, but pleased to wind Charlie up while it did. A compromise was agreed later in the day, in that I would have half the morning off for cargo supervision and then split the rest of the cargo watches with Charlie. As things turned out, I had patted myself on the back too soon, because the mornings turned into a joint planning and assessment enterprise with the supercargo, the Flounder sticking his nose in from time to time. Even so, it wasn't demanding work.

In the late afternoon of the first day, I went ashore with a good-size crowd. We walked as far as the Great Northern Hotel, a well-known colonial landmark, and spent the rest of the afternoon and evening in there, guzzling Leopard beer. Pub etiquette in New Zealand was to buy large jugs of beer which were used to fill smaller drinking glasses. We bought a round of jugs. Everyone had their own jug; some even dispensed with the tooth glass and drunk straight from the jug. The locals frowned and thought us vulgar. We drifted around town, we met girls galore. Officers and crew alike accosted me for gate passes, which I dished out without hesitation. We feasted in an Italian restaurant, then went back to the Great Northern again. Later, much later, we went back to the ship, the group a lot smaller by now. The *Benstac* was rocking, the noise could be heard from the dock gatehouse. Girls were all over the ship, ordinary girls from the suburbs on a night out and rougher ones, prostitutes, who worked the docks and ships as a regular beat. Even the rough ones seemed smooth, though, when compared to the monstrous hags from Birkenhead and Hull and the other big UK ports. The parties went on, night after night.

In the working day we had three gangs of wharfies who worked from eight until five, Monday to Friday; on Saturday they worked the mornings only. They started by unloading the ruined combine harvesters and other battered deck machinery, and then worked their way down into the holds. The loading from Auckland was mainly wool, frozen lamb, some light manufactured goods and a lot of transhipped cargo from South America.

We had a fracas with the wharfies one afternoon. They were heavily unionised, and one of the shop stewards discovered that we were going to be loading transhipped wine from Chile. The right-wing dictator General Pinochet was running Chile at the time, and he was a hate figure for the left. To demonstrate their solidarity with the oppressed Chilean workers, the wharfies decided they would not handle fascist wine and walked off the ship. I telephoned the golf club to break the news to the supercargo, who had to be fetched from the ninth hole where he was paired with the chief officer. The shop steward and I were playing cards in the ship's office when the two of them came back, grumbling. The shop steward went away and returned with two of his colleagues to even the numbers, I brought in a case of beer to ease the discussion and the six of us had a round-table conference to agree the best way to resolve the situation. After an hour of negotiation it was agreed that the wharfies would get a dirty bonus by way of double time for having to soil their hands with fascist goods, and the shop steward and his two pals would each get a case of finest Chilean red. We drank to that.

Auckland is the largest city in New Zealand, built on a dormant volcanic field – dormant but not dead. In antipodean terms the place is quite bustling, if not to the eyes of a European. It had an almost old-world charm, which the New Zealanders called laid-back but which I felt was sleepy. I liked it nonetheless and I liked the people. I never felt I had to rush anywhere and everywhere I went seemed welcoming. For the first few days we rarely made it any further than the Great Northern Hotel, where we sat with our jugs of Leopard beer and whiled away the afternoon or the evening, or both. We were usually in groups of between four or five, usually with a plan to meet others. I tended to go ashore on my own if I was intent on seeing something that I thought would be spoilt by having company. A couple of years previously I had been in Piraeus, the port for Athens, and had talked several people from the ship into going to visit the Acropolis with me. It turned out to be a mistake. I wanted to wander the ruins and picture the ancient world, but everyone else wanted to get it over with quickly so they could go down to Syntagma Square and sit in the sun and drink retsina. They kept hassling me to hurry up because the Acropolis was 'only a load of old stones'. They became more and more impatient, and I became more and more obstinate in taking my time until they finally got fed up and left me to it. It was an unenjoyable day for everyone. But in Auckland there were no great ancient stones, and I just wanted to amble round the town, which I was happy to do in the company of others. We ventured out from the Great Northern later in the evening to a few late night bars and clubs in the vicinity, although we didn't stray far from the general area of Queen Street and Albert Street.

I hired a car with Charlie and the third engineer one Sunday to see a bit more than the streets that were within walking distance of the docks. We drove around the sprawling Auckland suburbs, past street names and place names that could have been plucked from an English atlas: Chelsea, Greenhithe, Royal Oak, Hillsborough. It was clean and calm and pleasant. One of the wharfies had told us that parts of South Auckland could be a bit dicey, but we drove down there first and the place seemed fine, a lot smarter than many of the better areas of most British cities. After an hour motoring gently around the city, we went out of town and clattered round the countryside, which we found as green as England, stopping at small villages from time to time. We spent the afternoon in Kawakawa Bay, where we walked on the beach and swam in the cool of the sea and strived to impress the local girls, with little result.

At one o'clock in the morning, after we had been in Auckland for a week, there was a furious pounding on my cabin door, accompanied by the angry roar of the Old Man, Big Dennis.

'Second Mate! Second Mate! Are you in there?'

I was sitting in my chair in my cabin, reading the *New Zealand Herald* and sucking on a bottle of cold Leopard. I looked across at Marie and Janey, who were sitting on the deck, sucking on a marijuana joint. They had asked for somewhere to smoke their dope, and I was babysitting them before we all went back to the bar. Marie and Janey worked at the telephone exchange and had been out on the town one evening a few days beforehand when Charlie and I invited them back. They had now become regular visitors. Empty bottles of Leopard beer littered the table. It didn't seem a good time to invite the Old Man in. I kept quiet. I wondered why he was so exercised.

'Second Mate! Open this door! Open this door! I know you're in there!'

Marie and Janey looked at me and gave spaced-out grins. I put my finger over my lips and looked at them appealingly. Marie nodded and waved her hands like a minstrel, doing some sort of parody that I couldn't understand, but they seemed to get the idea that we needed to keep quiet. I was sobering fast and wondering about the consequences if the Old Man used his master key to come in: my debauched state would be a poor career signpost. The pounding resumed.

'Open this door! Open this door now! The ship is alive with women, they're everywhere. Someone has been giving out gate passes like confetti and they've all got your signature on them! I want an explanation, and I want it now!'

I thought: 'Whew.' It didn't sound like a capital crime. I crept silently across the cabin and switched the light out.

Janey said, 'Ooooo-ooo, spooky.'

I whispered, 'Shssshhh.'

She hiccupped.

Thump, thump on the door again: 'Open this damned door now!' he howled.

We sat in the dark listening to the Old Man's threats, waiting for him to go away. I was confident that he didn't have a master key, otherwise he would have used it by now. I didn't dismiss the possibility that he might go and wake the chief officer, though, who had all the keys to the kingdom. After a while the Old Man calmed down. I hoped he was coming to the conclusion that he was shouting at an empty space and that I must still be ashore. Then I heard a muttered conversation taking place. I tiptoed to the door and put my ear against it. He was speaking to Ross the cadet, demanding to know where I was. Ross was responding as a simpleton, affecting to know nothing. I gave him silent thanks and then listened to the Old Man give him a roasting for no real reason before stomping off down the alleyway. I waited a few minutes before sticking my head out. The coast was clear, so I hustled Marie and Janey out and sent them back to the bar. I opened my portholes, ran the shower as hot as it would go to generate some steam into the cabin, dumped all the empty bottles in the bin and walked around flapping a towel. All of this was intended to get rid of the waft of marijuana in case Big Dennis returned. It was hopelessly ineffective, the place still reeked. I went in the nearby pantry and found an industrial-size aerosol of insect spray in a drawer and emptied the whole can, which did a better job but the atmosphere was then too poisonous to remain in, so I went back down to the bar to feign that I had only just returned. The Old Man wasn't there, though, just the other officers and a lot of shore visitors, all loaded with their gate passes signed by me, no doubt. Charlie told me that the Old Man had looked in a while ago and appeared to be in a rage, but had left without saying anything. I thought: 'Tomorrow he might have calmed down.'

Tomorrow he hadn't calmed down. His angry face was mottled with fury, the normal pallid complexion blotched with red in a piebald pattern. The steward had given me a message to go up to his cabin after breakfast. I trudged up to the boat deck like a man ascending the gallows. When I arrived, he was near speechless, almost spitting with venom. He looked furious enough to kill me.

'How dare you! How dare you!'

'What is it, Captain?' I affected innocence.

'You know what it is! You know! You let those … you let those … women on board; those … whores! Whores!'

'I did not, sir!' I countered. 'I did not let any whores on board. I wasn't even duty officer last night. I was ashore until late.' I felt genuinely insulted.

'The ship was full of women, they were everywhere. I came back on board after having dinner ashore with the agent, and I bumped into a group of them. I asked them what they thought they were doing, and they showed me their dock passes… all signed by you! Explain yourself!'

'Ah.'

'Ah, indeed! What do you mean by it?'

'Well, we did have a few nice young ladies from the telephone exchange come aboard as the officer's guests, plus a few nurses from the hospital. But they were decent girls.'

'I'm not talking about those, Second Mate, I'm talking about the prostitutes down in the crew's mess. I went down there with the chief engineer to find out what all the noise was, and it was like walking into Sodom and Gomorrah!'

I thought: 'Oh.' I remembered the signed book of passes I had given it to the bosun, who obviously hadn't been as discreet as I would have liked.

'I did give the bosun a few signed passes,' I said weakly. I hung my head in shame.

The Old Man berated me for several minutes before telling me to get out and scour the ship and turf off all the women I found. He asked me to give him back any unsigned passes, although I'd told him that I had given them all out. As I retreated, he shouted at my back that he would be holding me responsible for any further problems of this type and he would be taking steps to make sure it could never happen again. That seemed a contradictory threat, although I didn't think it would be wise of me to point that out.

I went down to the crew deck to seek out the bosun. He was drinking tea in the mess. Two coarse-looking Maori women were in the corner drinking beer and playing with Tom the broken-backed cat. I motioned the bosun outside and we went out on the poop deck to have a parley. I explained my problem. I asked for the passes back, but he used the same lie to me as I had used earlier to the Old Man, saying that he had given all his passes out. I asked him to act on his honour and keep any women off the ship or at least out of sight if by chance any found their way on board. He gave me his solemn assurance and said he would brief the crew. I told him to make sure a few women left the ship in the next ten minutes, as the Old Man would be up on the boat deck watching. I walked off. It was the best that I could do. I kept a low profile for the rest of the stay in Auckland.

✯   ✯   ✯

After a fortnight, we sailed down the coast to Wellington, the capital of New Zealand. New Zealand is made up of two main islands, the North Island and the South Island, which are separated by the Cook Strait. The North Island is smaller but more populated. Wellington sits at the bottom end of North Island and was nicknamed Windy Wellington by the sailors because of the strong winds that blow in along the Cook Strait. The place was named after Arthur Wellesley, the first Duke of Wellington, he of the Battle of Waterloo fame.

The crew encountered problems with a Maori gang in Wellington. The Maoris are the indigenous people of New Zealand, a warlike Polynesian race. After the Europeans started to settle en masse in the eighteenth century, tension developed with the Maoris, and a series of armed conflicts took place, known as the Maori Wars. The Maoris put up a good fight, but it was hopelessly one-sided, spears and clubs against a modern army, and they were gunned into submission. As more and more Europeans packed into the country, Maori control and influence declined, and, like dispossessed peoples all over the world, the spirit dropped out of them and they fell into alcohol and self-pity. The Maoris were abused by the white settlers for over 100 years, although by the 1970s they were being treated with more respect, even though they existed mostly on the fringes of society, carried the main burden of social ills and were involved in a disproportionate amount of crime. Europeans, mainly of British stock, formed the major part of the population of New Zealand; the Maoris comprised less than 15 per cent.

A couple of the *Benstac* crew had gone into a bar in town that was mostly frequented by people from the lower fringe of life: pimps, pushers, muggers, thieves and general bad types. Very few of the bar's clientele were upstanding citizens, a large number were Maoris, or had Maori blood. The two able seamen who had gone into the bar, both Scots who liked a good drink and never ran from a fight, found themselves in argument with a couple of Maoris over the use of the pool table. The Maoris were the size of refrigerators and the ABs came off the worse. They were given a good beating and tossed out into the street. The next evening the *Benstac* crew returned, a ten-strong group this time, led by the bosun, to seek satisfaction. The bosun was short and square and as tough as they come. The Maoris laughed when he asked them to step outside, so he leapt up and head-butted one of them so hard he sent him crashing through the juke box The deck storekeeper split the second Maori's face open with a pool cue. At that point, the bosun made a tactical mistake. He should have led his men back to the ship, but they stayed in the bar to celebrate, which they came to regret. A dozen mean Maoris burst in two hours later, by which time the crew were half drunk and stood little chance. They took a bad thrashing; there were several broken fingers, a number of teeth knocked out, one broken hand and one man hospitalised with concussion for two days.

After Wellington, we received orders to go north again, up the coast to Napier, to take on board some more transhipped cargo. We were due to be there for three days. Napier turned out to be the port of the crew mutiny. The Old Man hadn't mentioned the gate pass incident again, and I was under the impression that it had blown over. The dock security in Wellington had been almost non-existent, and so people could come back to the ship without hindrance. But in Napier, things changed: the Old Man had a major clamp-down. He had a notice placed on the ship's gangway, which read: 'Entry to this ship strictly prohibited unless engaged in cargo handling or expressly invited by a senior officer.' It was a pompous notice, and we junior officers sneered at it; we were irked that we had been decided as unfit to vet the shore visitors.

The crew were livid. A delegation went to see the chief mate, but he sent them on their way. The bosun came to see me, warning that there was going to be a lot of trouble if Big Dennis didn't back down. I shrugged my shoulders and told him that orders were orders and there was nothing I could do to change the situation. That night, several girls tried to come on board and the sailor on gangway watch sent them up to see the chief mate to ask for permission, which was refused. Someone ripped the notice off the gangway and flung it in the dock. The Flounder had a new one fitted.

The next morning the crew walked off in protest, some with suitcases. Most of the deck crew went, together all the engine room crew and two of the three stewards. The bosun and the deck storekeeper stayed. The Flounder went wild with rage, the bosun showed ignorance as to where the crew might be. The Old Man called me up to his cabin and asked me if I had planned this. I was outraged – real outrage, not faux. I robustly denied any involvement and stamped off, fuming. The crew stayed away. They were sighted in a bar near the port, a couple of them slipping back at night for a change of clothes. When the ship was ready to sail, they all trooped back up the gangway to man the fore and aft stations and pull the ropes in, then they went down to the crew's mess and stayed there. One of the cadets had to take the wheel. The chief mate demanded a full return to work; the crew refused. On the bridge the Old Man raged, he ranted, his face went blotched, he glared at me, but didn't accuse me again. He screamed at the Flounder, telling him that it was all his fault for running the crew badly. The Flounder sulked. The Old Man asked me to mediate with the bosun; he hated asking, he spat the words out bitterly. The bosun told me the men would work going in and out of port, but that was it. They wouldn't turn to again until the ship left the New Zealand coast. The Old Man was in a quandary: he didn't want the shame of having to order a fresh crew from Leith because they would have questioned his competence, but he didn't want to command a ship where he might lose control. It was too late; he had lost control.

The lack of crew was a disadvantage but not a disaster. They all turned up to get a lift to the next port along the cost, paying their fare by dealing with the unmooring and mooring. The cook and one of the stewards had stayed, along with the bosun and the storekeeper. Another steward abandoned the protest after a day, and so we had food and people to serve it and people to deal with the cleaning. The bosun and storekeeper were able to cope with the changing of any of the ship's working gear, and we had three cadets to do everything else. The cadets felt the most put-upon, as their life changed from one of the relative ease of general cargo duties to deck crew slaves. The shore gangs dealt with the actual discharging and loading of cargo, and so the ship's work went on mostly unimpeded. At every port, the crew would traipse down the gangway with their bags and set themselves up in a nearby bar, keeping an eye on the ship so they could be back before departure.

Big Dennis, the Old Man, became so constantly furious I thought he was going insane. He would rage around the boat deck talking to himself, mumbling threats and occasionally giving a loud roar. In Lyttelton, we could see the crew partying in the Royal Hotel, right opposite the ship. In Timaru, they could be seen a few hundred feet away on the balcony of another hotel called the Royal, having a whale of a time. Big Dennis would study them from the boat deck through his binoculars, snorting and muttering and scribbling evidence in his notebook. In Bluff, at the foot of South Island, they disappeared upcountry for a few days, returning just before the ship was due to sail. Bluff is not far from Invercargill, which is a settlement full of people with Scots blood; several of the crew apparently had relatives there and had gone to stay with them. In all of the other ports, though, they positioned themselves in a place where they could be seen, flaunting their independence.

Big Dennis despatched me as an emissary when we arrived in Dunedin, once we had established where the crew were encamped. The mutiny had weakened by then; half of them had come back to work, either having run out of money or fearing the consequences of what they had done. My message was an ultimatum: we now had enough men to sail back to Europe, and unless they came back now they would be signed off and they could find their own way home. There were only ten mutineers remaining, a sorry-looking crowd, too. They were virtually broke, unable to pay for board and having to sleep rough, eking out their money with meagre food and a few drinks. I met them in a cheap and dingy pub in south Dunedin. They started in defiant mood, I listened: they gradually ran out of steam and fell into sullen silence.

I delivered my ultimatum. 'You look hungry and I can see you're broke. I'll buy you all a feed now and a beer, and then you'll come back to the ship with me. Either that or you're on your own; the Old Man will sign you off.'

There were predictable protests: 'It's not fair, Second Mate. The Old Man shouldn't act like this, banning parties on board; no one else does that. It's not fair.'

'I'm not here to discuss fairness. I'm here to tell you that you're either coming back with me now or not at all.'

The braver ones tried to argue me up: 'We'll come back tomorrow morning.'

'It's now or never. Take it or leave it.'

They took it. I fed them pies from the bar, and we ended up having a few beers and chatting for an hour or so, after which I led them back to the *Benstac*; they trailed behind me in a defeated crocodile. Big Dennis watched from the boat deck as we climbed the gangway, his mottled face a mix of rage and triumph.

We sailed from New Zealand after a week in Dunedin. Our freezer lockers were full of lamb, the holds and tween decks mostly loaded with wool and hides, sundry transhipped cargo was scattered about in different areas. We had four large yachts as deck cargo. The New Zealand coast was agreed by all as one of the best places in the world for a British ship to go. I had enjoyed myself tremendously, as had most of the officers. The crew had a mixed experience, and most were wishing they hadn't bothered with their protest. They would be given a DR when they signed off, it had meant a month's lost wages and thus no money to do the things they said the Old Man was preventing them from doing anyway. Still, they would have a good tale to tell in years to come. We started our voyage back across the Indian Ocean; next stop Suez, then Piraeus.

# 7

# Death of a Giant

We had entertained hopes that we would see Christmas in New Zealand, which would have meant a shutdown of work for most of the period between Christmas and New Year. That was not to be, though, and we sailed away from Dunedin on the evening of 23 December, to head west across the Tasman Sea on the start of our long voyage back to Europe. Although we all affected huge disappointment, there was an undercurrent of relief. We had been on the New Zealand coast for nearly two months, and a further week of intense partying would have been too much to bear. A fool thinks he can drink wine forever, but a wise man knows himself to be a fool, to paraphrase Mr Shakespeare.

That said, we had a grand Christmas bash on board. The meal itself was mighty: six courses over three hours. By the end I felt as stuffed as the three turkeys we had been wolfing. Normally, I wouldn't have been at the midday meal because of my twelve-to-four watch-keeping duties. The twelve-to-four men ate early, at 1130, but in a rare burst of festive generosity Big Dennis had re-arranged the watches in a way that favoured me. Ross, the senior cadet, was given the twelve–to-four watch on Christmas Day, leaving me free. I couldn't believe my luck, and put it down to Big Dennis repaying me for getting the crew back on board in Dunedin. He still disliked me intensely, and I him – but this released him of any debt, and he would be free to hound me again without holding back. The Flounder looked ill with envy, having assumed that he would be completely freed of his four-to-eight for some high-level eating and drinking. I goaded him by talking up Big Dennis as a generous man, which made the Flounder's face twist with bitterness.

The pre-lunch Christmas drinks started at 1045 and followed a ritual of formal jollity. At 1040 the officers who were not on duty had assembled in the Old Man's cabin, along with the petty officers: the bosun, the deck storekeeper, the engine room storekeeper and the cook. Big Dennis was not happy about the engine room storekeeper being there as he had been one of the mutineers, although he managed to put on an appropriate mask to avoid spoiling the party. At 1115 the Old Man's reception wound up, and the officers were then due to pay a visit to the crew bar. When it came to it, though, the Old Man simply couldn't bring himself to go and drink with the crew after their treachery in New Zealand, and he abrogated his duty, passing it to the chief engineer and the chief officer. They both felt the same as the Old Man, as did the second engineer, so the baton was passed on to me. I briefly considered declining, but rejected the idea and went down with the third engineer and a few others. The crew were irked by the snub from the senior officers, although I was not unpopular with them and they recovered quickly. We had a decent enough half hour, and I could tell they were secretly glad the full brigade hadn't turned up.

I had taken a sun sight at 0930 on Christmas morning, after which the sky had clouded over. I welcomed the overcast conditions because it meant there would be no noon sight to take. I ran up my morning sight to produce a dead reckoning noon position, then calculated the day's speed and ETA calculations in advance and wrote everything up on the noon chit. I was comfortable doing this because the morning star sights had been good and given us an accurate position, we were in clear seas with no dangers in the vicinity, and there was no great current drift. This meant that I could quickly nip up to the bridge at midday, have a quick check and then be back again clutching the noon chit for Big Dennis's attention before much time had passed.

Everyone drank too much, naturally, before we trooped into the dining saloon and ate too much. After the meal we lay around in the bar, sluggish and bloated, nursing glasses of wine. A few of the others started on the scotch, but whisky was always too brutal for me. So I continued to keep company with the New Zealand red wine I had brought in from the saloon, while I played cards with the engineers. As the afternoon drifted into evening, a few people, mostly the married men, became maudlin about missing their loved ones. The electrical officer started weeping, for which he was either commiserated or derided, depending upon how the audience felt. I found it difficult to connect with that sort of behaviour, having no loved ones to miss apart from my parents and brothers, who I didn't think counted in that context. A festive war of words ignited between two parties: the emotional philistines, who were the young and the unmarried, against those who were moved by the sobbing electrician, the old and the wed. We mocked them as pitiful weepies who ought to buck up, whereas in turn they sneered at us for being sad bastards who had nobody in our lives. There was a bit of truth of both sides. The day ended flatly, as such days often do.

The Flounder had a heart attack as we were arriving in Piraeus. I was on the poop deck supervising the lowering of the ropes to the mooring boat when Ross arrived and told me the Flounder had collapsed on the bridge and I was to go up there immediately. I passed him the walkie-talkie so he could take over, and went up the ladders to the bridge, stopping in at the dispensary to pick up the *Ship Captain's Medical Guide*. The Flounder was lying on the daybed in the chartroom, clammy, sweating, his eyes were wandering. The Old Man was standing over him. He turned when I came in.

'He just collapsed, I think it's a heart attack.'

The second mate had the role of dealing with medical matters although my medical expertise, such as it was, was mostly geared towards blood loss trauma through shipboard accidents, diagnosing and treating venereal disease and spotting malingerers. Heart attacks were not my speciality. Big Dennis knew this; his experience and knowledge was more extensive than mine, although still very amateur. We loosened the Flounder's clothing, wiped his face with a wet cloth, told him to lie still and told him he looked fine. We were liars, he looked at death's door. The *Ship Captain's Medical Guide* told us what we suspected: he had probably had a heart attack.

Big Dennis said loudly: 'He eats and drinks far too much and he's hugely overweight. This is what happens!'

I thought this was an unnecessary comment, and said: 'Hmm.' I wiped the Flounder's face down again. He smiled at me gratefully, like a sick child.

The Old Man went back out onto the bridge to see the ship safely brought to her berth, and left me to deal with the cure.

We radioed the agent and told him to organise an ambulance, and by the time we received quarantine clearance it was waiting at the foot of the gangway. They took the Flounder off on a stretcher he looked dreadful. I thought of his thirty years' service to the company that he had now resigned from, with this his reward. I thought of his dream of sailing as master next trip, now finally shattered. I thought of him now out of a job with nowhere to go. Three of the crew behaved disgracefully as he was being taken off the ship, grabbing their hearts and making choking noises in simulation of his attack. They hurled jeering comments after him. I told them to shut up and get back to work. They shuffled away, sniggering.

With the chief officer invalided off the ship, the cargo work that I had been doing a lot of anyway was passed to me more officially, until his replacement flew out to take over. I was appointed acting chief officer. My stint got off to an ignominious start with an unseemly brawl with the cadets later that night. I had stayed up late, working on the loading plan. It was fairly straightforward, as Piraeus was primarily a discharge port and we were only picking up a few hundred tons of wine and engine parts to take to Italy. The engine parts fitted nicely in one of the tween decks that would be free after the discharging, and the wine would go into a couple of the lockers. I produced several colour-coded plans and did a few sums on the Ralston to make sure the ship was going to remain stable. The Ralston was the ship stability calculator in common use at the time. It comprised a flat aluminium tray on a system of pivots, modelled on the ship itself, on which weights were distributed in positions representing the various areas on the ship. If 200 tons was to be loaded in Number 3 tween deck, then a brass weight representing 200 tons was placed in the compartment on the Ralston marked Number 3 tween deck. Once the Ralston was loaded according to the plan and the model was balanced by means of slides, the stability factors were automatically calculated and it could be seen whether or not the ship was going to topple over. I didn't really need to do the exercise for the relatively small amount of cargo discharge and load that was going to be carried out in Piraeus, but I knew the Old Man would be on my back if I didn't do a check. It was ten in the evening when I finished. We had berthed before breakfast I'd had only had three hours sleep

*The author as Second Officer.*

following the midnight-to-four watch. I was tired and went to my cabin to climb into my bunk.

At one o'clock there was a tremendous shouting and crashing in the alleyway outside my cabin. I got up and went out to see what was going on. The three cadets were fighting, Ferdie and Mark were locked together, gripping each other by the hair and clothes, swinging punches as best they could, snarling. Ross was siting dazed on the deck, holding his nose, blood welling over his hand. Sparks was dancing around ineffectually, shouting at them. I joined in the shouting, to no avail. The two of them crashed about, bouncing off the bulkheads. As they came near me, I tried to bang their heads together but couldn't get a decent hold of their hair, so I kicked Mark in the back of the knees and they both went down in a heap, Ferdie on top. I grabbed Ferdie by both shoulders and heaved him off. He hung on grimly, then suddenly let go and the two of us rocketed backwards, I slammed into the fire-hose casing and yelped with pain as the sharp corner dug into my back. I banged Ferdie's face into the bulkhead, trying to daze him and blunt his aggression. He went mad with rage, spun round and butted me in the mouth. I fell back, I spat blood, a dark mist dropped over my eyes and there was a roaring in my ears, and I rushed at him. Sparks inserted himself between us. We all shouted and threatened. Ferdie realised what he had done and quietened down; soon it was only me shouting. Sparks calmed me. A couple of engineers arrived, the cadets were packed off to their cabins. I went to mine and fumed.

The next day my lip was swollen and purple. Ferdie apologised abjectly, saying that he didn't know what was going on. His apology may have had the ring of sincerity, but I could see a glint of victory in the depth of his eye. I accepted his remorse with bad grace and gave him the worst jobs I could think of for the rest of the day, putting him on gangway watch in the evening. I had to suffer the jokes of the other officers for the next few days, the sailors smirked when I was around. I knew Ferdie would achieve high status for having head-butted the acting chief officer. A week passed before I felt able to laugh about it.

During our stay in Piraeus, the cargo went according to plan, and I even managed to spend half a day seeing the Acropolis in nearby Athens. I went on my own this time, not wishing to have the event marred by companions straining to get to the cafés of Syntagma Square. The Acropolis, high above the city of Athens on its rocky plateau, was a levelling experience. It wasn't that I was impressed by the birthplace of democracy, which it wasn't anyway, nor by the impressiveness of the structure, which is impressive, although there a plenty of structures that are more so. It was one of the rare places where you feel the footprints are still there, where you could turn around and see Pericles, the statesman and architect of everything that made Athens pre-eminent in the world, striding down the steps of the Parthenon, his cloak streaming behind him.

I had read somewhere that the building of the Parthenon was exquisite and exact beyond anything constructed today. The columns were angled marginally inwards so that if they had been continued skywards they would have converged exactly ten stadions, approximately a mile, above the very centre point. Imagine such a construction now, let alone 2,500 years ago. The Acropolis was a place where the ghosts seem very close. After a couple of hours, I decamped to Syntagma Square and met the others.

We sailed from Piraeus with me as acting chief officer pending the arrival of a replacement. The Old Man took the four–to-eight watch. The new chief mate arrived in Marseilles ten days later, an Island Scot called Ian who I knew from before. I handed over the cargo management to him, then went to my cabin to reflect. I thought: it's time to move on.

☆　　☆　　☆

The Old Man was as huffy as I'd expected him to be when I knocked on his cabin door after finishing my watch one afternoon to hand in my resignation. We were approaching the English Channel and were two days out of Flushing, where the ship's complement would all be paying off. Big Dennis had disliked me throughout the voyage, even more so after the crew had walked off the ship in Napier. He had made it plain that he held me mostly responsible for the event; a part of him still suspected that I had orchestrated it.

He shouted irritably: 'What's this? What's this?' waving the letter of resignation at me that he had just read.

'It's my letter of resignation, sir,' I replied.

'I can see that, man! Why are you resigning?'

'I want to broaden my experience … blah, blah, blah …'

'This is an excellent company, you know! One of the best; probably *the* best!'

'Aye, it is, sir, but it's time to move on.'

'You're a fool to leave. You should be grateful that they even gave you a position in the first place.'

'I'm very grateful, Captain.'

'You barely deserve it! You're not the best second mate I've sailed with!'

I felt my blood rise and didn't trust myself to answer.

'You'll regret it, you know! They won't take you back! You'll regret it!' He was getting mottled with rage and his face was stretched as tight as a drum.

'I might well regret it, sir.'

He glowered at me for a moment, then thrust the letter back at me.

'I don't want your damn letter. Give it to Head Office when you get off the ship.'

He turned his back on me; I stood there for a few seconds and then turned and walked out of his cabin. I don't know what I was expecting after serving on six company ships over two and a half years. A gold watch? Hardly. I suppose a 'Good Luck' would have been welcome, or perhaps a 'I hope it goes well for you,' or something of that nature. I wasn't expecting: 'I don't want your damn letter!'

When a whole ship's complement leaves a ship after many months, there is a generally good feeling. All the internal political manoeuvring is long done and the relationships are formed, for better or worse. In the early stages of the trip, I would identify those who I thought I would get along with well, those who I would tolerate and those I would have less time for. By the end of the voyage, there would have been movement within those three groupings, because some personal characteristics always take longer to break through the surface. Sometimes those who I thought I liked would become tiresome, and those who I had resolved to avoid showed depths that made me enjoy their company. In any event, by the time the end of the voyage approached, we were all in good spirits with each other, and the common feeling, the camaraderie, kept any negative feelings at bay. We were a happy band. As we neared the final port, each last gathering acquired a special poignancy. The last film night was hugely enjoyable, despite us having seen the film before and despite it being a rotten and badly dubbed spaghetti Western. We laughed and cheered all the way through. The last dinner before we arrived in Flushing was a special effort by the cook, poached salmon followed by *filet mignon*. The Old Man made a speech, surprisingly full of humour, although he made a mildly unpleasant joke about me leaving the company, saying that he had finally succeeded in driving me out. I thought: 'There's a small bit of truth in that.'

My last handover on the bridge to Ian the chief mate was at four o'clock in the morning. He had done a good job in the short time he had been on board, and the crew were much better behaved, although it was too late for them to avoid the bad discharge stamp that a lot of them were heading for. The traffic was heavy in the approaches to the Dover Strait, the sea was a blanket of lights and the Old Man was making periodic visits to the bridge. We were three hours away from picking up the pilot at Flushing. Leaving the *Benstac* had a special tug for me because I wouldn't be coming back with the Leith company. I wouldn't see these people again, or if I did it would be an unrelated coincidence.

We were securely moored in Flushing by mid-morning. Flushing sat at the head of the River Schlect on the Dutch side; it was a busy port, the waterway made busier by the constant flow of vessels entering the Schlect for the port of Antwerp, sixty miles upriver. Cargo discharge would be commencing after lunch. We set the crew to opening the hatches and swinging the derricks over to the harbour side so as to give a clear working space for the shore cranes. I spent an hour on the bridge, rubbing off all the pencil markings for the trip we had just completed, winding the chronometers, making sure the log book was fully written up, laying out the charts for the next voyage, putting everything in neat order for the new second mate. Ferdie the cadet came up with mail. I had one from my mother. It was curiously short, the briefest of news round-up, culminating with her asking me to telephone when I got off the ship and before I arrived home. I thought this strange.

We all left the *Benstac* in Flushing. The Old Man said the officers had to stay until the evening to give a proper handover, although the crew could go straight away. There was a general feeling that he simply didn't want the full ship's complement travelling together on the ferry, which made sense, I suppose. The crew weren't going to complain, because they were getting away first. We ended up leaving late at night for a fractured journey: a train to the Hook of Holland, then the midnight ferry to Harwich, after which we needed to make our separate ways home. We arrived in the early morning hours at Harwich. I had tried to sleep on the way across although I didn't have a cabin on the ferry and just slumped on a bench in the main lounge where I dozed fitfully. I said my goodbyes to everyone as they all headed for the railway station to take the train to London. I was going to hire a car but it was too early for the office to be open so I went to find a place for breakfast and kill a couple of hours.

When I thought the hour was decent enough I telephoned my mother. She seemed strained, over-talkative, slightly shrill. We batted pleasantries back and forward.

After a while I said: 'What's wrong, Mum?'

She said: 'Your father has cancer.'

There was a long silence, but a drumming in my head.

'Has he got long to live?'

'Perhaps six months. Come home.'

'I'll be home by lunchtime, Mum.'

I drove back across the flatlands of East Anglia in a daze, gripping the wheel tightly while an ethereal presence clung to my shoulder and whispered hallowed tales in my ear.

Pilot Officer Robert Hall, 'Bob' to his friends, was a bomber pilot in the middle years of the Second World War. He had joined the Royal Air Force in 1942, aged nineteen, was evaluated as appropriate for pilot and officer training, and sent on a troop ship to Arizona to learn how to fly. He passed with a satisfactory standard and was awarded his wings. After returning to England, he went to an RAF finishing school in the Midlands, flying Oxfords, Stearmans, Defiants and other trainers. Bob was rated as a good pilot and assigned to Bomber Command. He felt lucky: he was an RAF officer, he had his wings, he had a smart uniform, and all the girls loved him. He grew a moustache.

Bob was posted to Palestine where he did a fortnight with his new crew on the Initial Training Wing; the ITW was designed to make sure that a newly trained crew could fly together, as well as ensuring that everyone knew their job. It was also to see if anyone showed any undue sign of strain as the time approached for them to close with the enemy for the first time. Not all planes lost were hit by flak or shot down by German fighters. A great many crews were killed when they crashed in training or they were killed on their first mission because they just didn't know what was going on, they couldn't act properly under the pressure and collided with other planes in the crowded skies.

Bob was stationed at RAF Qastina, where he flew Wellington bombers on night sorties with other nineteen-year-olds to the Balkans, to bomb Romanian oil fields and German bases. The Vickers Wellington had a crew of six: the pilot, the navigator/bomb aimer, the radio operator and three gunners. It carried Browning machine guns: two in the nose turret, two in the tail turret, two in the waist. But the Wellington was vulnerable to attack from both above and below, it only had a top speed of 235 mph and a weak rate of climb – too slow for the German fighters, which came at them at speeds nearer 400 mph. The Wellington also lacked self-sealing fuel tanks, which meant that not only was it a compliant target, but one which burned and blew up very easily. The crews spent twelve hours in the aeroplane; Bomber Command fed them Benzedrine to keep them wired, they ate carrots because they believed carrots were good for night vision.

The flak was always heavy when they arrived at their target. They headed for the coloured flares that had been dropped by the pathfinder squadron to guide them in so that they could unleash their payload of bombs effectively, the Wellingtons lined up to go in one by one. The 30-second passage over the target, when Bob had to fly in straight and level while the bomb aimer brought the aircraft to position for the bombs to be dropped, was the most harrowing time of all. They were totally exposed. The flak exploded around them, hurling shrapnel through the paper-thin fuselage of any nearby plane. They prayed the night fighters wouldn't come howling in from above, raining fire down on them.

When darkness fell on the night of a bombing mission, the Wellingtons flew north-west from Qastina to the Balkans, and everyone knew that they might not come back. The crews were always told before lunchtime if they would be flying that night, so they could rest and get themselves prepared. Like most of them, Bob's crew left farewell letters in their lockers to be passed to their loved ones if they didn't return from a sortie.

People only have a certain reservoir of courage, and RAF Bomber Command measured this in operational missions. If you completed thirty missions, then your tour of duty was over and you were withdrawn from active service for six months. Over 1,300 Wellingtons were lost in action in the war. The overall losses of Bomber Command were immense: 55,000 men lost out of 125,000; nearly one in two. Bob and his crew made the magic number of thirty missions; his plane was shot up badly on two occasions, but he was never shot down. Once, he limped back to Qastina on one engine, the second engine trailing black smoke, the fuselage raked by bullets; the waist gunner was badly hurt, shot in the legs. On another occasion Bob had to land in a fierce crosswind, one aileron partially shot away; the Wellington lurched as it touched the desert runway, the undercarriage buckled, the plane sledged to a halt.

After his tour of duty in the Middle East, Pilot Officer Bob Hall was promoted to Flying Officer, was withdrawn from active service and was sent back to England. He was posted to the Ministry of Defence in London in 1943 to do intelligence work, mostly evaluation of aerial photographs, studying them to spot unusual topography which might flag some enemy subterfuge. His MoD tour was for six months.

He whiled away his time in the MoD, not enjoying the work. Every night he went home to his house off the Fulham Road, and then went out in the blacked-out streets of London to the blacked-out pubs with their strips of tape across the windows and drank and sang with all the other young men at war. Bob longed to be back in the skies. As the fifth month at the MoD passed, he applied to Fighter Command. He was accepted. He was elated.

In the late summer of 1944, the skies over Europe belonged to the RAF more than the Luftwaffe. Paris had been liberated the previous month, and the papers in Britain said the war would all be over by Christmas. On a bright September day, Bob was flying east, 10,000 feet above the green fields of the Champagne-Ardennes region of eastern France. He was in a flight of seven Spitfires, on patrol towards the Saar to maintain the air superiority enjoyed by the Allies. His flight had just exchanged their old Mark V Spitfires for the newer Mark IX. The Mark V had been the backbone of Fighter Command for the middle years of the war, but the Mark IX was a step up in speed, firepower and manoeuvrability. Bob loved flying his Spitfire. On that bright summer day over France, his flight was jumped by a group of Messerschmitt 109s. A Spitfire pilot screamed into the radio, and Bob saw them coming fast out of the sun. He flipped his aeroplane sideways and down into a tight turn. Bullets raked the tail end of his fuselage, passing straight through the light metal skin, he felt the plane judder. The 109 blasted past him and began to bank, but the Mark IX could turn inside its pursuer, could outfly it, could outgun it. Bob came out of the turn and flicked back towards the Messerschmitt. Both planes engaged fire as they powered towards each other with a closing speed of nearly 800 mph. Bob shot the Messerschmitt out of the sky, a clean kill: smoke, fire, explosion. He flew through the smoke and flame, and roared. It was his fourth kill, his best yet. The elation and relief of shooting down an enemy aircraft was the best feeling in the world.

1947: the war had been over in Europe for two years. Bob was a flight lieutenant based in northern Germany flying Mark 24 Spitfires. When flying in close formation, he had a mid-air collision with his wingman; his wing sliced through the tail of the other plane, they both baled out and parachuted to earth. They were both unhurt, Bob was found to be at fault. It was a stain on his service record from which he would never recover. He remained a flight lieutenant for twenty years.

1958: Germany, with a group of other RAF pilots training Germans how to fly modern jet fighters. All the students were their former adversaries, former Luftwaffe fighter pilots. The cold war was chilling down further, and the Western allies realised they needed to get the Germans back into the game. Bob cartwheeled over the skies of Germany with his students. They flew French Fouga Magisters, fast, modern two-seater trainer jets. They rarely talked about the war.

1964: Gloucestershire. Bob received a commendation for staying with his Jet Provost plane after engine failure. He was told to eject, but he stayed in the plane and pulled it up, missing the roof of a building by an estimated six feet.

1965: Scotland. Bob was awarded his ten-ton tie after taking the Lockheed Lightning to 1,000 mph.

1966: Singapore. Bob finally gained promotion to squadron leader. He was posted to Singapore to fly Twin Pioneers, short take-off and landing planes, taking supplies to remote jungle air strips in Malaya and Borneo. He flew with caution in case the remnants of Chin Peng's communist insurgents, still fighting a lost-cause war in the Malayan jungles, tried for some newspaper headlines. He was always armed.

1972: London. Bob's flying days were over; his eyes were too tired, his blood pressure was too high, he was overweight. He was sent back to the Ministry of Defence in central London, assessing aerial photographs for unusual topography: 1943 all over again.

☆   ☆   ☆

My father was dying, he had lung cancer; the ravages were too deep and too widespread to arrest. They told my mother he had up to six months to live. He had smoked heavily all his adult life and had been starting to cough more and more. He went to the doctor, the doctor sent him for tests, my mother went with him. After the tests had been done, my father was sent away to have a sample taken. It was a ruse; the consultant just wanted to speak to my mother alone. He told her of the cancer, he said she had a choice: tell him he was going to die or pretend that everything was fine so he could enjoy looking ahead. She chose not to tell him he was dying. She told him he had a chest infection and he should cut down on his smoking. On the way home from hospital, he said to her: 'I'm so relieved. I thought I might have had cancer.' She had to hold back her tears.

She explained all this to me when I arrived home. I stopped in the next village and telephoned ahead. She came out and met me in the drive before I went into the house. I had always thought of her as a timid woman, but as we stood outside the house and she explained things to me, she was a lion. She said: 'He'll realise soon enough, he'll know what's happening, but I think it's better if he has a few weeks of relief and happiness first.' I thought: 'Wow, Mum. Good for you.'

My father looked fragile, he had lost weight. He had always been a big man, confident, the loudest in the room. His voice had boomed, he'd had a direct gaze, he'd laughed easily, he had been good company, he had always been smartly dressed. But now: he looked frail, thin, his hair was wispy, he was unkempt, he looked old; he was fifty-four. Every father is his son's hero, at least for a while. Every son wants his father to approve of him when a child and when in adulthood. I was no different, I wanted my father to approve of me. I knew he was immensely proud of me, although I didn't feel I warranted this, I felt undeserving, I felt a fraud, but I tried not to shatter his illusions. I suggested we go to the pub, so he smartened himself up in suit and tie and we went round to the Wheatsheaf and stood at the bar in the lounge and drank pints of Morland bitter and smoked Rothmans cigarettes together.

He was a big drinker, he drank too much, he had been told to slow down in the past, he had been told to stop, the worm of alcoholism swam in his blood. But now it didn't matter, it just didn't matter any more. My father could always outdrink me. But not this time, he refused the third pint, saying, 'I couldn't take another one.' Inanely, that was just as shocking to me as his cancer. My father had never refused a pint of bitter. He would be on his eighth or ninth pint, drinking steadily, while everyone else was falling by the wayside. His smoking didn't matter either, not now. As we stood there, I led the conversation, he followed. He smiled at what I was saying and when I paused in the interrogative, for him to take the conversation, he just nodded in agreement. It wasn't like him. I wanted to hear his loud laughter, I wanted to hear him trump my stories with tales of his own wild youth. But he didn't, he nodded at me and smiled weakly and didn't really say that much. I sipped my last drink and we walked home together slowly.

My brother Peter came home from work that evening. We went out and discussed the matter. We both agreed that Dad should stay in ignorance until it was obvious and undeniable what was happening. I would shelve my plans to go out to Hong Kong and work in the Far East. I would work on the coast and stay close to home.

I did the rounds, looking for a position with a coastal carrier. I wanted something where I could be home within a few hours if need be. The cross-channel ferries were out of reach; there was always a waiting list because newly married deep sea officers were forever seeking a berth that was more conducive to domestic life. I tried for a job on a waste disposal boat, carrying hundreds of tons of toilet effluent up the Thames to dump it out in the estuary, where it hopefully wouldn't float back into the beaches near Southend. All the waste boats were all full up, though, with a long waiting list: constipated with ships' officers so to speak. A couple of coastal tankers offered me work, but I had resolved not to sail on another tanker and I wanted to stick by that. I took a position with a Kent-based company that had a large coastal fleet around the UK. They gave me a berth as chief officer and I picked up the ship in Gravesend. Chief officer sounds grand for a twenty-three year-old, but on these little ships there was only a captain, chief mate and second mate. In the engine room there was a chief engineer and a second engineer. There was a bosun and three ABs, an engine room hand, cook and steward. This was a long cry from the big ocean-going ships I had known.

My first coaster was an odd-shaped vessel that carried milk powder. The cargo would get blasted in by pneumatic shore pumps through big hoses. When we discharged, we had our own strange air-pumping system which was a sort of suck-and-blow mechanism. The second mate was bitter because he had been serving as chief mate on a dispensation, not being properly qualified, when I came aboard and displaced him. He knew the ship back to front, and understood the intricacies of the pumping system, unlike me who was learning as I went along. He gleaned enjoyment by watching me flounder, waiting for me to ask him what needed to be done next before replying with condescension. After a few days I finally lost patience, grabbed him by his shirt-front and told him to give it his best effort to get the job done as a team and stop acting the clever dick, or get off the ship. He changed for the better.

The hours were hard. At sea, the second mate and I worked a watch system of five hours on and five hours off; the Old Man was on the bridge for a lot of the time, often catnapping on the daybed in the chartroom. We went to small ports up rivers in Holland and Belgium to load, crossing the channel to Rainham in Essex before heading up the east coast to Goole. These two places were our main ports in England, although we called at a slew of other little ports as our orders demanded. The pace of work was sometimes shattering. Five hours on five hours off, and everyone up when we went into and out of port. Often we were only tied up for a couple of hours, and the next call was only a few hours away. The ship was small and cramped, the food was poor. When the sea was up the ship was tossed around as if she was a toy, and I was thrown out of my bunk on a number of occasions.

After eight weeks I came home for a month's leave; my father's deterioration shocked me. He was stick-thin, his face was sunken, he had no strength, his legs were like pins, he could hardly walk. I could feel my lip quiver when I spoke to him. He tried to act so normally. I told him of my exploits on the coast, it was all so surreal. I railed inside at the rottenness of the world.

I quizzed my mother: 'Does he know?'

She said: 'He's so brave. He's never complained once. He must know, but we all pretend that he's just a bit under the weather. We can't tell him. If we did, he would just collapse and die. It's going as best it can.'

✶   ✶   ✶

I was on the deck in Rotterdam, on a 1,600-ton coaster loading coal for a power station in Odense; two huge grabs were throwing the cargo into the holds, ten tons at a time, one every sixty seconds, the ship swayed and rolled with each dump. The Old Man walked down the deck and beckoned me over. I saw the expression on his face and knew what was coming.

'I'm sorry, Simon.'

I said nothing.

'The agent is booking a flight for you this afternoon.'

'Thanks,' I said.

'The message from your mother is that you should come home now because your dad is going.'

'Thanks.'

'Hand over to the second mate and pack.'

'I'd rather not,' I replied. 'The loading will be finished in twenty minutes and it would take me longer to explain everything to Julian. My packing will only take a few minutes.' Julian was the second mate. I walked off before he could reply, before my voice started to break in my throat.

My father wasn't going when I arrived home eight hours later, he was gone. They had carried him out a few minutes before I drove in. I must have passed the ambulance or hearse or whatever it was, on the road. My mother was stunned with grief, my brother Peter was mute. My younger brother Anthony, only twelve, looked glum and wounded. I felt wretched, but my wretchedness was sorrow for my mother, not for me, not for my dead father.

The next morning, all the ills of the world descended. I fell into a crushing pit. Nothing I had was worth a sou, my past was as worthless as my prospects, my talents were void. It was easier to slump and stare than eat. If someone brought me tea I would drink it when cold, otherwise I didn't care, I just sat. Uneaten food stayed on the plate beside me. The television flared in front of me but I focussed on the wall; sometimes I would move my eyes at great effort, and focus on the window. All the

*The author's father as an RAF officer.*

trees and birds outside were grey. Then, as if through a curtain, I heard my mother weeping from another room. I pulled the curtain aside and climbed through, I clambered out of the self-serving clutch of depression. I had only been there two days but it felt like half a lifetime.

Peter and I did the rounds, each conversation was profoundly sad: the optician, to say the replacement reading glasses were no longer needed; the Wheatsheaf pub to pay his bar bill; the funeral parlour to make the arrangements; the vicar for the service; all the phone calls to all the people who cared or who should care, or who would want to be seen to care. All the sympathy, real and faux. We placed a notice in the *Daily Telegraph*, which was important to my mother.

The funeral was my first. I didn't know what to expect. I was a pallbearer with Peter, my Uncle John and someone else. We buried him near an ash tree at the edge of the graveyard, I dropped earth on the coffin, it fell like thunder in my ears. Afterwards there was a grand party and we made a great effort to be cheerful. My father had spent his adult life enjoying pubs and bars and parties, and it would have been disrespectful to have sat around miserably. Everyone toasted him and his contribution to life. My cousins patted me on the back, but I didn't milk their kindness. Later, four hours later, full of alcohol but still sober, we went for a drive in a convoy and stopped at a pub and drunk more toasts. When we were home again, just the four of us – me, my mother, Peter, Anthony – we talked in a stilted way until the early hours before quietly going to my bed. As I sank into sleep I sensed my father's avatar gently tapping at the door, through my closed eyes I saw his bright smile, it was decades before I understood what I had lost.

I stayed home for another three weeks, dealing with all the closures: the pension, the mortgage, the disposal of clothes, the sale of the car. A man from the RAF Benevolent Fund visited with reams of paper. The finances were not good, but life would still be reasonable for my mother.

It was May. I decided to stay working on the coast for the rest of the year and then go east again. I took short trips, eight weeks on, four weeks off, all around northern Europe, the Baltic, southern and eastern England. I was chief officer, but it was a different world from deep sea; the two-hatch ships were only 1,600 gross tons. We wore casual clothes, there was no bar, just a crude officer's mess where we ate and gathered when time allowed. The sailors were mostly lazy and disobedient, the cook was incompetent and the food was dire.

I had an unpleasant experience in Odense, a port on the Danish island of Fyn. One of the ABs wouldn't get out of his bunk to work one morning after spending a heavy night in the local bar. The bosun failed to rouse him after several attempts, so I went into his cabin and found him lying there snoring. I shook him roughly by the shoulder and shouted in his ear to get up. He woke up with a start, sat up and threw his fist at me, whether by instinct or by deliberation I didn't know or care. I stepped out of the way of the wild swing then thumped him twice while he was sitting there. He slid down into his bunk, bleeding. I told him to get up and get out on deck to work, he groaned in agreement. I don't think much more about the incident until the bosun told me a couple of days later that the AB was going to make a brutality complaint to the British Shipping Federation about me. I paid it no heed, I had other things on my mind.

We carried whatever cargo the company could rustle up: coal, timber, grain, iron ingots, containers, sometimes bagged goods. Apart from a small stores derrick, we had no lifting gear and relied on shore cranes in port. In my early days on the coast I had found the waters unnerving because of the congestion, the constant traffic, the constant hazards; but after a while it settled as the norm.

I turned twenty-five. I reflected on my situation, which made me feel inadequate. No wife, no steady girlfriend, no friends beyond fleeting shipboard acquaintances, not much money building up, no hobbies, no skills beyond what I needed for my job, no artistic talents, no achievements. In my defence, I read a lot of books, I was interested in ancient history, I respected old people and I didn't let my mother down. Not much of a defence really. On the Ralston of life, the balance was poor.

During my four-week leave I hired a car to ensure my freedom. I took my mother and Anthony to Scotland for a holiday in the summer. We stayed at Loch Ness and visited the monster museum, we went to Oban to see McCaig's Tower, we took the ferry to Skye, we drove on narrow roads as far as John o'Groats and stayed in small hotels and inns. We enjoyed ourselves in a forced and brittle way, avoiding any talk of death and loss. When we got back I spent long spells in pubs, always at the bar, standing, or sitting on a stool, staring at the upside-down optics, drinking myself insensible, wishing I had said all the things to my father that I hadn't said, wanting to know so much more about his young life. Now I never would. I used drink to mask my grief.

As winter arrived, I wanted to get away. I wanted to get away from the tightness of close water navigation, of being on small, cramped ships in small, cramped ports. I wanted the deep blue of the deep sea on a big ship in the sun. I resolved to carry on until Christmas, but I started my quest for a new employer. Deck officers were still in short supply, but we all knew times would be changing sooner or later. I wanted to get away from Britain, I needed a cleansing change. Hong Kong. I contacted several shipping companies; most were fronts for foreign owners – most, but not all. I spoke to the taipan companies, Hong Kong's biggest and most important trading houses; they were the real McCoy. The word 'taipan' is the anglicisation of a Chinese word that described a European entrepreneur in the nineteenth century. Taipan companies were sometimes associated with the opium trade. Although the name had been in common usage for decades, it only gained currency when Somerset Maugham wrote a story called *The Taipan*. Taipans were the swashbuckling businesses of the day. The heads of the big Hong Kong trading houses liked to be called 'Taipan'.

I accepted a position with an old-established Hong Kong taipan company. I had two meetings with the London personnel man in his big office in King William Street, and he seduced me with tales of the East and stories of the trade routes. I was an easy person to sell to. He warned me I would visit places off the beaten track and could expect to be away for a long time. I lapped it up. We agreed terms, and he said I could expect to fly out in the New Year. Everything was subject to a full medical examination: fitness, blood test, chest X-ray, A1 eyesight verification. They wanted to make sure I was fit and strong enough to stand the grind.

I went home and broke the news to my mother. She said she was pleased for me, and told me I should go because I was like a trapped bird. I could see the injury in her eyes. I promised to write. I looked at her back as she walked away, I felt as empty as a blown egg.

# 8

# *Chasing Conrad*

I sat in the shade of the tin veranda of a tin pub opposite the Seaman's Mission in Port Moresby, the capital of Papua New Guinea, sipping Castlemaine XXXX beer and reading my copy of Joseph Conrad's *Mirror of the Sea*. The bar was full of local Papuans when I went in, and most had nodded in a friendly manner, or at least in a not unfriendly manner. A group of three looked slightly hostile. The Papuans of the western Pacific are Melanesians, darker-skinned and thicker-set than the Polynesians of the central Pacific. They looked solid, chunky, almost invincible, not menacing but as people to treat with respect. I took heed of those that were glowering at me and thought it best to go outside. The hotel I was staying in was one of a forgettable chain situated a few streets up from the port and was full of Australians.

Port Moresby was acquiring a reputation as an unsafe place since independence from Australia governance a couple of years beforehand. It wasn't that unsafe, really; the Australians had just lost the upper hand and the locals weren't as cowed as they had been under colonial rule. From time to time, some Papuans would catch a white man and thrash him to prove that they were no longer dominated, but that was rare. Papuans in a state of drink needed to be watched, though, their eyes would get dark with blood as they drank more and more, and a special rage could sometimes unwind. In my hotel they told me to stay away from the local bars, but I thought a couple of cold ones in the height of the day shouldn't present too much of a problem.

Papua New Guinea is the eastern half of the huge jungle island that lies off the north-east coast of Australia. The western half of the island was then known as Irian Jaya, a province of Indonesia. The island is largely unexplored; huge swathes of the interior remain as they have been for thousands of years. Port Moresby is the capital of Papua New Guinea, hot and sleepy; people emerge from the interior to work there, although many just loaf when they arrive.

I was waiting for my ship, the *Poyang*, to berth. She was due in later in the day, after lunch, the agent said. He had said he would pick me up from the hotel at three o'clock, so I finished my beer and walked back for lunch. He arrived at four as I sat on my Globetrotter suitcase outside the hotel. We took a launch out to the ship, which was drifting half a mile off the coast awaiting clearance. When the Q flag was lowered and pratique granted, I clambered up the pilot ladder and my gear was heaved aboard by a grinning Chinese deckhand.

The *Poyang* was a smart ship, built in the early 1960s as a conventional general cargo liner. She was registered in Hong Kong after being changed from the London register the previous year. Hong Kong was still British at the time, so we flew the Red Ensign. The *Poyang* had originally been built for a Finnish company and was intended to be used for diplomatic receptions in different parts of the world from time to time. This meant that the internal decor was of a far higher standard that would usually be expected. The bar and dining saloon were wood-panelled and the senior officers had sumptuous cabins, not that I was a senior officer of course. I discovered that I was in fact more junior than I had anticipated. I had been told that I was joining as junior second officer, which led me to believe that there were two second officers. Not so. There was a chief mate, a second mate and a third mate. The third mate was leaving; he handed over to me, which made me the new third mate in everyone's eyes. I suppose it wasn't that important but I felt disheartened at my diminished status.

I didn't know what to expect of the people when joining an old style Far East taipan company. I suppose I thought those on board would probably be a bit more adrift than the typical officer complement crowd. They were. There were only four other British officers on board: the captain, the chief engineer, the chief officer and the second officer. All the other officers were Hong Kong Chinese, as were the deck crew, engine room crew and stewards.

The British officers were an odd bunch. The Old Man was eccentric, he acted both timidly and petulantly. One moment he had a whispering voice and was nodding in habitual agreement, the next he was stamping his foot and shouting. He seemed to find it difficult to cope with any pressure.

The chief engineer was from Leeds or thereabouts, although had since moved to Australia and had little good to say about Britain. He was a snob with little reason. He spoke sneeringly of most people below him, although he seemed himself both poorly educated and badly spoken. I had met similar people who had raised themselves up in life while remaining insecure about their humble origins. It caused their personality to morph into exaggerated snobbery. The chief also had a dreadful memory, often even forgetting who he was talking to. I had to reintroduce myself on countless occasions. I started to suspect he had some sort of early-onset dementia, although later decided that he evidenced so little interest in others that they just failed to register with him.

The chief mate was due to leave in Lae the following week, he had been on board for eighteen months. He was a pleasant enough man, although I never got to know him properly. He told me he hadn't been back to England for five years, and was now going to take six months' leave in the Caribbean.

Last, there was Franz the second mate, a German-Englishman, who was due to take over as chief mate. I assumed that I would be moved up to second mate, but learnt to my dismay that a new second mate was due to arrive in a few days' time and I was to stay rooted as the most junior officer. Franz and I got on well enough in the few days he was serving as second mate, although he underwent a personality change when he was promoted to chief officer, becoming pompous and over-serious and prone to lecture people at the slightest opportunity.

After the chief mate had left and Franz took over, the three of them formed a troika that stayed together: the mildly eccentric Old Man, the amnemonic chief engineer and the pompously aloof chief officer. I was left right out in the cold.

The majority of the cargo we discharged in the Pacific Islands was textiles and light manufactured goods from Singapore and Hong Kong. We would then load copra, chests of tea, bags of coffee and scrap iron. We also took on board bags of dried sea-cucumber and other south sea delicacies to excite the palates of discerning diners in Hong Kong. These goodies were always stowed in one of the lock-ups, to keep the Chinese crew from snaffling portions for their mess. Overall, the *Poyang* was in good order; she was well painted, with a conventional rig of derricks and hatches, each hatch divided into three decks, with cages and lock-ups for valuable goods.

On the second day there was a moment that I found deeply poignant. We were discharging personal effects from one of the lockers when the Australian stevedore in charge of the shore gangs came to see me because he wanted to record some pre-discharge damage to the personal effects. I went along to look. I unlocked the secure cage and we could see that several of the suitcases had been pried open. Boxes of photographs and all the little personal trinkets of a lifetime's accumulation lay scattered and damaged and trampled in the dirt. These things had no intrinsic value as such, although at the same time they were priceless. A framed black-and-white photograph taken in the 1950s of a young couple arm in arm in Venice, the Bridge of Sighs in the background, the glass cracked. What lovers they? Other pictures of the same couple, older now, with three young children, most of the pictures were ripped and scuffed. A cigar box, broken. A Murano glass vase, broken. A wooden giraffe, broken. A string of fake pearls, mostly stripped bare. A straw hat, flattened and wrecked. We stuffed everything back into the cases as best we could. I couldn't bear to think of this now old couple when they received all their accumulated lifetime treasures.

Over the next few days, I settled into the ship. The crew were mostly ancient long-service Hong Kong Chinese men. The youngster was the deck boy, although he must have been in his mid-twenties, whereas the rest of the crew were all north of fifty. They were competent, although patronising to me, which I found irritating. When I gave them an order they would look at each other before doing it, going off laughing and talking loudly and expressively in Cantonese.

I could imagine them saying: 'Just listen to that stupid round-eye!'

'Yeah! I've forgotten more than he knows.'

'Me too! He's just a stupid kid! Let's do it our way, anyway; it doesn't matter what he says!'

'Yeah!'

'Yeah! Let's do it our way, he knows nothing!'

And do it their way they usually did, which I let go if it was of no import, although in the big things I had to battle to win, which was hard work sometimes. The situation improved as the trip progressed, after I had gone through a proving process and demonstrated that I had some knowledge of seamanship. One night, I found the gangway watchman passed out on Samsu rice wine, but I declined to send him up before the Old Man, instead telling the bosun to replace him with someone who could stand up. That brought me respect and gratitude from the crew, and things improved further from then on.

We left Port Moresby after five days and sailed round to Lae on the opposite north-east coast, a four-day trip through the narrow Jomard Passage that separates the Coral Sea from the Solomon Sea, through mostly deserted island waters. We kept ten miles off the New Guinea coast, the deep green of the jungle slid by, an occasional group of outrigger canoes our only sightings on the sea. When we arrived at our berth in Lae, the chief mate was off like a shot, having carried out a gradual handover to Franz over the previous couple of weeks. Franz was elevated. Tommy Mak joined as the new second mate. Tommy was Chinese from Hong Kong. I wasn't sure how we would get on. Tommy tended to keep his distance socially, but he was decent enough and not afraid to get his hands dirty when he needed to.

Lae was the second-largest port in Papua New Guinea and was preferred by most visiting ships to Port Moresby because it was more laid-back and generally friendlier, although the Australian stevedore in charge of the shore gangs and the troika alike said it was now unsafe, like the rest of Papua New Guinea. They spoke fondly of the good old days, although I felt like shouting to their faces: 'What's wrong with you? These *are* the good old days!'

After two evenings in Lae spent in the ship's bar with the troika, I could stand it no more and went ashore. They gave me sage advice to avoid going anywhere remotely connected with enjoyment and predicted my death if I acted foolishly. I acted foolishly. The chief stevedore had told me of a party at the nearby hotel, which was where I headed, my pockets stuffed with kina, the local currency. The party was fairly stuffy, although it seemed that anyone could join in. It was hosted by an Australian engineering firm, and was mostly attended by loosely dressed Australians who lived in the area, with a sprinkling of Papuans in smart clothes. When asked, I told people I was from the British ship *Poyang*; they seemed pleased that I had come along. I drank South Pacific lager, which wasn't bad, being brewed at the South Pacific Brewery just opposite the port. I moved from group to group as the evening progressed, chatting, eating the plates of food on offer, enjoying the free drink and not needing to spend my kina. At one point I found myself penned in by a pair of married missionaries. They were nice enough people although they were wasting their time with a sinner like me and I had difficulty escaping. At midnight, the party started to wind down. I was far from ready to go and fell in with a couple of overdressed Papuan girls who had been lurking at the bar. Two years ago they would have been turfed out, but it was their country now. They invited me to another party, which seemed a good idea. Their names were Grace and Bobo.

We drove off in a wreck of a car, heading out of Lae and into the green unknown, I sat in the front with Bobo, who was driving, Grace sat in the back. They shared a joint, passing it back and forward although I declined to join in. It smelled disgusting, a fetid smell as if someone was cooking garbage. The roads were bad as we banged and bumped along. Our plan was to load up with supplies of beer from a roadside stall they knew, then head off for the party. We stopped at a roadside stall, which brought me to sobriety with a jolt. It was a built from old wood and sheets of tin, and lit by hissing naphtha lamps. Half a dozen large Papuan men leaned against it and looked at us. The girls looked worried and whispered to each other. I could sense the tension in the air. Bobo wound down the window and called the stall holder over, jabbering at him in Tok Pisin, the English pidgin most widely spoken of the 800 Papuan languages. The stallholder came over, bearing a plastic bag full of large bottles of SP lager. I passed some kina to Bobo, who thrust it at the man. A couple of the loafers started walking towards the car, Grace shouted, we roared off without waiting for change. The girls shrieked in relief, they told me the men were 'very bad' and we were lucky to get away. They said the men didn't like Australians. I apparently had Australian status. After a while we turned off the road onto a track and then off the track onto a smaller track that was just flattened dirt and grass. It was as black as pitch, the beams from the headlights bounced through the trees. I started quizzing them where we were going, they assured me it was to a good party. We came to a clearing, two huts, no lights, nothing, no-one. I wound down my window. There were no sounds, just the rumbling of our engine and the clicks and snaps of small night creatures.

Grace said, 'Let's go.'

I said: 'Good idea.'

Bobo said: 'I think the party must be off.'

They came at us in a rush. Twenty or so men, partially clothed, hitting the car in a wave. Bobo screamed, 'Lock the doors!' We slammed the locks down. Bobo drove round the clearing in a reckless circle, the mob running with us, two were hanging on the back. One leapt on the side as I was trying to wind the window up, he clung on and stuck his monstrous head through. It was the size of a water melon. Bobo and Grace were screaming, I punched the face, it was like hitting a water melon, he barely blinked. Bobo managed to turn the car and we bumped off down the track. The mob started to drop behind, I kept punching the face, he eventually fell off, we drove away to safety. We went back to Bobo's place, a hut on the edge of Lae. We were stone cold sober, we discussed our escape while we drank the SP lager and repaired our shattered nerves. Bobo drove me back to the *Poyang* as first light crept across the treetops.

Sunday was a day of rest; all work ceased in the port. I was lying low and feeling grim when the steward came into my cabin and told me that my guests had arrived. This baffled me. I went out to find the husband and wife missionaries chatting to the Old Man by the gangway. They reminded me that we had agreed to go for a walk through the jungle together. My heart sank. I mined my memory and unearthed a dim recollection.

'The wife said: 'You asked if you could come, remember?' Her US accent was grating mid-western.

'Good for you,' the Old Man said, clapping me on the back.

I grimaced.

'We have the picnic, and we're all ready to go,' said the wife.

'And I've brought you a copy of *The Guardian* newspaper to read for when we rest up,' said the husband, in what I thought was a Canadian voice, judging by the way he pronounced brought as 'brawt' rather than 'braat'. I hated *The Guardian*, wherever he was from.

We had a six-hour tramp into the wilds and back, with a one-hour stop in a clearing by a lake for a picnic lunch. The meal was made of strange items I hadn't eaten before: pumpernickel, peanut butter and honey sandwiches, clumps of strange lettuce-like greenery, liquorice squares, a brown fizzy drink that tasted of antiseptic. I started wolfing food until I noticed they were both silently praying. I stopped chewing out of respect, the heavy pumpernickel bread sat in my mouth, oozing sweetness. I bowed my head slightly and pretended I was joining in, although didn't. Religion had fled from me in my mid-teens, although the guilt remained. No one carries guilt more readily than a lapsed Catholic. When we finished eating, I read my *Guardian* so as not to offend them. After lunch we set off again. The husband and wife missionaries were wearing shorts and stout walking boots and carried staffs, whereas I was dressed inappropriately for walking the Papuan jungle: desert boots, light slacks and a casual shirt. I was more dressed for a stroll in the town, which I wished was the case. From time to time we passed a file of Papuans, who all smiled brightly, and the missionaries paused to jabber with them for a few minutes in Tok Pisin. I don't deny that some of the jungle flora was beautiful, and once we passed a waterfall that travel writers would fight for. All things considered, though, I hated the trek. It was not an experience I needed at that time. By the end, I was peppered with bites from savage insects because I didn't have any insect repellent. The missionaries asked me if I would like to go to church with them that evening, but I lied by saying that I couldn't because I would be on duty.

I developed an interest in the tropical fish we kept in large tanks in the bar. We had several dozen in two tanks, one next to the bar itself and a second that we kept as a segregation unit across by the aft bulkhead. There was a great calming effect from the fish, and I often found my eyes drifting towards the tank in mid-conversation. When I was on my own I would stare at them and become lost in their world. In the tank were all the characters we expect in our own society: the ebullient, the flash, the risk takers, the inquisitive, the greedy, the lazy, the bullies, the cautious, the meek, the cowards. Some mixed with each other, some stayed aloof, and they all had a personality of their own. We had a lot of tetras, small flashy fish that mixed with most of the others, as did the distinctively striped loaches and the oddly shaped guppies. The angel fish needed watching, as they would sometimes eat the smaller ones, as did the aggressive red fin sharks. We often had to move the sharks and the angel fish into the segregation tank, although we would then throw in a few of the faster tetras to give a good mix. We also had a small pet crocodile in a third tank that was much larger than the others, which someone had bought in the islands. It was a dull reptile and no one liked it particularly although it had become a fixture. In the islands, tropical fish were difficult to come by and we would be badgered by people who wanted to buy some of ours. The habit had been to stock up on more in Singapore from the big fish emporium near the Thieves' Market in Rochor Canal Road, where they cost a fraction of the price someone would have to pay in the islands. The profits made went into the bar fund.

I took over as master of fish, which no one protested against, with the ambition of turning what was a hobby trade into a far bigger enterprise. After an uphill struggle, I convinced the troika that we should each invest HK$300 in the venture, about £30 pounds at the time, to buy an even bigger tank and a lot more fish, which I would then actively promote in the islands. I wanted to concentrate on the impressive lookers; the angel fish, loaches and red fin sharks. Without any effort we were selling fish at 200 per cent profit, and my plan was to ratchet this up to 500 per cent by careful selection of the right specimens. We would become tropical fish taipans. The troika stumped up their investment, and with the surplus money in the bar we had a fish fund of just under HK$2,000. We had great expectations. I spent hours studying the fish, taking notes, determining which were aggressive and which passive, finding out which fish mixed best and which should be kept apart. I experimented, moving different fish groups in and out of segregation to find the right mix of breeds. I kept the tanks clean and the water clear, and changed the feeding process. Up until then, anyone would just throw in a handful of fish food whenever they felt like it. I put a stop to that, locking the food away and then giving them carefully regulated feed at certain times. I wanted our fish to be in tip-top condition. I read all of our fish guides exhaustively. I talked fish, I bored the troika with my fish talk. I talked the troika into stumping up another HK$100 each so I could buy the right types of food and the right supplements to bring our fish to optimum health. They paid up to shut me up.

The cargo pattern on the *Poyang* was to load up in the big Far East ports of Singapore, Manila, Kaohsiung and Hong Kong, and then steam south and tramp round the islands for several weeks. The Far East end was hectic, the islands were sleepy. The ports we called into were mostly in the western Pacific, a lot of them in Papua New Guinea and the off-lying islands. On mainland Papua New Guinea, we always called at the bigger ports of Port Moresby and Lae. By bigger ports, I mean big in terms of New Guinea, although compared to world class ports they were backwaters. The smaller New Guinea ports on the north coast were Madang, Rabaul and Wewak, where we sometimes called before heading across the Solomon Sea to the Solomon Islands.

There was bad blood between New Guinea and the Solomons over the island of Bougainville, a paradise of a place that sat at the northern end of the island chain, named after the French explorer Louis de Bougainville in 1768. Louis is better known for having the colourful bougainvillea genus of plants from South America named after him. Bougainville Island was geographically part of the Solomons, although politically it was a part of New Guinea, which caused a festering resentment among the Solomon Islanders. Bougainville was constantly in a state of near-rebellion by the inhabitants, who considered themselves to be part of the Solomons. While not actively supporting the rebels, the Solomon Island government did little to help, which resulted in heavy-handed repression by Papua New Guinea, which in turn caused more rebellion, and so it went on. The main port in Bougainville was Kieta, a quiet place with a few Chinese trading stores, a couple of bars, the obligatory yacht club, a Chinese restaurant and not much else.

After leaving the Solomons, we would steam south through the edge of the Coral Sea to the New Hebrides. At the time, these islands were run as a condominium state jointly administered by the British and French, in comic opera style. The pilot boat that came out to greet us would fly both British and French flags, as would all government buildings. The place itself had a mix of opposing styles and influences vying for attention. If the French took an initiative that was seen by the British as promoting French culture, then the British would come back with a counter-initiative, and vice versa. For every French official there was a mirror British one, and the pair had to consult with each other to achieve any forward movement. There were in effect two separate governments, and each spent their time spying on the other, rather than governing the country. There were two police forces with different uniforms and even two prisons. Miscreants could elect to be tried under either British or French law. At the time, Britain was shedding its remaining colonies whenever it could, which was the opposite of the French plan, which was to grip onto theirs until they were thrown out of the country. Britain had already given independence to the majority of its Pacific Islands including the Solomons, Fiji and Samoa. In contrast, the French held onto Tahiti with determination, flooding it with money to keep the inhabitants happy, and would have almost certainly done the same with the New Hebrides if the British hadn't been there pushing in the opposite direction. The New Hebrides was due to become independent at the end of the decade, as were the British-governed Gilbert and Ellice Islands. The French were irritated that the British zeal for creating indigenous self-government was infecting the inhabitants of French New Caledonia, a group of islands that lay just north of the New Hebrides.

We drifted through these smaller islands as if in a different time warp. The days under the Pacific sun seemed long and tranquil, and it was rare for anyone to become agitated. From the New Hebrides and New Caledonia we sailed east to Samoa, calling at both newly independent Samoa and American Samoa. The Americans had adopted the same colonial tactic as the French; pumping the place with foodstuffs and gadgets inappropriate to its culture, while making the local chiefs rich men. This was largely successful in keeping the inhabitants from causing too much of a ruckus over their lost legacy.

From Samoa, we traipsed across to Tahiti and then north and west to the Gilbert and Ellice Islands and the guano island of Nauru. The western and central Pacific was our huge playground, and it was mostly devoid of shipping. On rare occasions we would encounter one of our own company ships, or a Bank Line ship or something up from Australia. Rarer still was a big ship down from the East under a Singapore or Taiwanese flag. Japanese and Korean fishing boats were not uncommon with their hot-bunk crews netting whatever came their way. Those apart, other shipping was mostly small inter-island ferries and a few coasters, along with the fishing canoes we would encounter near most islands.

Sea life was common: whales, dolphins, flying fish, big turtles, albatrosses and an array of sea birds. When the sea was flat calm and clear, we would sometimes catch sight of grey reef sharks circling around driftwood when we passed close. And the sea was always so blue.

There are over 20,000 islands in the Pacific, mostly in the west and central parts. In broad terms, the island groups that stream out between New Guinea and Fiji form what is known as Melanesia. To the north, the scattering of tiny islands between the Philippines and Christmas Island is Micronesia, and everything else in the central belt from Hawaii in the north to New Zealand in the south is Polynesia. The Melanesians are very black and hardy people, the Polynesians are lighter-skinned and tend to get chubby because of all the coconut oil that is such a feature of their diet. The Micronesians: well, there aren't many of them, although they are more akin to the Polynesians than the Melanesians.

For many thousands of years the peoples of the Pacific lived with each other and fought and killed each other. The traditional way of waging war was by invasion fleets of huge war canoes, whereby one island group would bear down on another with a battle plan of clubbing down the male inhabitants, stealing what possessions they had, and taking the women. In the sixteenth century, the European powers began poking their avaricious noses into the Pacific, the Spanish and Portuguese first, then the British and French. Between them, the Europeans brought sundry civilising traits to the Pacific region: religion, medicine, engineering, literacy, irregular verbs, table manners, shoes, parasols, alcoholism, smallpox, measles and syphilis. When compared to the other countries, the British came out on top in the Pacific land grab by first settling Australia and later New Zealand, then assuming governance of the majority of the South Pacific region. The lesser parts were taken by the French, Germans and Americans. The French ended up with French Polynesia – essentially Tahiti, New Caledonia and a few smaller islands – the Germans grabbed New Guinea, the Solomons and Samoa. But after their bad behaviour in the First World War, the Germans had their islands taken away from them by the victorious powers and handed over to be administered by Britain and Australia. The Americans came in from the east as late starters, and snaffled Hawaii, the Marshall Islands, some of Samoa and a few other bits in the North Pacific. In the 1960s, the British and Australians embarked on a programme of handing back the land to the indigenous peoples, although the French and the Americans remained determined to continue holding onto their islands as sovereign territories.

Bridge watches in the Pacific were lazy days. There were islands dotted all over the place and coral reefs were in abundance, both of which gave the need for tight navigation, although for the most part we would find ourselves steaming through quiet seas on sunny days with little or no traffic. The lookout was given jobs around the bridge area during the day, cleaning or painting. One of my duties was care of the lifeboats: Franz gave the watchmen to me for a fortnight and I set them to oiling the oars, greasing the wires, changing the fresh water, airing the sails, painting the thwarts and generally giving both boats a good freshening up.

Apart from morning sun sights and fixing our position by land if any was in the vicinity, I paced the bridge from wing to wing and talked to whoever visited, which was usually either Sparks or the Old Man. Sparks planned to stay at sea a few years and save money to eventually set up an electrical business in Hong Kong. We chatted about this and that, leaning on the bridge-wing dodger, watching the crew at work below on the main deck. The Old Man would come up after breakfast, potter in the chart room for ten minutes or so then come onto the bridge to light his foul-smelling pipe and tell me stories. He was perpetually nervous, fiddling and fidgeting, moving his head constantly. From things that were said, I ascertained that he found conning the ship difficult in the Singapore Strait, Manila Bay, the Hong Kong approaches and other high-traffic areas in the East. He was less nervous in the Pacific, because there was less to get nervous about. I steered him into telling me tales of the East from the 1940s and 1950s, when he was going up the Yangtse in river steamers, dodging bullets from the Kuomintang and the Communists alike. His stories were fine, and the years fell away from him as he talked.

The fish venture turned out to be a disaster. I went ashore with Tommy Mak in Singapore and we spent all of the money in the fish emporium. I bought a fine new tank and shoals of valuable new fish, together with boxes of specialist feeds and additives. When we went back to the ship, I spent several hours decanting the new tetras and loaches and guppies, the angel fish and red fin sharks and the various flashy bright ones I had fallen for. I segregated them into compatible groups and made sure the water was clean and at the right temperature in all three tanks. I fed them, then settled down to watch them. They were beautiful. Everyone liked the fish, the troika were very pleased, the Chinese officers used to come in and admire them, the stewards would nod their heads approvingly.

Two days out of Singapore, the first one died, it was a tetra. The body was floating on the surface in the morning, a bit nibbled by its colleagues. I used the net to get it out and thought nothing of it, fish died from time to time. A week later, five more had died. A fortnight after that, half of them were dead. Every time I went to look at the tanks, there were another two or three corpses bobbing on top of the water. I tried everything. I changed the water. I took out the stones and fake plants and shipwrecks and the model deep-sea diver and the rocks and boiled them all. I regrouped all the fish. I sterilised each tank in turn. I changed the feed. They kept dying. By the time we approached the first port in the islands we had a miserly collection of survivors together in one tank. The troika blamed me for bringing in diseased fish. They blamed me for losing the bar fund, they blamed me for talking them into a bad investment and losing them their money. I sold most of the fish in the islands; we didn't even recover the bar fund. I resigned as fish-keeper.

Noumea was the capital of New Caledonia and was my favourite island port in the South Pacific. The British had first arrived there in the 1770s, when Captain Cook named the island New Caledonia because parts of it reminded him of Scotland. The French claimed it a few years later, and the island became a source of sandalwood, which was then much sought after in Europe. When the sandalwood ran out, there was some regionalised slaving, with the local Kanak people being shipped out as labourers for the plantations of Northern Australia and Fiji. Nickel was discovered in New Caledonia in the middle of the nineteenth century, which brought a reversal of labour movement, with people being brought in from the other islands to help the depleted Kanaks tunnel under the ground. At the same time, France founded a penal colony, to which they shipped political prisoners, criminals and female delinquents from mainland France. The place was never as notorious as the penal colony in French Guiana, Devil's Island, and it only stayed open for forty years, but it was a cruel regime that spawned a web of smaller penal institutions. The land-grabbing that took place to build the institutions caused problems with the Kanaks, who were already upset from being excluded from the increasing Frenchification of society on the island. They were left with the choice of living on a reservation or working in the mines. There were a few revolts, including one that bordered on civil war, although the French colonial authorities finally brought the place into a state of order by gunning down any locals who acted too boisterously.

Noumea was clean and well-ordered when I visited. The streets were pretty, the landscape was gorgeous, the beaches were pristine and the people seemed contented. Along the front, there were several hotels and a decent selection of bars and restaurants. One evening, Franz and I went ashore for dinner to a place recommended by the agent. It had been opened the previous year: L'Eau Vive, a restaurant on a hilltop run by nuns. We ate jungle fowl and drank fine French wine. At the close of the meal, all the nuns came in into the room. They didn't look like nuns, they were dressed in brightly coloured smocks adorned with leaves and flowers. They stood around the edge of the room, one playing a guitar while they all sang 'Ave Maria' in voices as clear as the light of the world. It was the most hauntingly beautiful experience, and I felt tears prick the edges of my eyes. Every franc they make goes to the poor and needy. Neither of us felt able to talk afterwards; we cleared our throats with gruff sounds and signalled for another bottle of wine. Then we sat and smoked and looked out through the shutters at the coconut trees silhouetted against the moon. Life was so good; I felt like a chosen person.

Another night in Noumea, again with Franz, I almost drowned. We had spent the evening in the hotel bars along Anse Vata beach, a couple of miles south of the port, and we decided to freshen ourselves up with a swim in the bay. We crossed the promenade and went down to the water's edge. The sea was calm, reflected lights danced in the inky black water. We threw off our clothes and dived in. It was colder than I was expecting, but only for a few seconds. We splashed and horsed about, then Franz set out into the bay strongly, I followed. After a while I started to labour, I stopped swimming and floated on my back, looking up at the bright stars in the clear night sky. I looked around although I couldn't see or hear Franz. The lights of the shore looked far away and I began to wonder whether there were any sharks swimming in the dark depths beneath me. I started back to the shore, I swam and swam, then stopped and looked. The shore still seemed far off. I tamped down a rising jolt of panic and set off again, slower and more methodically this time, trying not to think of losing a leg to a grey reef shark or being swept away towards New Zealand, 1,500 miles south. My muscles started to tense, I prayed that I wouldn't get cramp. I stopped every fifty strokes, counted to twenty, then started swimming again. Eventually, I crawled up on the beach and slumped down on the sand like a shipwrecked man, thanking the gods for my deliverance. Franz, dressed again, was sitting on the sand, watching me. He said: 'I was starting to wonder if you were going to make it back.'

In Honiara, the capital of the Solomon Islands, we would go to the yacht club, where all the officers on taipan company ships had honorary membership. The place was mainly full of British and Australians, with a scattering of New Zealanders. A few were long-term residents, some were on secondment from their own governments on various funded projects, the rest were people who passed through on a regular basis as sales representatives for large corporate bodies. They spent their time mostly moaning about how standards had declined since independence had been granted the previous year. They snorted in derision at the pitiful efforts of the civil servants to take control, they sneered at the superior attitude shown by the new chief of police and the new port manager, they cackled at the poor education of the government ministers. They felt the manners exhibited by the locals were not what they should be. Manners were important to the members of the yacht club. We had to keep our manners about us when we were there, raucous behaviour was frowned upon, and I was told to behave with more decorum on a couple of occasions. From listening to their stories, they used to beat their servants before independence and often slept with each other's wives, but they never behaved raucously. I had observed that people who live outside of their own country adopted an exaggerated adherence to standards that had never existed back where they came from. Most expatriates did this to a greater or lesser extent, although the British were by far the biggest culprits.

I was in the yacht club in Honiara one day in June, drinking with a paint salesman from Wellington, when an old buffer, two sheets to the wind, came lurching over to our table.

'Do you know what day it is?' he shouted.

He was wearing a blazer and striped tie.

We shrugged. 'Saturday?'

'Yes! Yes! But which Saturday? Don't you know? Don't you know?' he said, impatiently, pompously.

'It's just a Saturday in June.'

He sucked in his breath and reared himself up.

'It's the Queen's birthday! How could you not know that? How could you not know?'

The paint salesman and I looked at each other, feeling inadequate.

'The Queen!' blazer and tie shouted, raising his glass.

'The Queen!' roared a dozen other members from the bar.

'The Queen!' we said, dutifully, and raised our glasses.

The Solomon Islanders had suffered badly in the nineteenth century, when many local men were forced into working in the plantations of Fiji and in Queensland, Northern Australia. It wasn't regarded as slavery, but was as near as you could get to it. The practice was known as 'blackbirding'. Eventually, Great Britain stepped in and formed a protectorate to wipe out the trade. At the time, the Solomons were under German administration as part of German governed New Guinea, although they were transferred to British control as part of a land swap.

If the nineteenth century was bad for the Solomons, the twentieth century brought much worse. Guadalcanal Island, the main island in the group, was the scene of a fierce land war between the Americans and the Japanese in 1942. Over six months, the Japanese lost 25,000 men in the land battles, the Americans, 2,000. The stretch of water to the north of Guadalcanal is known as Iron Bottom Sound, where twenty-four American warships and twenty-five Japanese lie on the sea bed following one of the biggest naval engagements of the Pacific war. The casualties of many thousand were roughly equal on both sides. Iron Bottom Sound is an official war grave site.

There wasn't a lot to see and do in Honiara. I took a trip out to Red Beach one afternoon, a few miles to the west of town. This was the beachhead where the US Marines had stormed ashore in 1942. There were various markers and memorials, and a few older men wandered

*The MV* Poyang.
*Oil painting by Robert Lloyd.*

about, their faces flat and devoid of all earthly expression. It was a place where no one spoke.

We carried textiles and light manufactured goods to Honiara, along with machinery, occasionally some cars, industrial goods, chemicals. We didn't take much away: copra, timber, personal effects of people leaving. Like so many South Pacific Islands, the Solomon Islands was a place that other countries sold to, not bought from.

I always found myself disappointed by the New Hebrides. It was a place I wanted to like, but every time we called there I left without having enjoyed the stay. The condominium status with the British and French mirror officials offered every comedy man could devise, and because of that I was probably expecting a more intense experience. I think the main reason I didn't like the place, though, was because of the rising tide of nationalism, which made a lot of the natives act unpleasantly towards Europeans. Father Walter Lini, the nationalist leader, was fronting the shout for independence. Lini was unpopular with the governing powers, Britain and France, and equally unpopular with the big regional aid donor, Australia. They all disliked Lini because they viewed him as a troublemaker due to his close relations with the USSR, Eastern Europe, Libya, China and several maverick countries who would make mischief in the South Pacific at any opportunity. They called him Linin behind his back. There was a concern that Lini might create a communist state if he obtained power, although it was probably a false fear to credit him with the ability to create the People's Republic of the New Hebrides or something similar. The reality was that the New Hebrides was a poor nation that needed propping up, it had little to give, and needed material assistance in economic and educational matters. It also needed the money that came with Western tourism, which was being developed. The people of the New Hebrides were overwhelmingly Christian while at the same time they conformed to age-old island hierarchal customs. In most of the villages, wealth was still measured in pigs. Given this as a backdrop, there was little chance of a communist state arising, Lini or no Lini.

The main port and capital was Port Vila, in one of the southernmost islands of the group. Vila Bay was as beautiful a South Sea inlet as you could find, blue crystal water against a backdrop of high green mountains. We tied up at the south side of the bay, about twenty minutes' walk into the centre. Although the port was beautiful, whenever I walked into town it was an unpleasant experience. Groups of loafing locals hung around near the wharfs and had the habit of jeering at any Europeans passing by. They stoned Tommy Mak and me on one occasion, and had a good laugh at us hot-footing it down the road. After we had made enough distance to slow down and discuss the matter, we couldn't decide whether the target was me, as a white imperialist colonialist running dog who had enslaved the native people, or Tommy as a Chinese neo-colonialist running dog who was now enslaving the natives further by capturing the local commerce. We thought it likely that we had been stoned on this occasion, rather than just jeered at, because the crowd was incensed at seeing representatives of the two despised oppressor classes in clear collaboration. Father Walter Lini was obviously doing a good job whipping up the fervour. The people in the town were more friendly, or at least not hostile, but it wasn't a place that drew me.

The other port in the New Hebrides was further north on Espiritu Santo Island. We referred to the port as Santo, although its actual name was Luganville. Santo was smaller than Port Vila, quieter and more relaxed. The locals liked us, everyone sat around a lot. On cargo duty I watched the stevedores discharge radios and gadgets from Hong Kong, before we then started to load bags of copra and cocoa. Off-duty there wasn't much to do, apart from drink cold beer in the sun and watch life drift by.

Tahiti. To me, the name Tahiti conjured up every image that made the South Pacific: flawless beaches, swaying palm trees, blue seas, coral reefs, beautiful island girls wearing necklaces of flowers, chunky men undertaking daring feats. It wasn't like that in reality of course, but it was still an impressive place to steam towards, with its towering green volcanic peaks and palm-fringed sand at the sea edge. Tahiti is the largest and most important island in the eastern part of the Society Islands, which is the major part of French Polynesia. The Society Islands are sub-divided into different groups: the Windward Group, the Leeward Group, the Disappointment Islands and several other scatterings.

Tahiti is imprinted on many people's minds as the place of ultimate temptation after the crew of Captain Bligh's ship, the Bounty, spent several months there in 1789 and became so enamoured that they mutinied later in the year and cast poor old Bligh off in a longboat. Captain Cook had called there twenty years before Bligh, as had the intrepid Frenchman Louis de Bougainville, and they were both complimentary about the island. In the 1840s, while Britain and France were squabbling in North Africa, a passing French admiral took advantage of the distraction to convince the Queen of Tahiti that it was best to become a French Protectorate. The place has remained under French control ever since. The arrival of the Europeans in Tahiti brought the same mixed blessings as it did to the rest of the Pacific islands. Victorian writers concentrated on the good and ignored the bad. The good was believed to be religion, education, medicine and morality. The undoubted bad was the introduction of alcoholism, venereal disease, smallpox, the loss of dignity, loss of birthright, loss of habitat. The painter Paul Gauguin lived and worked on Tahiti at the end of the nineteenth century, and a large body of his work depicts the unabashed simplicity of life there at the time. Monsieur Gauguin was no angel, though, and his antics in the grass huts are believed to have included a lot of cruel liaisons with very young Polynesian children.

We called at Papeete, the capital and largest settlement; the high peaks of Tahiti were visible fifty miles off as they cleared the horizon. When we actually arrived in Papeete, the mountains looked massive, looming over us. No wonder they were given the status of gods. Papeete was slick and clean and stylish. There were a few natives agitating for independence, but they were kept in check by Paris ensuring that plenty of money was pumped into the place. Tourism had been big in Tahiti for 100 years, and the island was geared towards those who visited it for its beauty, rather than people like us, who visited with the ring of commerce. Still, I enjoyed strolling round the streets and spending a civilised hour in one of the cafés. Sadly, we weren't allowed to remain in Papeete overnight, because the port authorities believed our cargo might be infected by rhinoceros beetle and so at the end of the afternoon we were cast out, like a leper, to drift around until daybreak. It was too deep for us to anchor. We were let back into the port again as the sun started to climb above the horizon. Our discharge cargo was light manufactured goods from Hong Kong, together with a ransom of transhipped French wine and brandy. Our loading was the usual fare from the South Pacific, mainly copra.

Samoa is a fractured island group 1,700 miles north-east of New Zealand. Western Samoa is the independent part, whereas the eastern islands are owned by the USA and known as American Samoa. When the Europeans started to arrive in the eighteenth century, they found the Samoans to be a fearsome, warlike people, often engaging in souvenir headhunting after they had killed their enemies. They were also much admired for their ability to navigate the Pacific without instruments or charts, just by using the stars and their own instincts. There was a lot of brawling between different Samoan factions in the late Victorian era, egged on by those powers that had an interest in the area: the British, Germans and Americans. Eventually, following some brinkmanship that almost caused fighting among the powers themselves, the Germans took ownership of Western Samoa and the Americans took Eastern Samoa. The British vacated any Samoan claim in exchange for the German-held Solomon Islands. After the First World War, Western Samoa was confiscated from the Germans by the British and administered by New Zealand until independence was granted in 1962. The USA, that beacon of liberty, has held onto Eastern Samoa.

First, we called into Apia, the capital of Western Samoa. I went up the steep path to the top of Mount Vaea to see Robert Louis Stevenson's tomb, which overlooks Apia harbour. RLS had sailed around the Pacific in the 1880s in his yacht, the *Casco*, calling into several islands before deciding to buy land and settle in Samoa, where he became a revered celebrity storyteller. There was great mourning in Samoa when he collapsed and died at the young age of forty-four. It was a hot walk up the hill, although when I got to the top I was impressed with the requiem he had requested be inscribed on his tomb:

> *Under the wide and starry sky*
> *Dig the grave and let me die:*
> *Glad did I live and gladly die,*
> *And I laid me down with a will.*
> *This be the verse you 'grave for me:*
> *Here he lies where he long'd to be;*
> *Home is the sailor, home from the sea,*
> *And the hunter home from the hill.*

I rather fancied that as my own epitaph, in an envious way. I sat around at the top of Mount Vaea for a while, looking down on Apia Bay, thinking great thoughts.

Another renowned author who called into Samoa was Jack London, when he was sailing round the South Pacific in own yacht, the *Snark*. Jack wasn't buried with any great monument to mark the spot, though; he lies unnamed, beneath a rock in California.

In American Samoa we called in at the main port of Pago Pago, which was known as 'Pango' by everybody. There is a clear difference between the two Samoas. Independent Samoa has strong links with New Zealand, and they play rugby and cricket and respect the Queen. In American Samoa, they play gridiron and baseball. Western Samoa was enjoying generous aid from Britain and New Zealand, although this was dwarfed by the funds poured into American Samoa. This placed the Samoans who lived in the eastern islands in a dilemma: they all wanted the money and the close links with the world's richest nation, but deep down they didn't want to be a kept dog. They weren't US citizens and had a strange US national status, which gave them local voting rights and travel rights to the USA but neither right of settlement on the mainland nor any national voting rights. The voice for independence was muted, and it seemed to me that it would probably stay that way until the time arrived when funds dried up, at which time the locals would probably demand that the Americans clear off.

The physical impact on the two parts of Samoa was apparent. Western Samoa was clean and organised enough; a bit down at heel, a bit shabby. American Samoa was flashier, full of cars and chocked with the franchises and corporate outlets you would find in any State of the Union. The people of both parts were universally large and still looked fearsome and warlike. I imagined they would probably still have hacked my head off for a souvenir if I angered them enough. I preferred Apia to Pago Pago, although that was because it was a better cultural fit for me.

My first visit to Tarawa remains in my memory at many different levels. Tarawa was the capital of the Gilbert Islands, which are in the central Pacific, just north of the equator. The place was best known for the fierce fighting in the Second World War when the US Marines stormed the beachhead and were cut down by the defending Japanese. It was the first time in the Pacific War that the Americans had faced strong resistance to a beach landing. Over 1,500 men were killed or wounded in the first day. The Tarawa atoll is a string of tiny islands, only a few of which are inhabited, on which there are a dozen or so small villages. The Gilbert

Islands were not deemed economically viable in their own right and existed on aid, mainly from Australia, New Zealand, Britain and Japan. The official currency was the Australian dollar. To get into the atoll, we had to go through a narrow entrance to the reef, an awe-inspiring passage. The Pacific waters were a shimmering blue-green and waves rolled and crashed over the reef on either side of us. The margin for error for a big ship like the *Poyang* was small. Once inside the reef, it was like being in some magical land where it was warm and bright and where we were surrounded by all things of beauty. Beautiful it may be, but not an awful lot happens on a Pacific atoll so our liner service was an event for the islanders and we were always warmly welcomed. We carried away the staple copra and pearl shell. We discharged all the other needs of life.

I had a good walk around the Tarawa atoll, as far as I could. I saw the guns still pointing out to sea and the beach where the young American marines had died all those years ago. Every now and again I would meet someone strolling along, and we would stop and converse as best we could, before each going on our way. There was hardly any noise, just the soft crash of surf.

We called there a few months before Princess Anne was due to arrive to grant independence. The Old Man knew the local dignitary, the senior tribal chief I believe, who was in charge of part of the ceremony. He invited us to his house that evening to watch the dancing that was to be put on for the princess. His house was a large wooden structure that was open to the elements in many places. I had been under the impression that we were going to be fed and hadn't eaten since lunchtime, although this proved a mistake because there was nothing to eat beyond bowls of peanuts. The dancing was enchanting, several young girls in grass skirts and garlands of flowers, swaying gently to murmured commands from the chief and a few elders. I sat on the floor with the Old Man and the chief and watched. I felt I was back in the days when schooners, not steamers, crested the reef wave. I could sense Joseph Conrad anchored in the lee while Robert Louis Stevenson sat on the beach sketching notes. The ghost of Jack London leant on a tree nearby. The hiss of the surf wafted over us in the warm Pacific night. I drank cold beer and ate peanuts from a bowl and didn't speak. The hours drifted by.

Mesmerising as the event was, I suddenly realised that I had drunk too many bottles of beer and eaten too many handfuls of peanuts. Sweat beaded on my forehead and I could feel a tell-tale twitching in my throat. I mumbled an excuse of needing the toilet and walked to the doorway, trying not to lurch and stagger. Once outside I rushed a suitable distance from the hut and vomited copiously into the sand. I strived to keep the noise down although was aware of a revolting rasping sound as I laid out a greasy carpet of semi-digested peanuts for the night insects to feast on. When I had finished my discharge, I turned round to see the Old Man standing there in the moonlight, watching.

'I expect you feel better after that, Second Mate?' he enquired.

I smiled weakly and said, 'Uhmm.'

'Let's go back inside then; got to keep up the right appearance.'

I said: 'Uhmm.'

We returned to the hut, where the dancing carried on relentlessly. It didn't seem so charming any more. I nursed a fresh bottle of beer that had been thrust into my hand and pretended to enjoy it. After another hour I pleaded tiredness, saying that I'd only had a couple of hours' sleep the previous night, and made my escape. A few yards down the road I was violently ill again. I blamed the peanuts for being too salty. It seemed a long trudge back to where the ship was, too long for me. The night was warm and the ground was soft and comfortable, so I lay under a coconut tree and fell into a slumber. I awoke some time later to a jolting and I looked around to find myself having been loaded into the back of a Land Rover, which was now crashing down the sandy road. I sat up and watched, wondering where I was being taken and by who. The Land Rover stopped near the ship, and I was helped out of the vehicle by two Gilbert Islanders who seemed to fulfil the role of policemen and port officials: and human refuse collectors, demonstrably. I managed the remaining journey unaided.

✶   ✶   ✶

The sea passages fell into three distinct areas: the Pacific days, the Far East days and the inner seas of the Indonesian archipelago. In our Pacific days, we hardly saw a ship, and the days drifted slowly as we sailed in a world of our own, far removed from other people. In the Far East, it was hectic, particularly around the entrances to the ports – Manila Bay, the Singapore Strait and the entrance to Hong Kong harbour – all of which called for us to be on top form. But it was the days in between when we sailed through the inner seas of the Indonesian archipelago that I enjoyed most of all. This was Conrad country.

Joseph Conrad was one of the most eminent of authors of the late nineteenth and early twentieth centuries. He had been born Józef Teodor Konrad to minor nobility in 1957 in what was then the Russian Empire and what is now Poland. His father was an activist against the Russian occupation who was imprisoned and exiled and eventually left the country for freer climes. Young Józef had flashes of brilliance, but he was a generally poor scholar, probably due to his fractured education as the family moved around Europe. His mother died of tuberculosis when he was young. The only area he really excelled in was languages, speaking Russian, Polish, French, German, Latin and Greek; his English came later. His father made sure he read all the great works of the day. Józef developed a taste for the sea and served on clippers and barques and steamers in the British Merchant Navy in the 1880s and 1890s, where he anglicised his name to Joseph Conrad.

This was during the high point of the British Imperialism, when the British Empire covered a quarter of the globe, the biggest empire the world had ever seen, held together by maritime power. Britain ruled the waves, the Royal Navy had the largest fleet of warships of any nation by a long way, and no other country was able to compete. The British Merchant fleet was equally dominant, with over 40 per cent of ships on the high seas flying the Red Ensign. Britain controlled a web of major sea ports across the world with London at the centre of the web, a Whitehall spider directing half of the world's commerce, puppet-masters despatching young men to govern half a billion souls in five continents. The main ports were at strategic locations, with deep water harbours and port facilities, all protected by the Royal Navy: Gibraltar, Suez, Aden, Durban, Cape Town, Bombay, Colombo, Calcutta, Rangoon, Singapore, Hong Kong, Sydney, the Indian Ocean islands, the Pacific islands, the Caribbean islands. The other major colonial powers, the French, the Dutch, the Germans, trailed in the wake of the British Empire. It was no small wonder that the British developed a sense of superiority, who wouldn't? Recalling empire builder Cecil Rhodes' seminal quote, *Remember that you are an Englishman, and have consequently won first prize in the lottery of life*, at the time Conrad was sailing the seven seas, Rhodes was spot on.

Conrad went to sea as a junior deckhand unable to speak English and left at the age of thirty-six with a British Master Mariner's Certificate of Competency, as an accomplished and recognised author and as a British subject. He spent most of his time on sailing ships and only a year on steamers. He was an enigmatic character. Although a Russian by birth, he always considered himself a Pole above all else, even though he was a fervent devotee and promoter of Britain. He became a British citizen in 1886. Through novels, some of which were semi-autobiographical, some of which were interpreted tales of other seafarers, some of which were pure fiction, Conrad wrote of the minutiae of shipboard life on ships of the day. He wrote of mad captains, damaged mates, interfering wives, overindulgence in drink, bad ship's food, avaricious ship owners, storms at sea, the trials of life, the obscure backwaters of the East. Conrad's stamping ground was the Far East, the western Pacific and the Dutch East Indies, modern Indonesia. He wrote about it in a powerful way that no one had done before and few have done since. I loved Conrad, I was a Conrad aficionado supreme. I had read all his works, I was a Conrad bore, I talked Conrad to anyone who would listen. For reasons I never understood then or since, Conrad fired me with a sense that I needed to go where he had gone, in the same way, doing the same thing. It was a kind of madness: *Conradius lunaticus*.

The true heart of Conrad country was the inner seas of the Dutch East Indies: the Java Sea, the Flores Sea, the Celebes Sea, the Sulu Sea, the Banda Sea, the Molucca Sea, the Strait of Makassar. These inland seas were all huge stretches of water between the islands, some took days to cross and I went through them all in my Far East and Pacific days. Our voyage from Singapore to the islands would take us right across the wide Java Sea, to the north of Java Island, past Bali and into the Flores Sea, leaving Timor to the south, into the Banda Sea, heading for the Torres Strait, the narrow stretch of water that separates Australia from Papua New Guinea. The Java and Flores Seas always seemed to be coloured a wasted green, thick-looking, foamy, with logs and clumps of stalky fronds drifting by. The ships we saw among the Indonesian Islands were mostly small and ancient coasters, belching sooty smoke, inter-island traffic plying their way, filled with people and spices and all manner of goods. Small canoes, fishing, sometimes several miles from land, appeared in groups. I would wave if we passed close, and the occupant would lift a hand in return salute. The islands were dark and green and the succulent smells reached out to us as we steamed by. The inner seas of the Indonesian archipelago were generally regarded as a safe area because they were well charted, the passages and straits were mostly wide and sea traffic was light. There was always something to see, and this made the bridge watches always interesting, but never that demanding. The passages through the inland seas gave me time to reflect, to take in the life that I had come out to live.

My favourite transit was when we returned to the Far East after calling at the northernmost Pacific islands on our voyage, Tarawa and Nauru. We steamed west across the stretch of the green Celebes Sea, through the Basilan Strait and into the blue Sulu Sea where we picked our way carefully through the smaller islands and rocks in the southern quarter towards the Balabak Strait, then out to creep north-east along the busy Palawan Passage in the Philippines before swinging into the wide reach of the South China Sea, heading north-north-west for Hong Kong. There was nothing finer than navigating a ship through these waters, nothing finer.

✯  ✯  ✯

I was promoted to true second officer after being on board for five months, and we had a number of other officer changes at the same time. Franz had been away at sea for eighteen months, and he was finally paid off in Hong Kong, with Tommy Mak being moved up to chief mate; I then took over from Tommy. I felt a surge of relief to move back to what I considered my true rank. The junior second officer position had just been a sales pitch by the personnel department in London to get me signed on the *Poyang* in the first place, and in truth I had only ever been the third mate. I didn't regard the chief mate position I had held while working on the coast as being a true chief officer's job, because coastal ships were so much smaller. Having said that, I had used what chief mate experience I had to try and diminish Franz's authority from time to time, when I judged there to be an advantage, or if I was feeling spiteful. In any event, on the *Poyang* I was now back as second mate, where I felt I belonged. The new third mate was a lanky, bearded lad from Devon called Carl, who was a welcome addition to the stew.

In Hong Kong, I also picked up a curious letter from Julian, the second mate of the last coastal ship I had sailed on before joining the taipan company. Julian had tracked me down through the London office. His letter was brief and asked me to read the enclosure and telephone him when I had the chance. He had enclosed a letter from the British Shipping Federation, addressed to me care of the coastal company. The language in the Federation letter was stern and referred to the 'brutality hearing' that had been held in my absence by the Federation Disciplinary Committee. The committee acknowledged the representations that had been made on my behalf, although they advised that they could not reach a proper conclusion in my continued absence because they felt that a lot of the questions were still unanswered. The letter concluded by saying that as they understood I was no longer serving on Federation ships they didn't propose to take any further action on this occasion, although they reserved the right to do so if I returned. I was baffled.

I caught the first boat ashore to Hong Kong Island after lunch, and went straight to the Seamen's Mission to telephone Julian.

In those days, international direct dial was a rare service and telephoning home entailed going through the international operator. The caller was then given a choice of making a person-to-person or a station-to-station call. Station-to-station was cheaper, although it meant that you paid for the call whoever answered it. Person-to-person meant that you didn't pay unless the person you wanted to speak to was there. I decided person-to-person was a better bet, in case Julian was back at sea. I reserved one of the telephone booths then went to the mission bar, picked up two cold San Miguels and a huge pile of change, then went back to the booth for what could be a long vigil. Hong Kong was eight hours ahead and it was now three in the afternoon, so if Julian was at home it would be early and he might still be in bed, although my call wouldn't be arriving at an obscene time. I gave the operator the number and was told in turn how much money to insert for a three-minute call. I loaded up the telephone accordingly and kept another pile in reserve for topping it up, then sat drinking my San Miguels and smoking until the operator called me back twenty minutes later with the connection. Julian had still been in bed.

Following an exchange of pleasantries, he told me the story, which was about the aftermath of me punching the AB on the last coaster I had sailed on. I hadn't even thought about the incident since it had happened. The situation had seemed quite clear to me: the AB was supposed to have been working on deck, he was still in his bunk, I shook him by the shoulder to wake him up, he swung his fist at me, I punched him, twice admittedly. The AB, said Julian, had painted a different picture to the Federation. In his version, I had crept into his cabin while he was asleep and given him a savage beating while he lay helpless in his bunk, knocking out his teeth, giving him concussion and causing him on-going nightmares. I hooted when Julian told me this. Julian agreed it was ridiculous, but that was the story the AB had been telling the Federation. Julian said he had been asked by the company to go along and attend the hearing and put in a good word for me. He did, and was horrified to see the AB, limping and with a bandage around his face eight months after the event no less, trot out his account, and even more horrified to see several crew members lining up to support him. The bosun was there, waiting to give his story. Julian collared him in the corridor and told him that he had better row back from the fiction when he was called to testify, otherwise there was little likelihood of the company inviting him back to serve on any of their ships. The potential damage to his prospects caused the bosun to give a more balanced explanation. He said that the AB wouldn't get out of his bunk, I had gone in to wake him and no one had actually seen what had happened. Julian gave a factual account in that there were no witnesses, plus a sterling defence of my character. The combination of the bosun and Julian evened the scales and caused the committee to put the whole issue in the long-term pending tray, until such time as I showed my face again. The AB was crestfallen in not getting the fat compensation payment he had been expecting, and went off on a rant about a psychopath being loose on the high seas, until he was told to shut up by the chairman. He stamped out, forgetting his limp, his fellow conspirators trailing behind looking equally crestfallen about losing their share of the spoils. The committee were unconvinced by the AB, although my absence caused them to shelve the matter until I returned.

As a result of Julian's account of events, I was angry and frustrated. The Hong Kong company I was working for was non-Federation so it didn't make any immediate difference to me that I was no longer able to sign on a Federation ship, although it could harm me in the future if I wanted to move back and work for a mainstream British-based shipping company again. I thanked Julian for his help, put the phone down, then went back to the bar and silently raged. Plans of revenge passed through my mind, although nothing that was practical. After a couple of hours, I made another call, this time to the MNAOA, the Merchant Navy and Airlines Officers' Association. I explained what had happened, they clucked in sympathy and asked when I could come in the office in London and discuss the matter in detail. I explained that I was in Hong Kong and wouldn't be home for some time. I was passed to another official who gave an explanation of the situation I was now in. Essentially, if there was an officer glut then no shipping company would take me on because they wouldn't want to invite the aggravation of dealing with the Federation. However, if there was an officer shortage then shipping companies would probably employ me and deal with the issue, because the main priority was manning the ships. The officer situation in the mid-to-late 1970s was in the early stages of moving from shortage to glut. There was nothing I could do, although I was irritated at the unwarranted stain on my record. I spent the rest of the afternoon day-dreaming nasty thoughts of meeting the AB one day and giving him a proper usage for his bogus bandage.

One of my subsidiary roles as second mate was to act as the ship's medical officer. The *Poyang* was not registered to carry more than twelve passengers and so we didn't need a doctor, just a designated medical officer. In actual fact the term 'medical officer' was far too grand; I kept the keys to the dispensary and patched up anyone who had an accident, as well as deciding upon appropriate medicine for those who were unwell. In the case of a major and traumatic operation, such as having to remove someone's appendix, we had recourse to consult with a real doctor via the General Post Office Coast Radio Station in Britain, which would link us with a hospital or doctor. Once connected with the competent authority, we would be able to receive instructions as to where to cut and what to take out. The patient would then be strapped to whatever we felt to be the best operating surface, usually the main table in the dining saloon, and we would do the best we could. In such cases, I would need to call on the greater expertise of the Old Man and the chief mate, both of whom had carried out the medical officer role in previous years, so that we would have a full operating team.

I never had a major operation to carry out and most of my cases fell under accidents, woundings or self-inflicted conditions. My training had been some fairly rudimentary medical courses ashore, during which we learnt all the usual accident control: cuts, burns, broken limbs, resuscitation and so forth. We were taught to inoculate people by injecting oranges, which was the closest texture to human flesh, apparently. We used pork to practise stitching wounds. Our basic brain surgery training had entailed understanding what part of the skull to drill in order to relieve pressure following a head injury. We were given a reasonable understanding of what drugs to use for what condition, with an emphasis on morphine.

Accidents could be anything: shipboard life offered plenty of hazards, although they were usually gashes and burns. I would anaesthetise the area with ethyl chloride spray and clean up the mess with antiseptic wash, stitching the wound if need be, then cover it with an appropriate dressing. It was quite common for me to treat damage caused by people fighting – bruises and loose teeth, usually, although sometimes broken fingers and the occasional slash from a knife.

Apart from conflict, the main self-inflicted illness was venereal disease, which was extremely commonplace; gonorrhoea mostly, as well as venereal warts. In the treatment of gonorrhoea, shipboard antibiotics had moved from penicillin to oxytetracycline, which

I usually found efficient at stopping the penile discharge and clearing up the condition. I always took a swab of the discharge and stored it between two glass slides, then gave these to the patient to take to the shore doctor for testing at the appointment I would make for him. Venereal warts were treated by applying a purple lotion, which I believe was some sort of mild acid. Syphilis was rare and couldn't be treated aboard ship, and all cases needed to be referred to a doctor at the next big port.

The other self-inflicted condition was from drink. This could be alcohol poisoning from overindulgence, gastric poisoning or blood poisoning from imbibing bad rotgut brews, temporary blindness and lunacy from drinking dangerous liquids such as compass alcohol, distilled shoe polish or homemade spirits, or perhaps just a physical injury from having fallen over drunk.

Last, there was always a bit of malingering to cope with, which I usually treated by making the patient drink the foulest-tasting concoction I could safely give him.

My biggest misdiagnosis was the crew cook's tuberculosis. He was a grossly fat and sweaty man, always coughing and spitting. He was also universally unpopular, spoke poor English, was in a permanent bad mood and disliked everyone. The chief steward brought the cook along to the dispensary one day and translated his rasping Cantonese. He was coughing more than usual, spitting up more phlegm, he was tired, he was out of breath and didn't feel well. I looked at his tongue, took his pulse, listened to his chest with my stethoscope, looked at his eyes and smelled his breath. After pretending to consult my copy of *The Ship Captain's Medical Guide*, I told him to cut down on his smoking, pay more attention to his personal hygiene, stop eating so much and get more sleep. I thought he was just being lazy and was looking for a few days off. I gave him some aspirins. I could see he wasn't pleased with my diagnosis, he argued with the chief steward for a couple of minutes before lumbering out, muttering to himself.

I kept an eye on him for the next few days although he seemed the same unpleasant person he had always been. I decided to send him ashore to the doctors in Hong Kong anyway. He never came back, he had TB. We all had to have chest X-rays after that, to see who else might have caught it. A few people were concerned that he might have been coughing up his phlegm into the soup. The X-rays resulted in two crew members also being paid off, and they were sent to the same sanatorium as the cook. I felt pretty bad over the incident: bad, sad and a very incomplete doctor.

I may have been a bad doctor but I was highly organised. The medical dispensary was clean and all the medicines were properly labelled and accounted for. One day, I found signs that someone else had been in there, which could only have been the Old Man, chief mate or chief engineer, who were the only people with master keys. The next day, someone had been in again, presumably helping themselves to the goods in 'my' dispensary. I concluded that one of the three senior officers was treating himself. I thought it was probably an embarrassing condition if he had to sneak in and give himself covert treatment, and made it my mission to find out who it was.

My immediate suspicion was that one of them had caught the clap and was taking oxytetracycline, but this would result in no drinking of alcohol. The Old Man and the chief engineer both drank gin as if it going out of fashion, and Tommy Mak had a healthy beer appetite. I counted every oxytet pill anyway, although the number stayed the same over the next few days. I then laboriously counted every pill and marked the level of every liquid in the dispensary and went in to check for any shortfall at the start and end of my watch. I soon found it was calamine lotion and cotton wool that was disappearing, lots of it. Someone had a rash in a place they wanted to keep private. I had two large litre bottles of calamine, and the open one was going down fast; the pilfering was being done while I was on the midday-to-four watch. My guess was that the theft was taking place after lunch and before the steward brought afternoon tea, probably between 1300 and 1500. I thought it more likely to be earlier rather than later, so the culprit could bathe their condition and then go for an afternoon snooze until tea was served.

I briefed Carl and he agreed to shadow each of the three suspects in turn. He glued himself to Tommy Mak first, leaving the dining saloon when he did, following him discreetly to his cabin and then lurking down the alleyway in case he came out. Tommy Mak was cleared, he didn't emerge until just before 1600 to go up to the bridge to relieve me. The next day it was the Old Man's turn. He turned out to be the one. Carl followed him back from the dining saloon and the Old Man went straight to the dispensary and stayed in there for ten minutes. Carl came to the bridge and told me. We discussed what to do. Putting pepper in the calamine seemed a bit extreme; we debated whether to hide the bottles. Carl wanted to piss in the one the Old Man was using but I vetoed that. I decided it would be more fun to bring the Old Man into the conspiracy so he could advise me how best to catch the thief.

The next time the Old Man came onto the bridge I put on my most serious face and told him that someone was stealing medicines and I was thinking of stationing a couple of people in the dispensary to catch whoever it was. The Old Man looked stricken, then quickly recovered.

'Ahh, is that necessary, Second Mate? What exactly's been taken?' he asked.

'Well, so far I've only found calamine and cotton wool, but who knows what else the thieving bastard's taking! He could be stealing all sorts of medicine!'

'What makes you think it might be anything more?' He was looking uneasy.

'It doesn't matter what he's stealing, sir. He's stealing and I'm going to catch him! Then you can log him and throw him off the ship.'

'Hmmm, I don't know.'

I let the silence stretch out.

I said: 'My God, Captain! I've just realised something!'

'What's that, Second Mate?'

'There's only you, me, the chief and the mate who have keys to the dispensary. It's not you or me, so it must be one of them! How are we going to handle that? Shall I tackle the mate and you speak to the chief?'

He went very quiet for a while, then shuffled from one foot to another, like a guilty small boy.

'Well … actually, Second Mate …'

The Old Man gave a long and detailed explanation about the dhobie rash he had around his groin. Dhobie is the seaman's term for laundry and dhobie rash is the painful itching caused

# 9

# Gazing into the Abyss

After nearly nine months on the *Poyang*, I was due to pay off in Hong Kong in September, at which time I would be due over four months' leave, although our arrival in port was threatened by a typhoon scare. The tropical revolving storm labelled Typhoon Hope had slammed into Hong Kong four weeks previously; it was one of the biggest storms to hit Hong Kong for years and had caused massive destruction. The 150-mph winds had ripped ships off their anchorages, flung cars around the streets, blown flimsy houses away completely. Another storm was now on its way and the authorities were jittery, having not yet cleared up after the last one. We were steaming up from Manila, and the Old Man decided to slow down and keep well south until the typhoon either passed ahead of us or curved away to the north and east. Sometimes a typhoon would swing south, but only very rarely once it had entered the South China Sea. If this happened, we would just have to run for the equator. Tropical revolving storms cannot cross the equator and will turn away before they get too near. We should be safe once we got south of Palawan, once we were below the 10-degree line of latitude.

We made the ship typhoon-ready, battening everything down as thoroughly as we could, closing every hatch and watertight door, and knocking all the dogs tight shut. We put extra lashings on the deck cargo and went down the hatches to walk below decks, securing anything that looked as if it had the potential to shift. The derricks were all lashed down, extra securing chains were put on the anchors, extra lashings on the lifeboats. Ropes were rigged at strategic points along the decks in case we had to venture out to secure anything that came loose. In the dining saloon, the storm boards were raised on the tables to prevent plates ending up in people's laps when the ship started moving about, the table cloths were damped down and the chairs were clipped to the restraining rings on the deck. The chief steward took steps to ensure that the cook and his men secured everything in the galley, fridge locks were put on in the bar to keep the contents from spilling out, everyone had responsibility for securing their own cabin.

A tropical revolving storm has different names in different parts of the world. Atlantic storms that hit the Caribbean, Central America and the United States are known as hurricanes. In Australia and the Indian Ocean they tend to be called tropical cyclones (although in some parts of Australia they are known as willy-willies). In the Far East they are typhoons, which translates from the Chinese *tai feng*, meaning supreme wind or devil wind. Tropical revolving storms form near the equator, where the warm water heats the air above it, forming a tropical depression. The moist air rises and starts to swirl, and is fuelled by more warm, moist air being drawn in, becoming a tropical revolving storm. The storm starts to move west, sucking up more moist air, the pressure dropping, the storm intensifying, the winds blowing harder and harder, swirling around the central eye. Typhoons start their journey in the North Pacific, moving west towards the Philippines and Taiwan. The typhoon will either track west all the way to the coast of China, or will swing north and east, sometimes heading for Japan. Very occasionally they will dip south. When they hit land they are often at their most intense, smashing though everything in their path, discharging torrents of water. As they cross the land, they start to lose power quickly because the supply of warm moist air is cut off. Those that travel north encounter cooler seas and also become less powerful.

Typhoon Hope didn't swing to the north. From her birthplace south of the Mariana Islands in the Pacific, she tracked west, did a feint north, then swung west again and rushed forward resolutely, picking up speed and power, being upgraded from storm to cyclone, being upgraded to a major category event, screaming through the Luzon Strait between Taiwan and the Philippines and slamming into the Chinese coast, right into Hong Kong. A typhoon causes uprooted trees, flying cars, grounded ships, destroyed houses, injury, death, wanton destruction in a rage of noise. No one who has been in a typhoon ever forgets the experience.

Typhoon Hope was bad, but by no means the worst in Hong Kong's long history of suffering these storms. Deaths tended to be much more numerous in days gone by because of less preparation, lower standards of safety and poorer medical facilities to deal with the injured. The unnamed typhoons that came through in 1874 and 1906 each killed 2,000 people, as opposed to the notable typhoons that came after the middle of the twentieth century, Mary in 1960 and Ruby in 1964, which were big category storms although only killing sixty-five and thirty-eight people respectively. Typhoon Wanda in 1964 was a nasty one, taking nearly 400 to their grave. Typhoon Rose in 1971 sits in many people's memories as one of the worst of all time, but the death toll was comparatively low at just over 100 souls. The worst tropical revolving storm ever recorded, the most monstrous typhoon ever to smash into the South China coast and rip through Hong Kong, was the unnamed storm that arrived on the morning of 2 September 1937, which caught the colony on the hop and slayed 11,000 people. The deaths were aggravated by the massive influx of refugees that had arrived to flee the instability of China, caused by the increasing communist insurgency and the Sino-Japanese war. The refugees were living in temporary shanty conditions with little protection against the forces. The deaths amounted to nearly one and a half per cent of the population. In comparative terms, there has never been another like it before or since.

When the Hong Kong Observatory saw a typhoon approaching and concluded that it was a danger to the colony, a typhoon warning signal was raised. Typhoon warning signals have been hoisted on Hong Kong since the 1880s, using a system of balls, cones, lights and flags to indicate the level of threat and the direction from which the storm is expected. The design of these warnings has changed several times, although the message is always the same: take cover, typhoon approaching. Since the 1930s, in additional to the physical hoisting of the typhoon warning signal, warnings were broadcast on the radio. Television warnings started in the 1960s. Once a tropical depression was upgraded to a tropical revolving storm, it was given a name. In days gone by, typhoons were mostly un-named, although tended to be casually and informally named after mythological creatures and sometimes after contemporary figures, often politicians, usually hated people. A system was finally settled in the mid twentieth century, giving such storms female names although, in the spirit of equality, this was changed in the late 1970s so as to alternate between female and male names. Typhoon parties were common among expatriates in Hong Kong. This involved them battening themselves down in a secure location, usually someone's house or apartment, with friends and copious amounts of alcohol, to then party out the storm.

When Typhoon Hope hit, the damage was immense. Statistically, a damaging typhoon can be expected to pass near or over Hong Kong every four years. But that is only an average, and the period between strikes can be much less. A typhoon can erupt at any time throughout the year but the typhoon season, the period when they are most expected, is from May to October.

With memories fresh from Typhoon Hope, the Old Man was acting cautiously and we crawled across the South China Sea at less than half revs, listening to the reports, waiting for the storm to swing to the north. We didn't want to be caught at anchor in Hong Kong harbour with a typhoon passing through. We would be safer if we could get on one of the big mooring buoys that were anchored to the sea bed with heavy chains, but we wouldn't know if we would be able to get a buoy until we arrived, and either way we would be safer still at sea. When a typhoon was headed for Hong Kong, a lot of ships slipped their buoys or weighed anchor and fled for the open sea to ride out the storm in open waters. Eventually, the storm swung north, then east, petering out well before it reached any land mass. Once it was clear that the storm no longer presented a danger, we wound the *Poyang's* engines back up to full revs and steamed north-west for Hong Kong.

Although I had been initially interviewed by the taipan company in London, the personnel department in the main office in Hong Kong wanted to meet me when I paid off and sent a message that I was to come in and see them for a chat and debrief.

We tied up to a buoy in the harbour and I took a bumboat across to the island, where I went over to the company office in Queensway, not far back from the Hong Kong waterfront. I then spent half an hour talking to two personnel wallahs about those things that people working in personnel departments like to talk about: career, prospects, opportunities, obligations and all such similar guff. They told me my report from the Old Man was good and offered me a return airline ticket to anywhere in the world, provided I paid any cost over and above that of a return flight to London. They said they wanted me back in Hong

Kong in four months. I had been mulling over taking a fortnight in Brazil, but had decided against it. I wanted to push on and to get my sea time in as quickly as I could so I could sit for my Master's Certificate. I needed another nine months at sea to get my qualifying time. I asked Personnel if I could just take a couple of weeks' local leave and roll the rest of my accumulated leave forward. They reacted as if they couldn't believe their luck and quickly offered me a position as second mate on the *Kwangsi*, a general cargo liner that was due to call at Manila in twelve days on her way south to New Zealand.

My immediate future agreed, they took me out to lunch at Ho Choy's before I changed my mind. I told them I had booked into the Grand Hotel in Kowloon and intended to stretch my legs for a couple of days in Hong Kong, after which I would fly to Manila. The airline ticket would be delivered to my hotel that afternoon, with some expense money to get to and from the airport. They even offered to pay the cost of four nights in a hotel, which was unexpected; they baulked at paying four days subsistence, which was not, although they did agree to give me the standard subsistence rate for two days. All in all, I ended up with more than I had hoped for. Lunch in Ho Choy's ended up as a boozy affair that went on longer than planned and the personnel department runner ended up delivering the airline ticket to me while we were still at the table, together with a fat wad of Hong Kong dollars that I had to sign for. Later, bloated and light-headed and feeling good, I walked back to the Star Ferry terminal and caught the first boat across to Kowloon.

The Grand Hotel was a good place to stay, an old, white-painted colonial-style building, crushed among post-war giants off Nathan Road, big rooms, good staff, a quiet old-fashioned bar. Rumours were that the Grand was going to be demolished to make way for a new shopping centre but I didn't choose to believe them. I met Carl in the evening and we made a night of it, finishing at the Bottoms-up bar in Hankow Road in the early hours, drinking typhoons, a lethal gin-based cocktail, trying to chat up the Chinese girls and making fools of ourselves.

I spent the next two days unwinding as a sightseer, eating on a floating restaurant at Aberdeen, riding the hydrofoil to Macau, taking the train into the New Territories to look across the border at China. I got off the train at Lo Wu, the end of the line, the last station before the border. Locals tried to gyp me as I walked around town, and I remained on the defensive. Back in Kowloon I went to Goh Kwok the tailor and ordered four new shirts and two pairs of trousers to be delivered to the Grand the next day, then treated myself to a new Seiko watch from a shop in Mong Kok.

Most of the time, though, I just walked, I wandered at a slow amble, usually finding myself around the waterfront areas. Hong Kong is an ever-fascinating part of the world, everything revolves around the harbour, the commercial heart. Throughout the day the water is a constant buzz of small craft, cargo lighters, bumboats, ferries, small inter-island ships and junks, keeping the commercial flame alight. Deep sea ships are either moored to buoys or anchored in the roads, the ships come and go, come and go. I took the Star Ferry from Kowloon to Hong Kong Island several times a day, leaning over the stern, the wake carving a foam trail behind us. I took full advantage of my world-class view of the never-ending harbour activity. On the third day, I took a taxi to Kai Tak airport to catch the afternoon Cathay Pacific flight to Manila.

\* \* \*

My break in the Philippines turned out to be testing, a watermark, a low watermark, it drained me, it sapped my reserves. It caused me to gaze into the abyss and, as Nietzsche warned, 'if you gaze into the abyss, the abyss also gazes into you'. I could feel felt myself slipping down the moral ladder even as I stepped onto the tarmac at Manila airport into the darkening day. I had wrapped myself in a mantle of my own self-indulgence, HK$15,000 in my pocket and heading for one of the world's great centres of decadence. Everything I had in the world was in my Globetrotter suitcase. I had made no hotel arrangements, I had made no arrangements at all in fact. I just had the local agent's address in my pocket with an agreement to call there in a few days to make sure I didn't miss the *Kwangsi* going south. I changed some Hong Kong dollars for Philippine pesos, deciding that 20,000 pesos would be enough to start.

Cab drivers argued angrily for me at the stand outside the airport building: I went with the victor, a noisy, aggressive little man. He hurtled through the early evening traffic, alternately shouting at me in American English and screaming at the other drivers in Tagalog. He drove as if possessed, as if he wanted to kill us both. I looked out the side window, being unable to bear looking ahead at my approaching death. The cab wasn't air-conditioned, sweat rolled off me. I wound down the window so I could lean into the fume-filled tropical air. The noise of the urban stew was painfully exciting. A carpet roar of motor traffic, horns shrieked, we

*Documents to travel the world with.*

raced furiously with other cars, our engines howled like tethered mad dogs, like junkyard hounds from hell, trucks laboured noisily as we swerved round them, motorcycles laden with three or more people spluttered along. Jeepneys, garish and loud, fought for road space with cars, bikes, motorbikes, trucks, people. Road manners were non-existent, no one cared for anyone except themselves. I felt sure that if the car in front ran over a stray child we would just run over the corpse in turn and carry on without pause. I had asked for a decent hotel in the bar area of Ermita. The driver said he knew just the place, and spent a large part of the journey screeching at me about how wonderful it was going to be.

The hotel was a dump, a two-storey building in a dim narrow street between Mabini Street and M. H. del Pilar. The outside area was strewn with rubbish, the drains reeked, rats scampered, people loafed, looking dangerous, smoking. A grinning lady stood behind the desk, welcoming me, an armed guard sat in the corner of the foyer. The driver had a machine-quick conversation with the grinning lady, she paid him for bringing me there, I paid him off and gave him an average tip he didn't deserve. She took me upstairs to my room, it was open to the outside although it had locked grilles on the windows and on the door to the balcony. A bed, a fridge, a chair, a desk, the ancient shower was down the corridor. The sheets looked grubby, the floor was dusty, small lizards ran around the ceiling, it was hot. The grinning lady gave me towels, and I gave her 1,000 pesos to fill up the fridge with beer.

Later, I sat on the balcony in the dark, drinking San Miguel and smoking, watching the outside streets. The area was profoundly unsafe. Groups of men slouched by and sometimes sat in front of the hotel and made a racket. On a couple of occasions, urchins came rushing down the street from M. H. del Pilar, then stopped and gathered themselves together in a circle, heads bent together, chattering. I worked out that they were probably dividing the spoils after mugging some unfortunate soul on the main street. I was worried about my gear, particularly my sextant and binoculars, which were the only items of value I owned apart from my watch. The room was safe enough from the outside with its metal grilles, although someone could easily kick in the door to the room from the landing. I went downstairs and dropped 1,000 pesos on the armed guard, who promised to keep a special eye on my room.

The next morning I woke hurting with savage insect bites, red lumps like small marbles travelled in a line from my right hip to my left shoulder, every two inches, where a creature had walked up me and stopped to bite every few steps: the grandfather of all bed-bugs. I flung the sheets off and turned the mattress, and the pain of the bites stayed with me for days.

I called the agent the next morning and found the *Kwangsi* was due to dock in ten days. Time enough. The next four days and nights passed in a blur. I lived in the bars, I burned money, I ate junk, I drank myself to near extinction. I woke every morning in my bug-ridden dump, feeling weak. I had a stash of codeines liberated from the *Poyang* dispensary. I wolfed them for breakfast. On the third day, I told the grinning lady I would be away for three days and she should keep my room for me. I tipped the guard another 500 pesos and he assured me he would be extra vigilant, then I went down to the waterfront, changed some more money and caught a bus to Angel City.

Angel City was a place that had evolved out of the weakness and lust of men. The city was situated fifty miles north-west of Manila, a two-hour bus journey along the clogged

MacArthur Highway. Angel City only existed because two miles to the north was Clark Air Base, the US command centre where B52 bombers had flown west to bomb Vietnam in the 1960s and early 1970s. Clark remained the largest US military base outside of mainland USA and was the hub of America's projected power in the Far East. Over 30,000 US Army, Air Force and associated military personnel were stationed there, overwhelmingly young men. Clark Air Base was a city in itself, with its own shops, sports teams, entertainment complexes, schools, hospitals, churches. Nearby Angel City was a sub-city that served the baser needs of the men.

Angel City made Ermita look tame. It was a cess of prostitution, exhibitionism and violence. Every taste could be catered for. Teenage girls were brought in from the provinces in their thousands to pursue new careers. Most of them started in bars as hostesses, hustling for drinks, carrying out some light whoring on the side as required. Many became dancers in bars, crashing round the raised stages in high heels to a cacophony of loud music and whoops from the clientele. They dressed in bikinis, sometimes only wearing bikini briefs; in several of the low-end bars they wore nothing at all. The blue movie industry was booming, and fledgling starlets queued. Girls with the right sort of talent went on and starred in live sex shows with men, with several men, with women, with men and women, with animals. Sadism, masochism, bestiality, every perversion and degradation known to man was on offer. Brothels and hotbed hotels were on every street alongside raucous gambling joints where men littered a year's wages on the turn of a card and the spin of the wheel. There were dog fights to bet on too, and cock fights and street fights where young Filipinos tried to kill each other with martial arts savagery. Drug dens were rife, where people could lose themselves in the cloud-lands of opium and heroin. Marijuana was as easy to buy as a packet of cigarettes. Angel City was a godless sprawl, abandoned children ran down polluted streets begging from servicemen, disease was virulent. Poverty of possession was matched by the poverty of the heart of those who ventured there.

For the right money, and not much of it, you could get anything you wanted in Angel City. Alcohol was the high octane fuel that propelled the place, thousands and thousands of gallons were dispensed twenty-four hours a day. The alcohol flushed out decency and imbued everyone with a harsh, false joy that inhibited pity and suppressed morals. Violence was constant, endemic, almost procedural, the oaths and thuds and crashes of glass were a background noise. Men lay outside bars, inert, or sometimes sat propped up against a wall bleeding and groaning. Military policemen sped through the streets in jeeps and patrolled the bars in packs of four, all with billy-clubs hanging on thongs from their wrists.

Places like Angel City appear over the centuries, wherever young men are gathered in large numbers without women. One of the best known was the Barbary Coast of San Francisco, which took shape in the 1840s during the California gold rush and continued until the 'Frisco earthquake of 1906 flattened the place. The Barbary Coast boomed in an age of growing literacy, and the activities of the dens of iniquity around Pacific Avenue were recorded in intimate detail. The place was peopled by press gangs, thieves and murderers, the populace and visitors drank bad liquor that could blind them, took opium that killed them. Prostitution was the biggest attraction and there was the vilest sexual exploitation imaginable.

Diseases ravaged those who strayed there and stayed there. Violence was consuming, death was commonplace.

Two hundred and fifty years before the Barbary Coast, a Caribbean island by the name of Tortuga, near Hispaniola, was a den of vice to make San Francisco look positively benign. This was a buccaneer island where the inhabitants sailed out to plunder passing shipping and slaughter the crews, and then sail on to attack and sack any lightly defended ports in their path. The nominal governor of the island, a Frenchman, imported 1,500 prostitutes to try and quieten the place down, but this was to no avail. Violence amongst rum-sodden cutthroats wasn't confined to the taverns, there were full-scale battles in the streets with cutlasses and pistols. Slavery, torture, brutality of every kind was the way of life, death was so commonplace it was expected. Dice and vice and desperate dissolute perversions were the order of the day, along with the disease and illness that went with it all.

Then to top that, go back 4,000 years before Tortuga, to Sodom and Gomorrah These twin cities were irredeemably evil and perverse, to the extent that God himself reputedly became so disgusted with the pursuits of the inhabitants that he had both places consumed by fire and brimstone.

Angel City wasn't Sodom or Tortuga or the Barbary Coast, but it was a brutal and unforgiving place all the same. I went there because I wanted to see it, telling myself that every young man would go there if he had the opportunity. I disembarked from the bus with an airline bag of clothes slung across my shoulder, a small amount of money in my pocket, the main stash in my underpants with some large bills for emergency in my socks. I found a marginally better hotel than the flop I was staying at in Ermita. I booked in and hit the town. Every aspect was Ermita magnified: more vice, more drunkenness, more human degradation, more menace, more violence. I trod carefully over the first couple of days. The American servicemen were sensitive to any perceived slight. The shadow of Vietnam hung darkly over the city, they were hyper-violent, using bottles and glasses without hesitation. My boozy days in dark bars on neon streets merged into the evenings and into the nights, the noise continued, the ambiance unchanged, the shows went on the same. On the second morning I woke with blood in my mouth and cuts on my hands and large bruises on my leg, my shirt was ripped. On the third morning I woke up on a bench in the Hallelujah Bar, my head pounding like a jack-hammer, my pockets empty, my new Seiko watch gone but my hidden stashes safe. Every morning I rebalanced my stash and set off for more. In my tour of the city, I met all manner of men, some of them were good company for an hour or an evening, some were so disturbed they should have been caged. I saw sights no one should witness.

On the fourth morning I got up late, crawled into the shower and sat there for ten minutes, then dressed in my soiled, stained, torn clothes and went out into the bright sunlight. I bought a complete new set of clothes in a nearby shop: shirt, slacks, underclothes, socks. I went back to the hotel and threw my rags away, then showered again and scrubbed myself and shaved and scoured my teeth. I bought a ham and egg breakfast, drunk four cups of black coffee and caught the bus back to Manila. Enough was enough.

When the bus arrived in Manila, I walked to the Sampaloc district and wandered the bookshops near the universities where I bought an eclectic stack to read: Edgar Allen Poe,

Sven Hassel, Somerset Maugham, Ed McBain and Robert Louis Stevenson. I retreated to my hotel room and cleared out the insects, then alternately lay on my bed and sat on the balcony in a cane chair with my feet on the rail, to read for three days until the *Kwangsi* arrived.

Things didn't work out quite as I'd planned. I finished my bout of autodidactism in two days, sitting up and reading through most of the night, slumping into occasional bites of fitful sleep from time to time, waking with a jolt as the book fell on the floor. I would then chase the cockroaches to their side of the bed and start reading again. I ploughed through the heavy books, sandwiching them with the lighter ones. Poe was followed by Sven Hassel, then Maugham and McBain and Stevenson. The pacey text of Hassel and McBain was a breather from the clunkier prose of the others. I kept out of the bars and ate properly, and was feeling good by the time I arose on the morning I was expecting to join the *Kwangsi*. Then the agent came to see me to advise that the ship had been delayed in Hong Kong and I would have to wait in Manila for another two days. I felt punished, I brooded. I was ready to be back at sea and didn't want to be stuck in Ermita for another hour, let alone a further two days. I needed the sea, I needed the clean air and the shipboard routine. Self-pity took a firm grip and I spent the rest of the day in one of the darker quieter places on the M. H. del Pilar strip, sitting on a stool at the bar, drinking San Miguel in iced glasses, gazing at myself in the mirror, warding off the cooing attention of the girls, ignoring the conversational overtures of men who passed through, listening to the tinny music, smoking one cigarette after the other, reflecting on myself and my values.

An alarm bell rang, faintly, in a distant corner of my mind and I worried that I might be falling into a dark place. I was enjoying my odyssey, but in my heart I knew that times were changing, had changed, and I was like the last soldier at the rear of the rearguard as the army retreated. The sun was setting on a way of life that I wanted to be there forever. I wanted to wander the world, making my journey in the trade of the sea, working as a ship's mate on a break bulk cargo ship that picked up interesting goods in interesting parts of the world and taking time to do so.

> *Apes and ivory, skulls and roses, in junks of old Hong-Kong*
> *Gliding over a sea of dreams to a haunted shore of song,*
> *Masts of gold and sails of satin, shimmering out of the East,*
> *O, Love has little need of you now to make his heart a feast.*

said Alfred Noyes. But there were no apes or ivory in the cargoes I carried, no saffron, roses of Sharon, cinnamon, calamus or myrrh. Just cheap plastic goods, engine parts, drums of oil and cases of memories, but it was the same in a way, it was just the end of the journey. I was a Luddite, an enemy of any advancement. I wanted the clock to stop, to go backwards even. I would squeeze another two, perhaps three, years out of the life, and then it would be finished, trickled away forever and only to be glimpsed in memories such as mine.

*Robed, crowned and throned, He wove His spell,*
*Where heart-blood beat or hearth-smoke curled,*
*With unconsidered miracle,*
*Hedged in a backward-gazing world;*
*Then taught His chosen bard to say:*
*'Our King was with us – yesterday!'*

said Rudyard Kipling. It was always so much better yesterday. Sometimes I felt I could have just sat in a rattan chair under an idle ceiling fan on the veranda of an Eastern bar and spent the days reading Noyes and Kipling and Stevenson and Maugham, who expressed the passing infinitely better than I could ever hope to do.

My life would take its own form and I would deal with the disappearance of the last tail of romance when the time arrived, but it made me sigh. What was starting to depress me even more, though, was my personal situation, my singular lack of development over the past ten years. The 1970s were coming to a close and I was twenty-six years old, but I sometimes felt that I hadn't taken a step forward since I'd been sixteen. My only personal advancement was dishonourable: I had shed the shyness that used to hobble me socially and replaced it with an oily smoothness that gave me reasonable success with the opposite sex, as long as I polished myself up first with a bit of inebriation. I had yet to find a serious girlfriend. I was quick to take advantage of a situation on offer, and just as quick to abandon it and move on. I was just the sort of person that parents warned their daughters to steer clear of. I had my deeper thoughts, of course, although I didn't choose to share them with anybody. Whenever someone started to probe below the surface, I moved on and left them behind me. With that as a backdrop, I had exactly what I deserved: absolutely nothing.

I probed deeper, my manners and morals were starting to repulse me. I organised my life to drink and to raucously enjoy myself, my ends were wholly self-serving. At times it seemed to me that I even regarded the ships I sailed on as convenient free transport between one set of selfish pursuits and the next, between one exotic and interesting part of the world and another. While many of my contemporaries were now settled, married, with children, prospects, money, a house, objectives and goals in life, I had nothing beyond a few hundred poundsworth of Hong Kong dollars in the Hong Kong and Shanghai Bank, my sextant and binoculars, a uniform and a motley collection of civilian clothes. After my visit to Angel City, I didn't even have a watch any more.

The more I reflected, the gloomier I became. The higher I ascended in my world, in status and rank and experience, the more immoral I became. I seemed to be in a spiral of degradation. I had no thoughts of the future, my behaviour was worse than that of a dog, but I didn't care because I was only interested in satisfying my own vacuous appetites. I could hear the whisper of a slow rising tide, it seemed as if I were sliding on slush, or on sliding ground, I was slipping , slithering towards a dark and rotten part of the world where I didn't belong and where I didn't deserve to be. I was first in and last out in any bar, any club, any night out, any party. I found good company in any drunk who spoke to me in any language. I was a hit with rough girls who were on the slide themselves. I was foolhardy to the point of idiocy when it came to visiting dangerous places. I did stupid things. I couldn't remember ever being frightened of anything, I was always more concerned with what people might think of me if I didn't carry out whatever foolish venture I embarked upon. Violence hovered near me. I drank recklessly, I smoked weed and took pills when they came my way. I abused my health. I never said no or stop or wait or let's not. I felt chained to a flight of moving stairs that was taking me relentlessly downward no matter how hard I tried to climb. I desperately needed someone to bring out the best in me, I knew the best was still to come, but the confines of my personality made this difficult to achieve, made it too difficult for me to engage with those who could lift me up.

It wasn't only my own shortcomings, of course, it was also my habits. My free time was spent in low bars and dives where I was hardly likely to find the gentler soul I needed. I sat in the bar in Ermita and grappled with this problem, finding no solution, feeling low, feeling low, in my low dive. My attempts at casuistry were so poorly constructed and self-serving they were laughable. I looked at my reflection in the mirror behind the bar and was disgusted, it seemed to be leering back at me. The bags under my eyes looked big enough to carry my meagre life's possessions. I ordered another cold beer and lit another cigarette, then sat with the ghost of my past dreams while the afternoon died around us, and together we surveyed the wreckage of all my hopes. I wanted to climb the walls of Camarillo.

# 10

# Hark the New Dawn

The *Kwangsi* eventually arrived. I watched her berth at Pier 15, sliding in through the polluted dock water in the early morning sun, one tug in attendance, as I sat on my Globetrotter suitcase feeling grim, waiting for Free Pratique to be granted so I would be allowed to go aboard. I sat and watched and waited for the Q flag to be pulled down. Manila docks were filthy, blackened, greasy, the air was gritty and unhealthy to breathe. The ancient cargo sheds looked as if they were falling down. There was a cocktail stink of oldness, of mould, of rot, of animal products, of engine exhaust and of things baked bad in the hot sun. My Globetrotter was the only thing I dared sit on.

I had worked myself into a state of melancholy, thinking that I was failing in all areas that were worthwhile. My two-week blast of leave, far from blowing away the cobwebs, had left me feeling low and listless, feeling bad about myself, feeling myself to be a sorry specimen. I had done nothing more than load another brick into the hod. I was however, incubating a hope that my antics in the Philippines represented a low point in my behaviour and from now on I would see an improvement and would find myself gravitating towards something better. I wasn't sure whether to believe this, although I clutched at the thought nonetheless, like a drowning man gripping hold of a twig.

And it was a twig worth gripping. It transpired that the *Kwangsi* proved to be the finest ship I ever sailed on. When I joined her she was a few years past her prime, although she was still a pleasure to work and the people on board were such a good crowd, they lifted me up. The ambiance of the ship and her trade route were the tonic I needed.

Aesthetically, the *Kwangsi* was a beautiful-looking vessel: she had sleek lines and tall accommodation, with a high rounded funnel that gave her a noble stance, slightly haughty. She was built for Alfred Holt & Co, owners of the Blue Funnel line. The Liverpool-based Blue Funnel still enjoyed the reputation of having the best-run ships in the British Merchant

Navy, and the standards imposed on the officers and crews were second to none. Built at the Vickers Armstrong yard in Newcastle in 1967 for Glen Line, another Alfred Holt company, she had been christened the *Radnorshire*. The *Radnorshire* was a Priam class general cargo ship, 12,000 gross tons, designed to crack along at 21 knots. Eight Priam class ships were built in the mid-1960s and were known as Super Ps; they were the most advanced of their day. A few years later the *Radnorshire* was given the distinctive blue and black funnel when the Glen Line name disappeared, and was renamed *Perseus*, before being sold on to the taipan company to become the *Kwangsi*. These ships only enjoyed a few short years at the top before they found their careers curtailed by the arrival of container ships, which pushed them off the prime routes.

The British merchant fleet had been declining for decades. At the end of the Victorian period, ships flying the Red Ensign had accounted for four out of ten vessels on the high seas, but by the end of the 1970s it was down to four out of a hundred. Until the 1950s, it was still the dominant world fleet, although countries gaining independence from the British Empire established their own register of ships, which caused a progressive drifting away. The twin killer blows to British maritime dominance were the post-war rise of Japan and the explosion of 'flags of convenience' in the 1950s. The flag of convenience states were countries, principally Liberia and Panama although with many more following in their wake, that tolerated lower standards, fewer safety requirements, less bureaucracy, lower taxes, no union interference. They represented a haven, a heaven, for ship owners and operators. The American fleet was over-regulated and heavily unionised, and fell apart very quickly as the owners fled to the new flags. The other established shipping countries, Britain, Norway, the Netherlands, suffered a slow but steady attrition. The quadrupling of the oil price in 1973 put further cost pressures on ship operators and caused them to seek savings wherever they could, and many more British companies changed to a foreign flag of convenience. The phenomenal rise of the Japanese phoenix after the Second World War sent the economic pendulum swinging to the east, and the Japanese shipping register took the Number 1 spot, with Liberia as Number 2.

These were problems faced by all the traditional maritime countries, not just Britain. In fact, the British fleet appeared strong right up to the late 1970s, even though it was a ticking bomb.

Containerisation of shipping accelerated, and general cargo fleets started to fall apart. A large container ship, where all the cargo was pre-loaded, could do the work of several conventional general ships in a fraction of the time. The big ports and the major shipping routes became containerised first, and then the practice spread around the world like a virus, changing the face of docklands forever, wiping whole fleets off the face of the earth. Greater competition from more countries, national protectionism of trade routes and increasing operating costs all added to the mix. Shipping companies that had been around for over 100 years, suffered, declined, died and disappeared.

These were changing times. Before the collapse of the UK fleet at the end of the 1970s there was a shortage of officers, and many ships were unable to find the full complement of certificates, with the consequence that people were taken on and ranked above their competency level. As the end of the decade approached, however, the situation reversed. Uncertificated officers disappeared, and over-qualified officers started signing on British ships, if they could find a ship at all. The officers followed the ships, followed the jobs, which meant signing on whatever foreign flag vessel they could find. Pay slumped, as did leave entitlement. Assisted study leave disappeared, safety standards fell, crew numbers reduced, conditions of service deteriorated. The life was no longer what it was. We all watched as our maritime heritage evaporated before our eyes.

The taipan company wasn't immune to the upheaval, but this was not the North Atlantic trade, nor any of the other prime routes. We were operating in areas that would take some time to change. The company was vibrant and well run, and there was no contraction. Life went on much the same for us, although it was dispiriting to see so many great shipping names disappear.

In amongst all of this change, human nature made us cling to traditions, hold on to what we had, however outdated it might seem. We ate our meals off white linen tablecloths, using silver service cutlery embossed with the company crest. Stewards in starched jackets served us our four courses for luncheon, five courses for dinner. We had bells in our cabins to summon a steward bearing a gin and tonic, our clothes were collected and laundered each day. If we wanted cigarettes, or cigars, or writing paper, or beer or other things, we would sign a chit and give it to the steward, and the things we ordered would appear. The dinner gong sounded before our meals, we wore our uniforms and maintained our discipline and carried out our working rituals unchanged. Every four hours the log book was written up in longhand, every two hours the officer of the watch was given a cup of tea, the lookout would call the lights as they appeared, the foc'sle bell would be rung as we heaved in the anchor. All these things were important, and we never took short cuts unless they were imposed upon us.

The Q flag was lowered and I climbed the *Kwangsi*'s gangway and made my way to the ship's office. The chief mate was there with the second, third and fourth mates. I introduced myself and we had the usual chitchat, then I went off with the second mate for a handover tour. The second mate looked mean-faced and surly, and I wondered what the problem was. Once we were outside the office and out of earshot of the others, he told me, in a controlled eruption, how much he resented me coming on board to take over his role because he had wanted to stay for another round trip to New Zealand and back. He had already been on board for a year. I ignored his charmless manner, told him I was here and that was that, and suggested he concentrate on the handover, which he did, grudgingly, gracelessly and in an incomplete way.

The next port was Singapore although he had only laid off the courses on the charts as far as the head of the Palawan Passage, still in the Philippine Islands, leaving the rest of the work for me to complete. I knew the route to Singapore anyway, but it was bad practice not to prepare all the charts. He told me he had been too busy and asked me if I wouldn't mind dealing with the rest of the work. I didn't give him the absolution he was seeking, I just grunted. Once he had finished explaining the bridge to me, I told him not to bother with the deck handover. I said I would walk around and learn the gear with the third and fourth mates. He then tried to overcompensate, becoming over-eager to show me things to assuage his guilt, but I told him I was happy and accepted the handover.

The *Kwangsi* stayed in Manila a week. The third mate, Mick, had been aboard for three months and knew the ship well. We walked round the decks and he explained the running gear, the cargo spaces, the fore and aft working stations and all the ship's idiosyncrasies. Everything seemed in good order. As I was walking along the deck a few days after signing on, I saw the previous second mate climbing up the gangway, looking furtive. I'd thought he would have been back in England by now. I asked the chief mate what was going on.

'He's begging the Old Man to sign him on again; that's the third time he's been back since he left,' said the mate. 'He should have flown home a couple of days ago, but he keeps delaying his flight.'

I was mystified. 'Why?'

'No idea. He just keeps coming back and asking to sign on again; he doesn't want to go home. He wasn't a very good second mate, anyway; he was lazy, and irritated most people. The Old Man keeps telling him to clear off.'

'Is there something going on that I don't know about, choff?' I asked.

'No, nothing. He just doesn't want to go home. He wants to stay on for another trip, and was hoping the Old Man would prefer him to you, but the Old Man doesn't like him and I don't like him, so he was never going to be asked back. The Old Man is going to be narked when the old second mate knocks on his door again. He'll be told to bugger off.'

I let it lie. Some people find change difficult to take, and after a long time aboard a ship some find it hard to leave, particularly if home is uninviting. The previous second mate was clearly finding it hard to let go. If I had liked the man I might have had some sympathy, but I didn't, so I hung around the gangway looking artificially happy, and waited until he scuttled off after his roasting from the Old Man. He left with his eyes downcast as he walked past, avoiding looking at me.

I had a difficult watch coming out of Manila Bay, my first sea watch on the *Kwangsi*. We left our berth at nine o'clock in the evening and by the time we dropped the pilot and crossed Manila Bay, it was midnight. The Old Man stayed on the bridge until we passed Corregidor Island and set out into the South China Sea, then wrote up some brief night orders and went below.

There were several ships in the vicinity as we left the bay, both inbound and outbound. I set the course for the three-hour transit to Lubang Island, after which we would turn further towards the south, heading for the Palawan Passage between the Spratly Islands and Palawan, down towards the coast of Sarawak and on to Singapore. None of the ships in sight were giving me cause for concern; we were overtaking one and would be leaving her down our port side before the end of the watch, but there was plenty of sea room. The sea was quiet, the night was clear, visibility was good. I plotted the position every thirty minutes, kept the radar on the twenty-four-mile range and leant on the dodger to look out into the night.

At two o'clock, pin-pricks of light started to appear ahead, right across the bow from two points either side.

The lookout wandered over to me: 'Plenty lights ahead, Second Mate.'

'Aye, thanks,' I answered.

Plenty lights indeed, and more appearing all the time. It was a big fleet, getting bigger as we approached. The fishing fleets off the Philippines were as big as they get, numbering in the hundreds. Each boat was a small open canoe with an outboard motor and a single occupant casting his net by hand, at night lit by bright naphtha lamps. Nothing showed on the radar, they were too low and too small and made of the wrong material to reflect a proper radar echo. In a calm sea with the radar range turned down to one mile, they just started to appear on the screen, although that was no use because at that range a radar reflection was of academic interest only.

I couldn't go round the fleet, it was too big, it was wrapping itself around me. I would have had to alter course more than 90 degrees, and that would have caused other problems. All I could do was pick my way through. I resorted to the time-tested tradition of heading for the biggest gaps, which was essentially the only way to get through a fleet of small fishing canoes unless there was sufficient sea room to go round the whole thing. The trouble with heading for the black gaps in a sea of lights is that more often than not there were only gaps because some canoes were saving their naphtha, not because there was an open expanse of clear water. As soon as they felt threatened by a big ship they would light the lamps, a series of bright sparkles would erupt to fill the darkness as we came closer. I put a man on the wheel. The more we moved into the fleet, the more tightly packed the boats became. If one was dead ahead I would have to wait until it started to dip below the sight line of the fo'c'sle head and then move 5 degrees one way to let it slide close down the ship's side. I tried to give them fifty yards or more of clearance, but sometimes it was impossible and the wash of our ship would buck the canoe and bounce water into it. If the fisherman was a cool customer, he would pull the rope on his outboard and motor away a bit further at the last minute. If he was cooler still, he would flick on the engine and just swing the bow round to the wash and ride the foam until it passed. If he was uncool, he would howl and scream and shake his fist up at us as our wake washed over the gunwales. I would lean over the bridge wing and wave to him in the gloom, to his fury.

I felt relieved when we finally approached the western edge of the fleet after thirty minutes of concentrated dodging, and was waving at a couple of howlers when the chief engineer come swarming up the bridge-wing ladder. He shouted at me, accusing me of mowing down innocent men. He had been drinking. I asked him to leave. He became abusive. I told him to leave in more certain language. He left. The Old Man arrived a few minutes later.

He said: 'Problems, Second Mate?'

'No problems, sir. A lot of fishing boats, but we're through them now.'

He walked back inside the wheelhouse to get his binoculars. We stood together and watched the last of the boats pass down either side of us.

'The chief said you were knocking them aside.'

'The chief's had too much to drink, Captain. I was passing close to a lot of them but we didn't hit any.'

'He said you swamped a couple and they sunk.'

'That's nonsense, sir. A couple of them were so close the wash went over the gunwales, but they didn't sink. You know those canoes wouldn't sink if they were half full with water anyway. The light went out in one of them, but I could still see it in the dark, it was fine.'

I was angry at the chief; there was no need for this. I could see his head looking over the top of the ladder, halfway up from the boat deck, eavesdropping. I walked towards him; he scuttled down the ladder.

I shouted: 'Will you please come up to the bridge, Chief!'

He disappeared aft. I stamped back over to the Old Man.

'I did not run down any fishing boats, Captain!'

He said. 'Calm down. I can see everything's fine.'

I snorted.

'Come down after your watch and have a drink with me and the chief.'

I thought: 'I certainly will.'

I banged on the captain's door at five past four, still seething. He was sitting in his dayroom on his own, a smile on his face.

'The chief's just left; have a beer, man.'

The people on board the *Kwangsi* raised me up. They were universally a good crowd. We existed in a bubble, living our lives immune from the rest of the world. There was Mick, the third mate, who became a good friend. Mick was from Birmingham, a big character, tough, bluff, bearded, teeth chipped and nose broken from rugby, a no-nonsense man. Mick never became angry or dispirited or disappointed, he never panicked, he never became concerned. He was good company, sharp and funny. He would often push the envelope of behaviour when we were out on the town. Mick was a good man to have on your side.

Frank the electrical officer, was further along the rowdiness scale, a scouser, manic, a fighter, a prodigious drinker, a *quidnunc*, an impatient man, borderline dangerous, he mocked people he didn't like. Frank was six foot four inches tall, lanky, girl-crazy, crazy for a wild time every time he went out. Frank acted outrageously as a matter of course, he had a brilliant mind. A night out with Frank was always going to be edgy.

Loma was different from anyone else I had ever met. He was from the Solomon Islands, although had been brought up in Fiji and was a naturalized Fijian. He was roguish, a habitual teller of tales so inflated they collapsed under their own weight. Loma was short, built like a bull, as mighty as a circus strongman. His weakness was drink, he had the islanders' curse. When he started he couldn't stop, he would become truly incomprehensible and would throw every caution to the wind. I had to send him off the bridge and back to his cabin on a couple of occasions because he was simply too inebriated to take over the watch. Loma was a hero in the islands.

The Old Man was an old man, closing sixty years of age. He was almost as bull-like as Loma. He wrestled with demons. Like Loma, he was cursed by his drinking appetite. For twenty-seven days out of thirty he was the very picture of a captain at sea, the very model of all that was right and good – clear-eyed, commanding, decisive, utterly in control. Then for three days he was a wreck of a man, hunched, glowering, accusatory, argumentative, reeking of gin, a dangerous glint in the depths of his eye. He was a good man for most of the time, but a truly frightening one when in his bad state.

There were two juniors, Chris and Mike. Chris was a cadet nearing the end of his time, regarded as a sort of junior fourth officer below Loma, ready to take over on one of Loma's occasional falls from grace. Chris was from a good family with a better background than most at sea; there was a hint of a black sheep about him, though, but he never elaborated. Mike was the other junior, a man in the final stages of service as a Royal Navy midshipman, and was on secondment to a merchant ship to gain experience. Mike was eccentric, he used long-winded phrases that no one understood, he sang at the top of his voice, he sometimes played the accordion on deck at night, he affected to be baffled at the loutishness of the Merchant Navy, and referred to us as 'targets'.

The chief officer was a pixie of a man, five foot three inches tall, married to a Spanish woman who couldn't speak English, nor could he speak Spanish. He read letters from home and wrote back with the help of a Collins dictionary. He had huge ears and was very correct in his speech and mannerisms, very prim, very easily shocked. He should have been a vicar. He was unforgiving, and insistent on the cargo work being carried out with an outdated sense of order and tradition and record-keeping that would have been unwarranted thirty years ago. Mick hated him, Frank mocked him, Mike worshipped him, Chris hid from him, the old man bullied him, I liked him. I liked his old-fashioned sense of honour and his refusal to bow to the modern world.

The second engineer was a benevolent tyrant who bullied the junior engineers mercilessly, laughing as he dished out punishment to some unfortunate soul. He was fabulous company. Even those he bullied liked him. A magnetic personality, a Welshman, a handsome man, a man who worked so hard it hurt to watch. He was one of those men who always made you feel good about yourself.

And the chief engineer. There always has to be one. I didn't like the chief, nor he me. A sly man, over-conscious of his position, a man always on the lookout for any perceived slight, mindful of any affront to his dignity. An Englishman who had relocated to Australia, overweight, an occasional liar, a tedious conversationalist. Others seemed to get on well with him, but I found it difficult to stay in the same circle. Once, only once, when we were the last two standing after a party in Auckland, the others all gone or collapsed, we fell to talking and the tension between us dissipated. He told me that he regretted not leaving the sea when he had been a younger man because he had missed his children growing up. I found his choice of language strange, it was almost as if he regarded the growing-up process of children as being for the entertainment of the parents, rather than their responsibility. I knew little of course, having neither children nor a partner to plan them with, so I nodded and murmured in sympathetic agreement. I confessed my own inadequacies, my motor of self-gratification and my consequent poor track record in attracting and sustaining any worthwhile relationship. He nodded and said: 'You don't need to worry, it will come.' I felt grateful for his words and willed them to be prophetic. The next day I tried to recapture the mood but it was gone. We despised each other again.

The other officers were all Chinese from Hong Kong, a good crowd who joined in but kept their distance more. Quite often, the Chinese officers mixed with the Chinese crew within a confusing structure of social deference that cut through ranks and which could make a junior deckhand more revered than a senior officer. The set of deferential rules that governed social values, family values, reputational values, age, clan, connections and background were unintelligible to Westerners, often positioning someone's status in a very different way. All in all, though, we had a good mix of officers, a lively bunch to be at sea with.

The crew members were all Hong Kong Chinese, as were all the crews of all the company's ships. A great many were long-serving company men, unswervingly loyal, wedded to traditions. They were not young, most being in their fifties, a scattering in their forties. Once signed on, they regarded the ship as being 'theirs', and expected to remain aboard for years. On arriving in Hong Kong they would go ashore after work to be with their family, and sometimes the family would come and live on the ship during its stay in port. This gave us the benefit of a crew who knew exactly what they were doing, even though this could sometimes be irksome in that they always felt they knew (and sometimes they did) more than the officers who were actually running the vessel.

The trade of the *Kwangsi* was between the big three Far East ports, Hong Kong, Manila and Singapore, together with a scattering of smaller places in the Philippines, then down to New Zealand and Fiji, with the occasional call at other South Pacific islands. In New Zealand we loaded milk powder, together with hides, frozen meat, animal products, wool, dairy goods, wine, forestry products, machinery and some hi-tech equipment. In the Far East we mostly took on board manufactured goods and transhipments, together with cars and machinery. Less came out of Fiji: sugar beet and sugar cane, fish and fish products and sundries.

In the East, I enjoyed the smaller ports in the Philippines, which were mostly in Mindanao, the second largest Philippine island after Luzon. Our regular calls there were at Bislig, Iligan and Cagayan. The docks in these places were slow in pace. Close to the waterfront there was a street of bars flanked by a couple of streets of shops, the buildings were all open-fronted and single-storey, which gave a temporary, street-market feel. The roads were grubby and noisy and crowded, the people shrieked a lot in Tagalog. In Mindanao, Muslim separatists had been killing officials and giving grief to the government for decades, with a brief respite during the Second World War, when they did their bit for the war effort by killing Japanese. We were only supposed to go ashore with an armed guard, although mostly we didn't bother. We didn't come across much trouble, although occasionally heard distant gunfire at night and saw tracer in the skies. There had been more intense separatist trouble in Zambuanga, on the nearby island of Negros, where the government was struggling to keep control. We were often scheduled to call into Zambuanga but always ended up with a change of orders at the last minute and passed it by. In these small ports, we mostly discharged crates of milk powder. The towns didn't have the bright lights of Manila or Singapore or Hong Kong, although they made up for that with an abundance of enthusiasm and they were always welcoming to us.

*The MV* Kwangsi.
*Oil painting by Robert Lloyd.*

Fiji was a new experience for me. It wasn't on the *Poyang*'s route. We called in at Suva, the capital, then Lautoka, the only other place of significance. Fiji had one of the most devolved economies in the South Pacific, although it was also a troubled place. The root of the problem was that the indigenous population, a mix of Melanesians and Polynesians, were becoming outnumbered by incoming peoples, mainly Indians, who at that time made up half the total population. When the Chinese, Europeans and sundry others were added to the mix, the indigenous peoples found themselves becoming a smaller and smaller percentage. This resulted in a lot of ill-feeling, mostly directed against the Indians. The atmosphere was strained at best, poisonous at worst.

As an environment, Fiji was a treat, with its gorgeous beaches falling into the bluest seas. When I was ashore with Mick and Frank, we would spend the afternoon on the veranda of the Grand Pacific Hotel on the Suva waterfront, drinking exotic cocktails and watching the blue sea and the blue sky until the sun went down. The Grand Pacific Hotel had been around since the Great War and had changed little since. In Lautoka there was less to see and do, but it was still a place to relax in the sun. Loma was sometimes with us, when he wasn't off visiting various relations. His legendary status had been brought about by him being the first Fijian deck officer of a British ship, together with some heroics in his youth that he wouldn't speak about. It was something to do with rescuing a child from the jaws of a shark or a killer whale, or something similar. The locals stood around open-mouthed when Loma was in town, and we rarely had to pay for a drink. This status of his, which was accepted as far as the

Gilbert and Ellice Islands just north of the equator, was one of the main reasons Loma was given so much latitude in his many falls from grace. Some said that his dismissal would have had economic consequences for our South Pacific trade.

New Zealand was altogether a different pace. After arrival, we would be on the New Zealand coast for four or five weeks, calling at half a dozen ports. Our staple cargo was crates of milk powder from Mount Maunganui, in the Bay of Plenty on the east coast of the North Island. We would spend a week in the Mount; the loading work was unchallenging, nine to five only, so we had plenty of time to explore. I hired a car on a couple of occasions and went to the hot springs at Rotorua and saw other local sights. The people were friendly, and we built up a good rapport with many. I fell in with a group of young New Zealanders that I then saw regularly in our visits to the Mount. There were a couple of girls in the group, which was a good thing and kept us out the pubs. I found myself being introduced to gentler activities, rather than my usual frantic boozing and making a spectacle of myself. In my time off, we walked, talked, visited the local sights, ate lunch. I started to learn more civilized pursuits. I even began to believe that maturity could finally be arriving, even though I was aware that these were early days and I still had plenty of time to let myself down.

After calling at the Mount, our next port was usually Auckland, the biggest city in New Zealand, sitting a bit further down the coast. This was our biggest discharge port and we were generally there a week, sometimes more. I liked Auckland, having been there before on the *Benstac*, because the wharfs came right up into the town and we could walk down the gangway and be in the city centre in a few minutes.

We had a bad incident during one visit to Auckland. Frank was arrested following a heated argument with the dock watchman who was preventing him from bringing his newly acquired girlfriend back to the ship because she didn't have a pass. The argument ended with Frank punching the watchman, the girlfriend left, we went back to the ship. A police car pulled up as we were climbing the gangway and Frank was hauled away. They wouldn't let me come for the ride, so I walked down to the police station to show moral support. I could see Frank's face looking through the barred window of a cell.

He called plaintively: 'Simon, they've been beating me.'

I asked to see him. The policeman on duty told me to sod off. I went back to the *Kwangsi* and reported it to the mate, who woke the old man, who called the agent, who went down to the station. Frank was released. He was chastened. He had several long bruises on his arms and back where he had been whacked with a truncheon. He told a story of a policeman coming into a cell to quieten him down and teach him a lesson. We clicked our tongues and sucked air through our teeth with sympathy, although we told Frank it was his own fault for punching the watchman in the first place and then making a ruckus with the police when he was taken away.

The matter escalated. Police visited the ship, Frank gave a statement, I gave a statement, an internal affairs officer told us he was looking for a reason to get rid of bad apples from the force and was going to prosecute the man who had beaten Frank. Mick and I told Frank to feign forgetfulness and drop it, we told him he'd deserved to get beaten, we told him we would have beaten him if we had been in the policeman's position. Frank was having none of it; he went along with the prosecution. The matter drifted on over several months, and each time the *Kwangsi* called at Auckland the internal affairs police officer came aboard to give us an update. The case finally came to court, by which time we were all fed up with the whole event, even Frank. I was called into the witness box and quizzed by the prosecuting attorney, who constructed his questions in a manner designed to damn the accused policeman. After the prosecutor had taken his fill of me, I was grilled by the defence barrister, who did his utmost to paint me as a biased fool who couldn't be relied upon as a witness, as well as being drunk at the time. I did my best to appear otherwise. The procedure was complex, and the end result, as far as we could make out, was that the policeman was found guilty of using unnecessary force, rather than unlawful assault, and was disciplined. He didn't lose his job, though, which we were pleased about.

Virtually all the New Zealand ports are on the east coast, which is sheltered from the rolling Pacific swell and which has the natural harbours. New Plymouth and Greymouth are the only ports on the west coast, both of which are quite small. Wellington, the capital of New Zealand, was a place I never warmed to. It had an industrial, impersonal feel that was at odds with the rest of the places we visited. We usually stayed in Wellington for a week, loading hides and animal products. The hides had a nasty smell that pervaded the ship, and we were always glad to leave and get some wind blowing through to clear away the stench. All the other ports only had our company for a couple of days, perhaps three. We grew friends in most places we visited, and had parties, large and small, as we worked our way round the coast. Occasionally we came across another British ship, usually Bank Line or Port Line or P&O, and we would visit and have inter-ship competitions, football or cricket, table tennis, whatever the organiser chose to organise.

In the Mount once, during a two-day break from cargo work while we waited for more milk powder to arrive, we played a football match against a scratch team from Air New Zealand. It can't have been much fun for the handful of spectators. For ninety minutes we all charged around the pitch, artlessly, twenty men chasing the ball in a herd while the referee ran after us screaming and the two goalies watched. It was a rough contest with minimal skill on both sides; some of the play was more akin to rugby. Small groups regularly broke off from the main herd to brawl, and even the referee joined in the fighting. The game ended in a seven-all draw. Most of us were injured after the event. Our supporters wiped the blood from us and we played up in heroic pose.

In all the smaller ports – Timaru, Napier, Whangarei, Nelson, New Plymouth, Dunedin, Bluff – we had our friends who welcomed us back, we visited our regular pubs where we drank jugs of Leopard beer into the night and then the next day we loaded our cargoes of animal products. My favourite port of call was Lyttelton, the entry point for Christchurch. There wasn't much there but it always felt special for some reason. Perhaps it was the harbour, wide and clear and wrapped in green hills, perhaps it was the people, who had an old-world courtesy, perhaps it was the feeling that I was near the end of civilisation, with just a few small settlements along the coast before the vast southern oceans, then into the high latitudes, the roaring forties and the screaming sixties, then the end of the world.

✯ ✯ ✯

I felt I was at last truly in the life I wanted. I loved the ship, I loved the trade, I loved the part of the world we traversed. I loved my fellow travellers. I knew the life wouldn't last, nor should it, but while it did I wanted to squeeze out every drop. I knew I was heading inexorably towards the end of the era, but I had now gained a spirit of acceptance. I accepted that the world I wanted was passing by forever.

In some ways, we existed in a time warp on the *Kwangsi*, while the world went on around us. To an extent, we kept up with what was happening by the newspapers. We read the *South China Morning Post* in Hong Kong, *The Straits Times* in Singapore, *The New Zealand Herald*, *The Fiji Times*. We listened to the BBC World Service. Anyone who came out from Britain would bring a good cross-section of British newspapers, we would phone home from time to time, and we always had our letters from our loved ones. In the main though, we were in a zone apart.

Navigation wasn't challenging after we left the East. It was really only the Singapore Strait, the Hong Kong approaches and Manila Bay that were testing in terms of maritime traffic. Occasionally we would encounter fleets of fisherman, as I had done leaving Manila Bay that first time, but for the most part the sailing through the islands and across the Pacific was more pleasurable than gruelling.

If our last port in the East was Singapore, then we would traverse the Indonesian archipelago, through the Java Sea, the Flores Sea, the Banda Sea, then across the Arafura Sea and through the Torres Strait between New Guinea and Australia.

Sometimes, the voyage was arranged so that the last port was Manila, in which case we crossed south-east through the Philippine Islands, north of Mindanao and out through the Hinatuan Passage into the Pacific. This meant that we then had a long voyage down to Fiji in the open sea, during which we wouldn't sight much for days on end. This was where the old man tended to show his bad side, making himself look foolish. He would call me on the bridge shortly before the end of my afternoon watch, telling me to come to his cabin after I had handed over. His voice was officious, but I could almost smell the gin through the phone line. When I went into his cabin he would order me to sit down, give me a cold beer and then proceed to air whatever was on his mind, usually tales from the past, recounted in a maudlin and sometimes resentful manner. Often he already had company, someone usually in a shattered state. The chief engineer was often there, occasionally Mick the third mate, who would desperately slip out when I arrived, so he could sober himself up for the evening watch. Once, I couldn't rouse Loma, and in the end the chief mate came up to relieve me. Loma was in with the old man, his eyes bloodshot, his voice slurred. They made a pretty pair, hunched over and growling at each other. Sometimes, when I couldn't bear the thought of two hours in his cabin listening to ever more nonsense, I would slip off the bridge and find a place to lie up until the evening dinner gong sounded, ignoring the occasional emissary that was dispatched to find me.

My twelve-to-four watch-keeping hours suited me well, all alone in a circular sea with nothing from horizon to horizon. In the afternoon I watched the gentle dip of the bow as we cleaved through the seas, resting my arms on the wooden taffrail under the Pacific sun. On the midnight-to-four watch, I paced the bridge and out onto the bridge wings under the wide tropical night. I navigated the ship using charts that had been drawn up over 100 years before, corrected and updated from time to time perhaps, but essentially the same guidance that had been used by wooden sailing ships that traded around the islands before the first aeroplane flew, before the quagga was extinct, before the Charge of the Light Brigade, before the Sulzer Brothers patented their steamship engines.

My days at sea had a set routine that was driven by the watch I was on. The bridge routine was the thread that joined the different parts of my life together. Having got to bed at about five o'clock in the morning, I would rise at 0930. I checked the chart to see the speed we were making. If we were out of sight of land then I would look at the fix from the morning star sight; if land was in sight then I would study the half-hour positions that had been fixed by compass bearings and radar. I then wound the two chronometers, six-and-a-half turns exactly, and chatted with Mick over a mug of coffee. Sun sights were taken if there was no land. I would take my Tamaron sextant out of its box, walk out onto the bridge wing and bounce the sun off the horizon through the sextant's telescope, calling out to Mick so he could read the exact time off the Number 1 chronometer. I would be on the bridge for forty-five minutes in the morning, going below to read and relax for an hour before heading for my early lunch at 1130. Early lunch was just me, the third engineer and his fiver, idly chatting together as we ate our meal in the quiet of the saloon.

At midday, I would take over the watch. Mick would stay and talk for fifteen minutes or so and then leave me to work out the noon run, calculating the distance we had steamed over the last twenty-four hours, the day's speed and the average voyage speed achieved so far. I would then work out the distance to our destination, and calculate an ETA at three different speeds: 14 knots, 14.5 knots and 15 knots. I would put all this information on the noon chit, which I would give to the watch sailor to take to the old man, with a copy to the chief engineer.

In the afternoon I would plot the course every half hour if we were in sight of land, otherwise I would estimate our position by DR. We were a weather ship, which meant that every four hours we would record extensive meteorological information: cloud types, wind speed and direction, visibility, air pressure, sea swell and the sea temperature, which we did by lowering a bucket over the side and testing the water with a thermometer. These meteorological log books would be collected periodically by the met office in the larger ports. At the end of the watch I would write up the main log book with details of our course and position, together with any salient comments. After the end of each watch the officer of the watch walked the ship to check for any problems: cargo shift, fire, anything out of the ordinary. The final log book entry on each watch would read 'Rounds Correct'.

My world on the bridge and chartroom was ordered by the library of almanacs and tables and guides that every deep sea ship held. *Norie's Nautical Tables*, *The Nautical Almanac*, *Brown's Almanac*, *Reed's Almanac*, *Admiralty Light Lists* (six volumes), *Star Sight Reduction Tables*, *Admiralty Sailing Directions* (all seventy-two volumes) *Admiralty Radio Signals* (four volumes), tide tables, speed and distance tables, ex-meridian tables, *Ocean Passages of the World*, *Notices to Mariners*, *The Mariner's Handbook*. None of these books was a good read in itself, apart from *Brown's Almanac*, possibly, which contained a miscellany of useful information. In the chartroom, however, surrounded by all these guides that provided the knowledge and the means to travel the seas, there was a comfort, a … completeness, which was only felt by the navigators who knew the secret of how to read them all.

At the end of my afternoon watch I would read in my cabin or on the monkey island for an hour or so, before going to the bar to sit and talk with the others until the steward walked along the alleyway beating the sonorous dinner gong at 1830. We all trooped in to the dining saloon to eat. Dinner was five courses, although I rarely ate more than three: soup, entrée, main course. I usually didn't bother with dessert or cheese, just the coffee. Afterwards, we lingered for a while, replete, smoking, occasionally quaffing liqueurs. Then I would retire to my cabin to catch four hours' sleep before being roused at a quarter to midnight. If I was very tired, or had stayed up late, I would arrange myself so that I went to sleep lying on my arm, which always caused me to wake up three hours later with a numbed limb. It was my alarm clock.

The midnight-to-four watch would be my time for reflection, for thinking great thoughts and making great plans between fixing the position of the ship. I paced across the width of the bridge, back and forward, back and forward. Every dozen transits or so, I would extend the pacing to the bridge wings, scanning the horizon over 360 degrees. At 0400, Loma would arrive to take the watch, and we would talk after the handover, not for long, perhaps five or ten minutes. I would then do my rounds before meeting up with the third engineer and fiver in the bar for a few drinks. We usually called it a night at about five in the morning, although

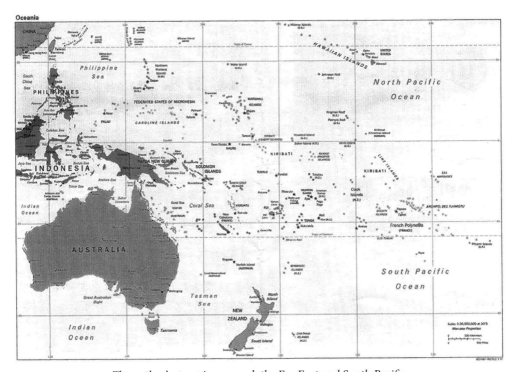

*The author's stamping ground: the Far East and South Pacific.*

189

sometimes we stayed up longer, if we felt in the mood. Then in the morning I rose again at 0930 and so it went on. There was great comfort in the routine.

Christmas found us in the middle of nowhere; it came and went in a cloud of too much food and too much drink. We had obtained a Christmas tree from New Zealand and hoisted it up to the mainmast truck, where it remained until a blow off Bougainville consigned it to the deep. We didn't exchange gifts or cards, because that wasn't the done thing, although we wished each other a Merry Christmas. There was a lot of exaggerated heartiness and bonhomie, and the bar opened earlier than usual. On New Year's Day, we were eighteen hours out of Fiji and the occasion passed with a similar flourish. The old man was happy to have a few blasts of the ship's horn at midnight to see in the new decade, although he baulked at setting off the out-of-date pyrotechnics for an impromptu firework display.

Chinese New Year was a big event, celebrated with a four-hour banquet, flushed down with Tiger beer and Chinese rice wine. The food kept coming, a dozen courses, mostly cooked in north Chinese style, which essentially meant that it was more stewed or baked than fried. The conversation was raucous, we smoked between courses while we drank our beer and rice wine. The Chinese petty officers were invited into the saloon to suffer a long-winded and embarrassing speech by the old man. They stood in a line with rictus grins, wishing they were elsewhere no doubt, while the old man rambled through a lot of sentimental guff that was only partly understandable to the British audience, let alone to the Chinese. There were then several *kung hei fat choy* toasts, which everyone joined in with enthusiasm, before they left us to our continuing gluttony.

As the second officer I was again the ship's medical officer. I ran a tight dispensary on the *Kwangsi*, cataloguing my medicines and carefully curing, or attempting to, whatever ills came my way. I always acted as if I knew much more than I did, which I felt was half the battle. I was forever waiting for my glory moment, an amputation or major operation of some kind, but it never came. On the *Kwangsi*, the only curative powers ever asked of me remained the patching of wounds caused by shipboard accidents, treating venereal disease and curing minor poisonings from overindulgence in alcohol and food. One day, though, I was given a lesson in rudimentary medicine by one of the stewards. I was in the bar when a bottle of beer exploded in my hand and a shard of glass sliced open the fleshy part of my finger. I raised my arm to shoulder level and walked down the alleyway to the dispensary to patch myself up. Blood was pouring out of the wound, my arm was red and I was leaving a crimson trail behind me. The cabin steward came round the corner, I made to move round him but he stepped in front of me. He opened his packet of cigarettes, took one out, tore off the paper and decanted the tobacco onto the wound. The bleeding stopped instantaneously. He advised me to leave the tobacco on for five minutes and then wash it clean. I did as he instructed: the wound was clean and clear, all bleeding ceased. I didn't go so far as keeping cigarettes in the dispensary, although it taught me a good lesson and made me realise that my practical knowledge was even sparser than I imagined.

There was an interesting incident with the radio officer one afternoon, which left me unable to speak for several minutes. The Sparks was a young and very serious Hong Kong Chinese, unwaveringly correct and precise in the way in which he spoke English. His diction and enunciation were perfect, with only the faintest trace of Chinese accent. It was as if he had carefully constructed each sentence before it came out of his mouth. Sometimes it could rebound on him, though, as things tend to do if you take them too seriously. Poor Sparks didn't have an ounce of humour in him. I don't think he knew how to laugh, so it was always crushing when he showed himself up.

He came up to me on the bridge after lunch and said: 'Simon, perhaps you might be able to tell me. How do you spell 'bee-con'?'

Thinking he was talking about radio beacons, I said: 'B-e-a-c-o-n.'

'No, no,' he said. 'Not that beacon, not a radio beacon. I mean the other sort of bee-con.'

'It's spelt the same. The spelling is the same whether you are talking about a radio beacon or any other sort of beacon. B-e-a-c-o-n.' I explained.

He looked impatient. 'You do not understand me. You do not understand what I am asking. I do not mean any sort of directional or guidance beacon, or any sort of signalling beacon, in fact. I mean the other type of bee-con, the different type entirely.'

'I don't know what other sort of beacon there is. What do you mean?' I asked.

'I mean as in bee-con and eggs for breakfast.'

I almost fell on the deck.

We had all become a bit concerned about the fall in value of the Hong Kong dollar against the pound, which was taking place at the time. Most of the officers had financial responsibilities and liabilities back home, and the cut in the value of their take-home pay was causing problems to some. I had no responsibilities or liabilities, and so it wasn't particularly damaging to me although, like anyone, I was disenchanted with the falling value of my earnings. After reading some wisdom in the *South China Morning Post* one day in Hong Kong, I thought I would take a punt on buying gold. I bought a dozen Krugerrands at US$231 at ounce from a gold merchant in Kowloon and opened a safe deposit box with the Hong Kong and Shanghai Bank with the intention of leaving them there until further received wisdom prompted me to cash them in. When that wisdom arrived later in the year, the price had risen to US$414 an ounce, an 80 per cent gain. I had made over US$2,000 in just a few months. I went ashore with Mick, Frank, the second engineer, Chris and Mike, all of whom were all keen to celebrate my good fortune. I picked up my Krugerrands from the safe deposit box and stuffed them in my pocket. We all headed to Nathan Road to sell them to one of the gold buyers there. On the way we passed the Australian Bar and decided to pop in for a quick beer.

'Your round, Simon,' the second engineer shouted. 'You can afford it.'

I could indeed. I said to the barmaid: 'Six beers,' then thrust my hand into my pocket and dumped a handle of notes and coins on the bar. The Krugerrands burst out of their plastic clip and scattered everywhere, a couple rolled off the bar and behind some crates of beer. I frantically gathered them together although could only find eleven. We searched every inch of the floor and behind the bar, we combed every corner, we took out all the crates from behind the bar, we stacked all the furniture at the far end. All the customers helped. I promised drinks on me for everyone as soon as the twelfth coin was found. Nothing. Eventually, we abandoned the search, thinking someone had managed to run off with the final Krugerrand. I was sitting there feeling glum, the beer sour in my throat, when Frank produced it from his pocket with a flourish, to the huge merriment of everyone else. I gave a sickly smile of relief, then left them at it and went and redeemed the whole lot with a gold merchant for a fat wad of Hong Kong dollars before anything else happened, putting most of the money in the bank before I returned.

At sea, we spiced up our evenings in the bar by inventing cocktails. Most were dreadful, and couldn't be drunk in any quantity due to our propensity to measure the quality by the alcohol content, rather than by the taste. The Hammer endured, which was a mix of gin, vermouth and lime juice in a long glass, filled with crushed ice and citrus. A variation was the Vammer, which was vodka-based but otherwise the same. Both drinks were ideal for the climate and became a regular tipple for many us. They were not lethal, although the Hammer had a sting in the tail that arrived the next morning. The Vammer was slightly kinder.

We had a very basic coffee maker in the bar that boiled water from a reservoir and steamed it through a filter filled with coffee, after which it dripped into the glass pot that sat on a hot plate. Mick took to filling the water reservoir with vodka to produce more interesting coffee. He swore it was a powerhouse brew even though it still tasted like ordinary coffee. The swots among us declared that the boiling and evaporation process only weakened the alcohol content, although Mick persevered anyway until people gave up protesting and it became the standard after-dinner brew.

An infantile joke ran uninterrupted throughout the whole of the time I was on the *Kwangsi*. The big fridge behind the bar was stocked mainly with cans or bottles of beer, together with a few mixers. There were a small number of soft drinks, for the rare occasions when someone wanted one. From time to time, when no one else was around, one of us would take a can or bottle of beer and shake it violently to guarantee a fountain of foam when opened. Our drinking then had a Russian roulette feel, no one knowing whether the next one was going to cause gouts of high pressure beer to burst forth. Each one of us went through a soaking at some time; the victim hopped around howling with rage while the onlookers howled with laughter, never failing to find it hilarious.

I never had a single regret about my change from tankers to general cargo ships. It was probably not the best career move, but in those days I was focused on aspects of life today, not career tomorrow. Once I settled into general cargo ship life, things proved to be as good as I thought they probably ever could be, although at the same time not as good as I really wanted. I remained shackled to a foolish romanticising of what used to be, and to an ultimately pointless quest for a way of life that had mostly disappeared between the wars. That regret apart, though, my life at sea was good.

At sea, best of all was the camaraderie. There is a commonality shared by men who live in extreme conditions, which can never be replicated by those living a more normal pattern of life and who spice up their existence with clubs and rituals and outings. I wondered if there were particular components that sparked the camaraderie and concluded it was just the act of men working together and living together for months on end in an environment beyond the norm. The main criterion was being in a place where it was simply not possible to go home, because you were home. This tends to restrict bonding of this type to those in uniform for the most part, although sometimes perhaps also to groups of explorers and researchers and the like, people who live in the wilds for months on end. The advance of modern communications has now cut into this. If someone can phone home every night, then there is no break with home, there is only an ongoing inconvenience.

The bond we generated brought out the good things in us and encouraged the better parts of our nature to emerge. We shared more, we cared more, we looked out for each other and never left anyone behind. We scrupulously observed traditions and made greater effort to enjoy ourselves more than the occasion probably warranted. We still squabbled and bickered and sometimes fought, as men do, and we formed our alliances and plotted against each other. But in all this there was a glue that was difficult to shake, even decades later. When someone had a telegram telling of their wife having given birth to a new baby we were genuinely delighted, not politely interested. When the bosun lost everything he had playing mah-jong, lost every last cent and every last possession beyond the clothes he stood up in, we were as distraught as if it were our own loss and organised a collection to put him back on his feet.

The slower pace of cargo ships lent greater romance to the trail, and the cargoes we carried gave evocation to what we did. Copra and coffee in the islands, factory goods from the sweatshops of the East, wool and hides from New Zealand, all added a scrawl to the postcard. Slow days tallying bags of dried fish or cases of wine as they were swung on board in nets, slow days steaming across balmy inland seas where we were the only ship on the planet, slow days watching the wake being carved out of the sea behind us.

In those days I served as a junior officer in the East and in the islands, I loved the life I lived, I could not think of anything better, I could not think of anything that I would rather do. I felt on borrowed time, which sometimes made me act more frantically than I should have done. I was too wild when I went ashore, I put aside no money for the future. Money either accumulated or it didn't, depending upon my spending pattern, which in turn depended upon the opportunities afforded to me.

I could see the life dying all around me, particularly at the end. Every time we took our wandering trader back to the hubs in the East, there were fewer and fewer ships like us, there were more big container ships, more small container ships, more car ferries, more bulk carriers, more drive-on-drive-off, roll-on-roll-off, float-on-float-off ships. More and more ships were built that changed the whole pattern of loading and unloading cargoes, with the owners seeking the ultimate commerciality, where the ships never stopped and those who sailed in them had no hand in the process; the screw just turned. But for now, the days went well and the approaching end added a piquancy that made them so much sharper.

My time on the *Kwangsi* was a fine voyage, the best since I had been at sea; the nine months served were well spent. The nights ashore were heady, but the time at sea calmed me down, prepared me for the next phase of my life. I made good friends, the days were long and sunny, and I was never tired. We all laughed a lot, at the life we led, at each other, at ourselves. When I had joined the ship in Manila, my hair hung down to my shoulders and I was wired, nervous, jittery. I cut my hair off on the second day then grew it long again over the next nine months. By the time I paid off, I felt calm and rested and wiser. I was strong and had the resilience that only young men have, I was deeply burnt by the sun, I had plenty of money in the bank because I had earned more than I managed to spend, even with my reckless ways.

I paid off the *Kwangsi* one morning in June in Auckland, eighteen months away from home including my trip on the *Poyang*, handing over to Mick, who was staying aboard, even though he had been on for a year already. He was to act as temporary second officer until my replacement arrived from the UK. Loma was bumped up to third mate, and Chris would take an uncertificated fourth mate role. Mike the midshipman was leaving at the same time as me, and we had a joint paying-off party that went on into the night. All the officers were there, together with half a dozen local friends. The following day was a Sunday, a non-working day, which meant that the party could rage all night: it did. It started in a good-humoured way with toasts and well-wishing all round, then deteriorated into wildness after a couple of hours, as more alcohol was consumed. We had had piggy-back jousts on each other's shoulders, armed with mops, striving to paste our opponent in the face with the wet mop-head. We fought Star Wars duels on the boat deck holding four-foot neon light tubes as our light sabres, which burst spectacularly as we battled. We played dambusters, rushing around the bar in fleets, singing. We drunk Hammers competitively. Later the mood turned maudlin as we swore undying friendship to each other; even the chief wished me well. Later still, we sat on the poop deck while Mike played his accordion and we sung along in murmured dirge, watching the sun come up over the harbour heads.

It was the southern winter when I boarded the Air New Zealand aircraft. I was carrying a heavy head cold. I went deaf after take-off and had a lot of pain in my ears. The airline staff were concerned and arranged for me to see the airport doctor at our stopover in Honolulu. I was even deafer when we landed, and my head felt as if it was exploding.

The doctor peered in my ears and shook his head. 'You're bleeding out of one eardrum and the other is inflamed and on its way. You're not flying anywhere.'

He gave me pills and told me to come back in five days. He also told me to keep out the sun and not take any alcohol. Telling a young man that he has been awarded a week's holiday in Hawaii, although he must avoid the sun and not drink, is a fruitless expectation. I flushed the pills down the toilet then booked into the Princess Kaiulani hotel on Waikiki beach, bronzed myself in the Hawaiian sun during the days and partied with strangers at night, until my hearing gradually came back. It was a good end to the trip.

I had been at sea for ten years, from joining a rusting tanker in Hamburg as a sixteen-year-old cadet and entering a world that was alien to me in every way, to flying back to England now, leaving behind the only world I knew. My personal ambitions were mostly sated, even though there was still an itch that wasn't fully scratched. I was due nine months' leave plus six months' study leave, but the shipping world was changing so fast now that I didn't know what I would be coming back to after that time. It wouldn't be the same, that was for sure. And when I did come back to sea, what then? Let's see.

Time moves forward in a parabola, every year goes past quicker than the last. When I was two days old, that second day lasted half of my lifetime. Imagine a day now that lasted half of my life, imagine how long that day would be. No wonder all those childhood summers seemed to last forever. In my ten years at sea, the first four were endless days in the sun; the subsequent six went by at a clip. In another four years I would be thirty, unimaginably old, how soon would that arrive? Herbert Spencer puts it best: *Time: that which man is always trying to kill, but which ends in killing him.*

Too much food for thought, probably. I was getting a decent bite out of life, more than most could ever conceive. And I was still young, still in my early summer, decades from the bleak midwinter. I was aware there were more worthy goals and greater pleasures than tramping the backwaters of the world in search of a life now mostly gone, but betterment is purchased by the deeds we do and my deeds would take me towards greater things if I deserved it. I had looked into the abyss and locked eyes with my moral nadir, and had pulled away. I was resolute in thinking that the best of me was yet to come. Although now, after 600 days away … home.

# The Ship's Epilogue

To those who have spent a part of their life at sea, every ship has a personality and is remembered for it. There is usually a polarity of feeling towards a ship, one of two extremes, either fondness or dislike. A ship is a 'good ship' or a 'bad ship'. Even so, whenever we hear of the end a ship we served on, at the hands of the breakers, or by sinking or fire or explosion or running aground, there is always a sadness, irrespective of whether we liked her or not. Apart from the VLCC, which I didn't enjoy, the deep sea ships I had sailed on were all good ships. But they didn't all go quietly to die of old age: -

SS *Horomya* – Light oil tanker built on South Tyneside at the Clark Hawthorn shipyard in 1956. Engines: steam turbine. Tonnage: 19,656 deadweight. Port of registry – London. Enjoyed 19 years' unbroken service with the same shipping company before being scrapped in Santander, Spain, in 1975.

SS *Medora* – Crude oil tanker, VLCC, built at the Mitsubishi shipyard in Nagasaki, Japan, in 1968. Engines: steam turbine. Tonnage: 210,658 deadweight. Port of registry – London. Sold in 1979 and converted to a Floating Storage Unit in the North Sea, renamed *Fulmar FSU*. Serviced the Fulmar oil field for several years. Replaced in 1996. Fate unknown.

SS *Benalbanach* – General cargo vessel built on the Clyde at the Barclay Curle shipyard for the British India Steam Navigation Company in 1957, launched as the SS *Woodarra*, renamed *Pando Gulf*. Engines: steam turbine. Tonnage: 8,753 gross. Bought by the Leith company in 1974 for the Far East trade, renamed *Benalbanach*. Port of registry – Leith. Scrapped in Inchon, South Korea, in 1978 after 17 years' service.

SS *Benlawers* – Cargo passenger vessel built on the Clyde by Upper Clyde Shipbuilders in 1970. Engines: steam turbine. Tonnage: 12,784 gross. Port of registry – Leith. Sold to a Singapore company in 1978 and renamed *Globe Express*, then sold on to Italian shipping interests and sold on again, eventually being converted to a livestock carrier. Engine room fire in the Indian Ocean when sailing from Australia to Jordan under a Panamanian flag. Abandoned, and sank with 67,000 sheep on board. 26 years' service.

SS *Benledi* – General cargo vessel built on the Clyde at the Alexander Stephen shipyard in 1954 for P&O as the SS *Ballarat*, renamed *Pando Cape*. Engines: steam turbine. Tonnage: 8,792 gross. Bought by the Leith company in 1972 for the Far East trade, renamed *Benledi*. Port of registry – Leith. Scrapped in Inchon, South Korea, in 1978 after 24 years' service.

SS *Benreoch* – General cargo vessel built on the Clyde at the Charles Connell shipyard in 1952 for the Far East trade. Engines: steam turbine. Tonnage: 10,142 gross. Port of registry – Leith. Sold to Greek owners in 1976 and renamed SS *Tusis*. Broken up in Kaohsiung, Taiwan, in 1979 after 27 years' service.

SS *Grey Hunter* – Black oil tanker built in the Hiroshima shipyard, Hiroshima, Japan, in 1974. Port of registry – London. Engines: steam turbine. Tonnage: 123,965 deadweight. Laid up in a Norwegian fjord from new due to the oil crisis. Sold to Greek owners in 1986, renamed SS *Phassa*, then SS *Kimolos*. Fate unknown.

SS *Bencruachan* – Cargo passenger vessel built on the Clyde at the Charles Connell shipyard in 1968, the last ship to be built at that yard. Engines: steam turbine. Tonnage: 12,092 gross tons. Port of registry – Leith. Broke her back after being hit by a freak wave off South Africa in 1973. Scrapped in Kaohsiung, Taiwan, in 1980 following only 12 years' service from launch to scrapyard.

SS *Benstac* – Cargo passenger vessel built on the Clyde at the Charles Connell shipyard in 1968 for the Far East trade. Engines: steam turbine. Tonnage: 8,327 gross. Port of registry – Leith. Sold to Greek owners in 1976. Sank in 1985 after an engine room explosion two days out of Buenos Aires, Argentina, while bound for Lobito in Angola. 17 years' service.

MV *Poyang* – General cargo vessel built at the Wärtsilä shipyard in Turku, Finland, for Finnlines in 1964. Launched as *Finneso*, renamed *Finnboston*. Engines: diesel. Tonnage: 9,047 gross. Bought by the taipan company in 1978 for the Far East South Pacific trade. Renamed *Poyang*. Port of Registry – Hong Kong. Sold to Chinese shipping interests in 1981. Broken up in Alung, China, in 1995 after 31 years' service.

MV *Kwangsi* – General cargo vessel built at the Vickers Armstrong shipyard in Newcastle in 1967 for Blue Funnel Shipping as an advanced design Priam Class ship. Launched as *Radnorshire*, renamed *Perseus*. Engines: diesel. Tonnage: 12,094 gross. Bought by the taipan company in 1978 for the Far East South Pacific trade. Renamed *Kwangsi*. Port of registry – Hong Kong. Sold to Saudi interests in 1982. Suffered serious damage by shellfire in the Iran–Iraq war in 1984; condemned and scrapped after 17 years' service.

…and let's raise a glass to all who sailed in them.

And so, my quest was over, my life chasing Conrad was done. And in doing so, I had witnessed the dying of the light on a way of life at sea that will not be seen again. Did I have any regrets? Certainly not then. Not on that last day, not when I walked down the gangway of the *Kwangsi*. I never even glanced over my shoulder. I just climbed into the agent's jeep and drove off. Looking back after all these years, though, do I have any regrets? No. No regrets, no regrets as such. My life has since been blessed with sweeter things: a loving wife, family. I am happy to a degree that would have been incomprehensible to me in my younger days. Of course, there were things I could have done better and should have done better, and I should have acted less foolishly at times. I should have paid my health more heed and drank less to avoid those mornings when I looked as if I had been visited by the wrath of God. And I should have taken more notes as I went along, rather than piecing things together all these

*The changing face of the author in 10 years at sea.*

years later, from old letters and log books and accounts and recollections of friends and my own memories. But no regrets. There is something though: a wistfulness that's gradually inflicted on every ageing man. I just … miss. I miss being young, I miss being strong, I miss being fearless, I miss being quick on my feet, I miss the lack of anxiety, I miss laughing at things that now give me concern, I miss the ability to work all day and play all night, I miss having all the appetites of a young man. Perhaps I miss the sea too, a bit. But regrets? *Rien.*

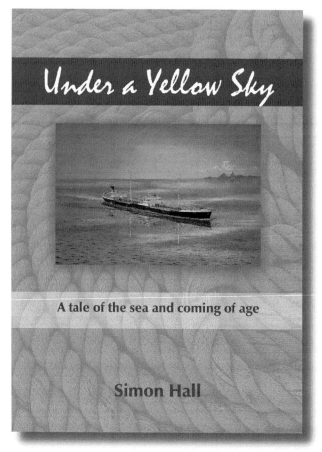